10-19-06

YANGTZE

A PORTABLE STANFORD BOOK

YANGTZE

NATURE ▾ HISTORY
AND ▾ THE ▾ RIVER

LYMAN P. VAN SLYKE

ADDISON-WESLEY PUBLISHING COMPANY, INC.

Reading, Massachusetts   Menlo Park, California   New York
Don Mills, Ontario   Wokingham, England   Amsterdam   Bonn
Sydney   Singapore   Tokyo   Madrid   San Juan

This edition is published by arrangement with the
Stanford Alumni Association.

Library of Congress Cataloging-in-Publication Data
Van Slyke, Lyman P.
  Yangtze: nature, history, and the river.

  (A Portable Stanford book)
  Includes index.
  1. Yangtze River—History. I. Title.
DS793.Y3V35 1988   951'.2   88-3378
ISBN 0-201-08894-0

Jacket design by Copenhaver Cumpston
Jacket illustration: detail from "The Great Yangtze River"
by Chang Dai-Chien, in the collection of Chang Chun.
Reproduced courtesy of Chang Chun and Eugene Wu,
director of Harvard-Yenching Library.
Text design by Jeffrey Whitten

ABCDEFGHIJ-DO-898
First printing, March 1988

To the memory
of
my father and my mother

CONTENTS

A NOTE ON ROMANIZATION

The rendering of Chinese words into the Western alphabet is called "romanization," and a messier situation could hardly be imagined. Several systems—each defective in some particulars—have been invented to handle this problem, and two of them are in wide use. The first was developed in the nineteenth century by two Englishmen: Thomas Wade (diplomat and linguist) and Herbert Giles (scholar). Despite its imperfections, the Wade-Giles system was the first to come into standard use and it remained standard until about a decade ago.

The other system has been adopted as official by the present government in Peking and has become increasingly common, particularly in writing about contemporary China. This system, called *pinyin*, is better than Wade-Giles in some regards, worse in others.

Wade-Giles and *pinyin* exist side by side, and each author must decide how to handle the romanization problem. My decisions are as follows: (1) in general, I use Wade-Giles, as more likely to appear familiar to most readers; (2) where certain place names—like Peking, Hankow, Canton, etc.—have a tradition of use, I use them also; and (3) in a very few instances, I use *pinyin* romanization. I think this hybrid practice will make it a little easier for the general reader than would an unnatural consistency.

ACKNOWLEDGMENTS

I remember the moment but not the year when the idea of a book on the Yangtze River was first implanted. Sometime in the mid-1970s, my colleague, Hal Kahn, and I were walking across the campus near History Corner, engaged in desultory academic conversation. I recall expressing the excitement I had felt in reading Fernand Braudel's *The Mediterranean and the Mediterranean World in the Age of Philip II*. A couple of blocks and several topics later, I described a new undergraduate seminar on the Yangtze River, with which I already felt a strong fascination. "Someone ought to write a book on the Yangtze along the lines of Braudel's book on the Mediterranean," Hal said, thus bringing together these two strands, which until that moment had been quite separate in my mind. The conjunction seemed so natural, so virtually inevitable, that I wondered how I had not thought of it myself.

Much time has passed, and the book will soon make its appearance, an occasion I seize happily to acknowledge how much Hal's friendship means to me personally, in my historian's role, and in the writing of this book. Second only to my debt to Hal Kahn is my debt to Albert Dien, from whose broad sinological erudition and scholarly integrity I have benefited for thirty years. I also wish to thank Professor Juhn G. Liou for reading the portions of the manuscript dealing with the geology of the river. And at the Stanford Alumni Association, thanks to Peter Voll of the Travel/Study Program for enabling me to make two trips on the Yangtze; to Della van Heyst for believing that I might someday produce such a book; to Miriam Miller, for her editorial care and judgment; to Gayle Hemenway for assistance with what must have seemed far too many maps, charts, and illustrations; and to Donna Salmon for her clear and careful cartography. Some of the work that went into this book was supported by grants from the American Council of Learned Societies, from Stanford's Center for East Asian Studies, and from the Dean of Humanities and Sciences.

Without steady encouragement, warm companionship, and occasional needling from my family, especially Barbara, and without the fellowship of many anonymous friends, I think this book would not have come into being. Needless to say, I am responsible for all infelicities and errors remaining in the book despite the best efforts of colleagues, editors, family, and friends.

PERSPECTIVES

This little book was inspired by a big book—Fernand Braudel's *The Mediterranean and the Mediterranean World in the Age of Philip II*. His big book (two volumes and 1375 pages in the Harper paperback edition) was first published in France in 1949 and later revised before finally being translated into English in 1972. In writing history, Braudel made history: because of his work, the world now looks different to most writers and many readers of history. Of course, no such change is achieved de novo, especially in historical studies, but is itself the culmination of earlier developments. In this case, the course of development was the French *Annales* school of historical writing, which turned away from the recounting of events and the traditional narratives of kings, generals, and ambassadors to the doings of ordinary people over long periods of time, *la longue durée*.

The first part of my debt to Braudel is in the very conception of my subject. For Braudel, the Mediterranean was not simply a body of water. It connoted all the traffic and all the travelers that sailed it on peaceful or warlike missions, the lands surrounding and thrusting into it, even the more distant lands in which its radiating influence was felt. Until the time of the Spanish Armada, this greater Mediterranean world was the center of Western civilization, and it included most of Europe, the Balkans, North Africa, and the Middle East. Thus the Mediterranean world, despite its great diversity, had for Braudel a kind of coherence imposed by the common arena toward which all were oriented.

My notion of the Yangtze River is a similar one: not simply the river itself, but also its tributaries and its watershed, which comprises a broad zone lying athwart central China, where nearly 350 million people live today. Like the Mediterranean world, though not to such an extreme degree, the world of the Yangtze River is also one of great physical, material, and cultural diversity, for China probably contains as much variety as Europe—a variety obscured by the Chinese tradition of political unity. And like the Mediterranean, the Yangtze basin became quite early one of the most strategic areas in all China. Economically, it had become the the most productive region of China by the eighth century, and it played almost equally important roles in social development, politics, and culture.

If my conception of historical and geographical space owes much to Braudel, so does my conception of time. Braudel viewed time from three perspectives. The first, he wrote, was a natural time "whose passage is almost imperceptible, that of man in his relationship to the environment, a history in which all change is slow, a history of constant repetition, ever-recurring cycles." Nor, he said, could he be content with the typically brief geographical remarks found in so many books, "as if the flowers did not come back every spring, the flocks of sheep migrate every year, or the ships sail on a real sea that changes with the seasons."

Braudel's second perspective is that of social time, "the history of groups and groupings." Here the pace is less deliberate, more varied than in the first. From this perspective, one sees family and community, migrations, the growth of cities, the organization of human labor, production, commerce and traffic of all kinds, conflict and war. Thus, for example, the pressure of population growth in China, gathering momentum from the eighteenth century, pushes into the present and is felt everywhere. New patterns of farming, of urban development, of trade and migration carry still the imprints of the past, and sometimes even reinforce old patterns. From the perspectives of these two kinds of time, China's recent revolutions appear less radical, and continuities or gradual changes stand out more boldly than abrupt breaks from the past.

Braudel's third perspective—and the one from which my own views and these essays most diverge—involves specific events, the events and personalities that occupy our attention from day to day, producing "rapid, nervous fluctuations . . . but the most exciting of all, the richest in human interest." I do not agree with Braudel that events are only "surface disturbances, crests of foam that the tides of history carry on their strong backs." It seems to me that events and individuals may impinge upon the course those tides take, which are themselves the accumulation of myriad human acts. Surely individuals and their deeds are conditioned, constrained, and limited by these deep currents of long duration. Yet there are times when the "tides of history" do not all flow in the same direction, when forces are in delicate balance. At such moments, the actions of an individual or a small group may have decisive consequences. To assert the opposite is to deny our individual human experience, and to deprive our acts of all significance.

Furthermore, these tides of history, these great social and economic currents, remain mere abstractions until their existence is embodied in actual and observable human action—in events, that is—of all kinds. Yet Braudel is surely right in saying that if we look at events only in the limited sense of conventional textbook histories, we will misunderstand both the past and the present because we will miss those forces that shape these events and give them their fullest meaning.

Running through these perspectives is a theme with which Braudel does not deal, except implicitly. Like all great geographical phenomena, they summon memories, attitudes, emotions, symbols. Who can think of the Mississippi without an instinctive sense of the continent divided in half, without Tom Sawyer and Huck Finn, without "Ol' Man River" (at least since 1927, when *Showboat* opened on Broadway)? In short, geographical facts also exist in the mind, a bundle of associations unique to each individual yet widely shared, cultural constructs which change as time passes and new layers of association are overlaid upon earlier ones. In China, where memories go back three thousand years or more, layers of time and memory lie like geological strata deep upon the land.

Natural time, social time, remembered time—these are the three kinds of time, the three lenses, through which I will try to view the Yangtzean world. These temporal lenses, of course, like all visions of a reality which we cannot view unmediated or see all at once, are an artifice of the mind. Such artifice, Joseph Levenson once said, is "only a method, an avenue of entry, not an end. 'Out there' in the history men make, the web is never rent, and the threads are interwoven. . . . One tampers with the unity of nature, but the end is to restore the whole in comprehensible form."

In attempting "to restore the whole in comprehensible form," I have followed my own interests, and I am acutely aware that each of the essays in this book is no more than a brief introduction to a subject that could well be pursued at much greater length. Despite their superficiality, I hope that the essays are sufficiently self-contained to be read separately, but I also hope that read together and in sequence they will build up a layered and faceted picture of this most fascinating and (outside of China) probably least well understood of the great rivers of the world.

PART I

NATURAL TIME

THE LAY
OF THE LAND

On June 20, 1985, a young photographer named Yao Mao-shu began a perilous journey. He had decided to raft the full length of the Yangtze River, from its source amongst glaciers over 20,000 feet high to its mouth, near Shanghai. Nothing of the sort had ever been attempted before. Yao was inspired, he said, by a Japanese adventurer who the year before had set a world's record by completing a similar effort on the Amazon, but Yao had also sought unsuccessfully to join a much larger Sino-American group which was then seeking permission from Chinese authorities to raft the Yangtze. Denied participation in that group, he decided to go it alone and try to claim first honors for China. About a month later, on July 26, his body and some of his effects were recovered. The current in the steep gorge he had just entered was about thirty-five miles per hour. He completed only one-sixth of the journey. In his futile effort, Yao Mao-shu became a national hero who galvanized Chinese efforts to emulate him.

On July 21, 1986, under the shadow of Mount Geladandong, a fourteen-member Sino-American team, led by a determined and experienced outdoorsman, Ken Warren of Portland, Oregon, began its journey. They were not alone. No less than six Chinese teams were already on the river, determined to memorialize their countryman Yao Mao-shu and to prevent a foreign-led first conquest of *their* river. (See Chapter 11 for more detail on these expeditions.)

By August 3, one of the Americans had died of pulmonary edema, and four others left the expedition in protest against its leadership. On August 26, their rafts severely damaged, the team was stranded in gorges so remote that it took Ken Warren five days to find his way out on foot and get help to rescue the group. Meanwhile, as the Sino-American group was reluctantly abandoning its efforts, the surviving Chinese expeditions reorganized themselves into two teams. Despite the loss of four men in the worst gorges and rapids, they pressed on, and upon their November arrival in Shanghai, they claimed successful completion of the journey.

Shaping the Land

As they began their journey, members of the rafting expeditions probably gave little more than passing thought to the geological origins of the river which would soon torment their fragile rafts. Geologically, the Tibet-Chinghai Plateau within which the Yangtze River takes its source at about 20,000 feet—about the same as the Amazon—is part of a vast arena of recent and violent deformation of the earth's crust. Geologists Peter Molnar and Paul Tapponier write that it is "the region of the earth that exhibits the greatest diversity of geology, topography, and climate, together with a strong susceptibility to major earthquakes." They go on to say that

> although the geology of Asia seems to present a chaotic jumble of land forms, much of the deformation of the surface, when it is viewed as a whole with the help of satellite photographs, seems to fall into a simple, coherent pattern attributable to a single cause: a geological collision between the Indian subcontinent and the rest of Eurasia.

This collision, caused by the northward drift of the Indian-Australian plate upon which India rides as though on a raft, began about 40 million years ago and continues to this day. The most obvious effects of this inexorable encroachment—still today averaging five centimeters per year—is the stacking up of the Himalaya Mountains and the lifting of the Tibetan Plateau. The line of collision—the "suture," as geologists call it—is along the crest of the Himalayas. This collision of continents also produced China's drainage pattern, in which all the major rivers flow from west to east and only tributaries to these major rivers flow north and south.

But this vertical uplift, this crumpling of continents against each other, has absorbed only part of an intrusion whose effects are felt throughout Central Asia, Siberia, and China. According to Molnar and Tapponier, the rest of the advance has been taken up by the displacement of China, which, it seems, is being pushed eastward to make room for India's northward push—"like toothpaste squeezed out of a tube" (see Figure 1-1). Near Peking—1,500 miles from the impact zone—the great T'ang-shan earthquake of 1976 (7.8 on the Richter scale) was probably caused by the effects

FIGURE 1-1 (facing page). The Indian continent, riding on a northward-drifting tectonic plate, made contact with Asia about 45 million years ago. The collision raised the Himalaya Mountains and the Tibetan Plateau. It also caused extensive faulting on both sides of the intrusion, and elsewhere as well.

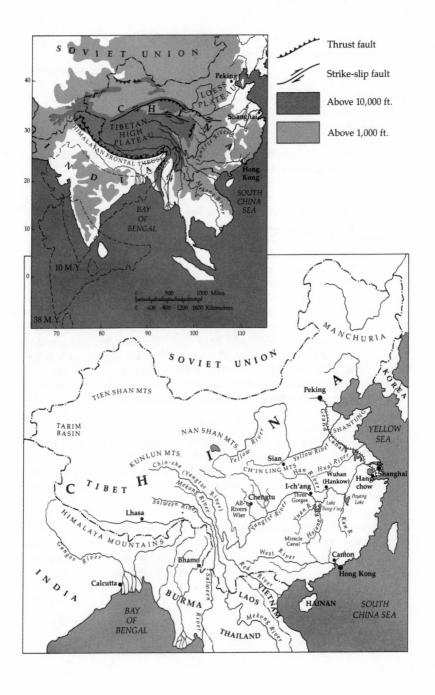

Thrust fault

Strike-slip fault

Above 10,000 ft.

Above 1,000 ft.

of this movement. By official count, 250,000 persons perished in this disaster; the actual toll may well have been higher.

Prior to the arrival of India, most of what is now Southeast Asia was ocean, an ocean that extended as far north into China as today's Szechwan province. As the collision of continents took place and the land was raised, this great sea, "the Chinese Tethys," was gradually reduced in size. Eventually, a large remnant was cut off entirely from the Indian Ocean, to occupy the Szechwan Basin. With further geologic change, this inland sea eventually disappeared as well, leaving behind underground deposits of salt and natural gas that the Chinese early learned to exploit (see Chapter 6).

In China, east of this recent Indo-Eurasian collision zone, is an older and less distinct pattern formed by mountains arcing untidily across East Asia from southwest to northeast, producing the great "Cathaysian geosyncline." (A "syncline" is a valley or trough in which the rock beds incline toward one another; its opposite, a ridge or arch formed by beds sloping away from each other, is an "anticline.") In south and southeast China, particularly, the pattern is jumbled and confused, a rugged, verdant landscape with only occasional tracts of level land, mainly in river valleys.

One result of this crosscut pattern is that China has more mountainous and upland terrain—less level land suitable for agriculture—than any of the large nations of the world: Russia, the United States, Australia, Brazil, India. China and the United States have about the same total area, but in the U.S. about 30 percent of that total is arable. China has less than half that much arable land (about 11 percent) but four times as many people. Another result of this geography is that most major regions of China are separated from one another by formidable barriers (see Chapter 4).

Climate

Climate is a long-term pattern. Weather is this season, this year. Societies adapt themselves to climate, then stand at the mercy of the weather. In contemporary America, most of us most of the time take climate for granted and find weather only occasionally troublesome—or worse. No agrarian society, as China still is, can take so much for granted.

China's climates, like those of most of Asia, are driven by the world's largest land mass and the world's largest ocean. This is the monsoon climate, which refers not simply to the rains of the wet season, but to the pattern of alternation between wet and dry seasons, separated by short transitional seasons (see Figure 1-2). This pattern was also created by the collision between India and Asia.

Prior to these eras, with the seas extending far north of present shorelines and with much flatter terrain across Asia, middle and higher latitudes were warmer and wetter year round than they are now. The collision, with its consequent rearrangement of land, water, and elevation, produced increas-

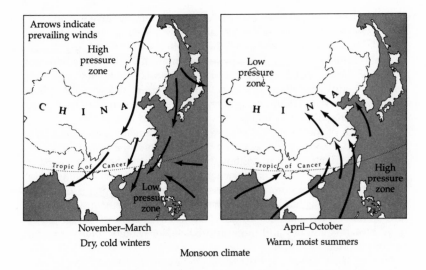

Arrows indicate
prevailing winds

High
pressure
zone

C H I N A

Tropic of Cancer

Low
pressure
zone

November–March
Dry, cold winters

Low
pressure
zone

C H I N A

Tropic of Cancer

High
pressure
zone

April–October
Warm, moist summers

Monsoon climate

FIGURE 1-2. The monsoon climate, showing the alternation of relatively dry, cold-air movement (winter) with moist, warm-air movement (summer).

ing dessication at higher latitudes, with the process moving gradually southward: the Gobi Desert was once grassy steppe or forest, and north China was a moist, densely forested region. Of this the archaeological record leaves no doubt, with clear remains of plants and animals to be found only in such an environment. Even into neolithic and early historic times, one can find such evidence. Moreover, by this time, man's actions were accelerating the slow pace of geologic process. Deforestation for agriculture, fuel, and building began early and continued without pause until most of north China was stripped of protective cover. This aggravated the processes by which north China was being made ever more arid.

With the modern topography of Asia in place, frigid air masses settle over central Asia and Siberia in the winter. This cold, heavy air creates a zone of persistent high atmospheric pressure flowing outward and under the warmer oceanic air masses. Conversely, in summer, air masses over the continent are readily warmed and caused to rise, forming a low pressure zone which draws in moisture-laden air from the Pacific. Within this overall pattern are, of course, many regional climates, and weather is more variable still. North China almost as far south as the Yangtze River is open to the expanses of Inner Asia, and consequently winters are bitter cold with relatively light snowfall, since continental air masses contain little moisture. For example, Peking is on about the same latitude as Washington, D.C., but its winter temperatures average about 15° (F) colder.

When the monsoon shifts, and winter's northwesterlies give way to summer, warm wet air moves across the land. Now it is south, southwest, and central China that most persistently feel its effects—abundant, usually dependable rainfall, and hot, humid weather. In north China, too, summer is the rainy season, but here it is much more unpredictable and of shorter duration. Long dry spells may be punctuated by torrential downpours which wash away crops and fields, bridges and villages. Meanwhile, other regions of north China may enjoy timely rains or lie parched in drought.

Just north of the Yangtze River is a rugged mountain chain, the Ch'in-ling Range—the straggling, easternmost extension of the mountain ranges flung off the Tibetan Plateau. Although few of its peaks reach beyond 6,000 feet, the Ch'in-ling is a climatic barrier, dividing north China from central and south China. As summer air masses move northward and rise to cross the mountains, they are cooled so that much of their remaining moisture falls as rain on the southern flanks of the Ch'in-ling. North of the Ch'in-ling, rainfall is scantier and more unpredictable, winters colder, growing seasons shorter.

Climate has also sculpted the land. One example must suffice, but it is an example that does much to explain the vast differences between the Yangtze River and the more northerly Yellow River, justly and sadly nicknamed "China's sorrow." Millennia of cyclones and winter monsoons, blowing across the Gobi and other arid expanses of Inner Asia, have picked up untold cubic miles of dust and fine sand, depositing this load over large areas of northwest and north China. This windborne soil, known as loess, is sometimes nearly as fine as talcum powder, yet it reaches a depth of up to 400 feet in some areas. As far east as Peking, every resident is familiar with winter dust storms that cut visibility to a few feet and make of the sun a disc of beaten copper.

Through the loess lands flow the Yellow River and its tributaries, carrying huge amounts of this easily eroded soil, mixed with other alluvium. This load the rivers deposit farther east. In time, wind and water together created the North China Plain, filling in primordial seas which once lapped at the feet of the Taihang Mountains. These rivers slow down as they reach the

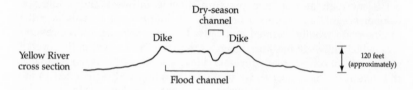

FIGURE 1-3. Cross section of the raised bed of the Yellow River as it crosses the North China Plain.

plains, depositing much of their burden along their beds. Since dredging is an impossible task, dikes are a necessity. The result, shown in cross section in Figure 1-3, is that the riverbeds eventually rise *above* the surrounding terrain and are confined only by man-made embankments. No tributaries can enter a river whose bed is already above the adjacent plain, and the Yellow River has none east of the great right-angle bend where its course changes from southward to eastward. When the dikes are broken out on the plains, whether by acts of nature or of man, the rivers simply flow through the gaps to flood enormous tracts of level plain.

Ten times in history—no one knows how many times before—the Yellow River has drastically changed its course, often from north to south of the Shantung Peninsula, as shown in Figure 1-4. With good reason indeed has the Yellow River been called "China's sorrow." These heavy burdens of silt coupled with unpredictable water levels account for another important difference between the Yellow and the Yangtze river systems: the Yellow River is almost useless for transport, while the Yangtze has been called "China's main street." These two rivers bear considerable resemblance to the superbly navigable Mississippi and the unpredictable Missouri, the "Big Muddy."

Yellow loess soil, an earthy ochre color, gives its name to the river, to the mythical culture hero—the Yellow Emperor, and to the imperial yellow reserved for the resplendent tiled roofs of the Forbidden City. Rammed earth walls, as durable as cement, can be formed of loess. Loess can be easily dug

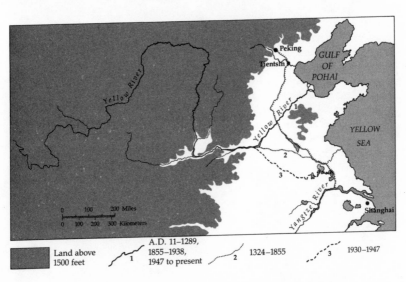

FIGURE 1-4. Principal changes in the course of the Yellow River in historical time.

to form dwellings: pit houses in neolithic times, and later—to the present day—by tunneling an inverted "U" shape into loess cliffs, then sometimes adding a freestanding exterior structure. Such were the cave dwellings occupied by Mao Tse-tung and other communist leaders in Yenan from 1936 to 1947. They are cool in summer and warm in winter, but are terribly vulnerable to collapse in earthquakes. In December 1920, a severe temblor centered in the loess highlands buried an estimated 300,000 people under avalanches and collapsed cave dwellings.

By contrast, the course of the Yangtze River has been much more stable than that of the Yellow River, and its volume of water far greater—nearly ten times as great. This volume of water comes partly from more abundant rainfall, and from a much greater volume of snow and glacier melt at high altitudes. But it also comes from the very large number of tributaries flowing into the the Yangtze, whereas the Yellow River has very few. Only the Amazon carries more water than the Yangtze. It is time to take a closer look at this great river.

OF TIME
AND THE RIVER

To the river we call "Yangtze," the Chinese give many names. The most common of these is *Ch'ang-chiang*, meaning simply "Long River," and I shall use this name interchangeably with Yangtze. It is a river like no other great river in the world. Only the Nile and the Amazon are longer. But for most of its course, the Nile is a strand, a narrow corridor thrown north from central Africa, and much of the huge Amazon Basin is uninhabited forest or jungle. In the regions through which the Long River and its major tributaries flow, some 350 million people live—considerably more than the population of the entire United States—and the lives of all of them are affected, deeply or more lightly, by these rivers (see Figure 2-1).

The Long River has a split personality. Before it reaches China proper, it has fallen by over 90 percent of the elevation from its source altitude to sea level, and it has traversed more than half its total distance. It is this steep and sparsely populated side of the Long River that Yao Mao-shu, Ken Warren, and the others sought to run in their kayaks and rafts, and it is only now being completely mapped. No famous explorers are associated with this part of the Long River. Chinese very rarely cared to enter high mountains, except under extreme necessity or extreme incentives, and—like most peoples—few had any drive to discovery for its own sake. For many centuries, it was generally assumed that the Min River was the headstream of the Yangtze, because it seemed a larger river than the River of Golden Sand at the point of their confluence.

From the Source to I-pin

Until very recently, the Yangtze River has been poorly understood. Only in the last decade have its exact source and its geological origins been satisfactorily identified. Although by the nineteenth century Chinese and foreign geographers understood that the River of Golden Sand was the true exten-

Some Basic Facts

Length: 3,900 miles (6,400 km.)
Altitude at source: 20,000 ft. (5,800 m.)
Tributaries: more than 700
Watershed area: 700,000 square miles (20% of China's total land area; 25% of total cropland)
Population in watershed area: 350,000,000 (33% of total)
Agricultural output: 40% of national total; *grain output:* 70%; *cotton output:* 50%
Industrial output: 40% of national total
Annual discharge: 350 cubic miles of water; 600 million tons of mud and silt
The river/canal network based on the Long River carries 80% of China's internal waterborne traffic

sion of the Long River, it was not until 1976 that a systematic effort was made to survey the origin of the Long River. Even so, a scientific party accompanying one of the Chinese rafting groups in 1986 conducted further investigations which suggested some further slight revisions in the accepted source attribution. And it was only as a result of dramatically new theories of continental drift and plate tectonics that the geological evolution of the Long River could be satisfactorily understood.

We now know that the upper half of the Yangtze River resulted from the collision of continents described in Chapter 1, an event so mammoth that the creation of rivers was a mere episode (see Figure 2-2). Once formed, the stream that will become the Yangtze meanders across the Tibet-Chinghai Plateau, fed by melting ice and snow coursing out of the surrounding mountains. This alpine plain is lightly inhabited by Tibetan peoples, with their flocks of sheep and yaks. Lamaseries occasionally rise above flat-roofed stone houses. Up onto this plateau runs the old tea road—surely one of the most arduous "roads" in the world—that brought brick tea and a few other products from China into Tibet and on to Lhasa.

Eventually, the river nears the edge of the plateau, then plunges southward off the "roof of the world," through sheer gorges few have ever seen. Here was where Yao Mao-shu lost his life and the Sino-American expedition was stranded. In this part of its course, the river is called by the lovely name "River of Golden Sand" (*Chin-sha Chiang*) from a coloration to which traces of fine gold sand do indeed contribute.

The glaciers and snows of the Tibetan and Chinghai mountains feed the headwaters not only of the Long River, but of other great rivers of southeast Asia. The Mekong and the Salween also have their sources in this same region. For about 200 miles, these three fall through nearly parallel north-south gorges, separated at one stretch by less than forty miles. These gorges owe their peculiar parallelism to the tectonic process already described; here, off to the side of the head-on Indian-Eurasian collision zone, the K'ang-ting fault system, shaped like an accordion, bends southward around the intruding mass. It is quite likely that at one time the Long River continued southward as an extension of the Red River, which enters the South China Sea in Vietnam at modern Hanoi and Haiphong. A glance at the map shows how close and how nearly aligned are the two rivers just before the Long River turns abruptly north, then south again, before setting a steadier course toward the northeast. This double hairpin bend is further evidence of violent faulting and displacement, which in this case altered the watershed pattern. Instead of continuing through Yunnan province and into the nearby Gulf of Tonkin via the Red River, the Long River now had to find its way more than 2,000 miles to the East China Sea. After its change of course, the Long River acquired many tributaries that had previously been independent rivers following their own southerly course; now they entered this upstart river on

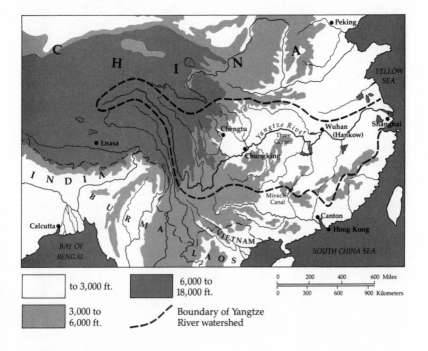

FIGURE 2-1. The Yangtze watershed.

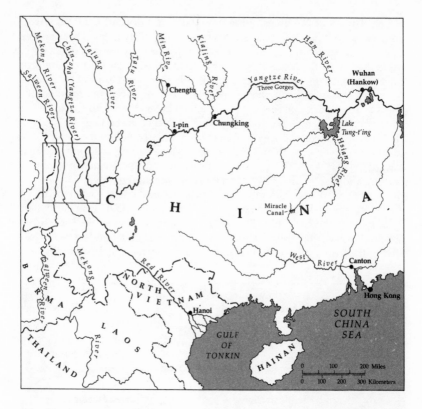

FIGURE 2-2. The upper Yangtze (Chin-sha Chiang), showing its capture of south-flowing rivers (Yalung River, Min River, etc.).

its left bank in what geographers call "river capture." It is this capture of major left-bank tributaries as well as its greater length that justifies calling this river the headstream of the Long River.

After crossing Yunnan province, the Long River reaches the sizeable city of I-pin, in southwest Szechwan province. Just above I-pin is the true head of navigation, beyond which no commercial craft can make their way. Here, where the Min River joins it, the Long River has already traversed 2,200 miles, well over half its total length, and it has fallen to an elevation of only 1,600 feet, less than 10 percent of its source altitude. About 300 river miles farther on, at hilly Chungking, the river is but 800 feet above sea level. For the remaining 1,100 miles to the sea, the Long River will drop an average of only a little over six inches per mile, most of it in the Three Gorges.

Through Szechwan and the Gorges

I-pin marks the beginning of the Long River's true entry into central arenas of human history. Here the river flows into the Red Basin of Szechwan, the first of the great regions through which it passes, and today the core of China's most populous province, with something over 100 million inhabitants—about the combined populations of England and France. During those geological eras when the Red Basin was an inland sea, fed by the ancestors of today's Long River and its tributaries, the fertile brick-colored soil that gives the hilly Red Basin its name was being laid down. In historical times, this good earth has produced those abundant crops which permit such dense population.

Throughout Chinese history encircling mountains created refuge in the Red Basin for local strongmen or exiles from the heartlands farther east: Chinese think at once of the heroic days of Liu Pei and Chu-ko Liang during the era of the Three Kingdoms in the second century A.D. (see Chapter 9), or of Chiang Kai-shek, holed up in Chungking during the war against Japan.

Szechwan means "Four Rivers," though there are so many waters feeding the Long River that there is some disagreement as to which four are intended. In late spring and through the summer, the melting of ice and snow at higher elevations joins the heavy monsoon-carried rains to add enormous amounts of water flowing from all directions toward the center of the basin and into the Long River: the Min, Yalung, Tatu, and T'o from the west and northwest; from the north, the Fu and the Ch'ü joining the Chia-ling and thence into the Long River at Chungking; the Heng and the Wu coming up from the south.

Only the Long River can carry the tremendous volume of water collecting in the Red Basin eastward and eventually to the sea. It does so through the most spectacular, dramatic, and fabled section of the river, the Three Gorges, a 150-mile passage which is like the narrow throat of an hourglass. At one point the river is no more than 350 feet wide. Yet through this gantlet must pass all the melt and all the rain collected by the Long River in all its previous flow. In full spate, as during the floods of 1931, 1954, and 1981—to name only recent years of high water—changes of water level in the gorges have sometimes reached twenty feet in twenty-four hours, seventy to eighty feet overall. The power and velocity of the water in the gorges comes less from any absolute drop in elevation than from enormous fluid pressure forcing the water through this constricted passage, like a huge venturi tube.

The Three Gorges—Ch'ü-t'ang Gorge, Wu (or Witches) Gorge, and Hsi-ling Gorge—lie on a west-to-east line between the cities of Wanhsien and I-ch'ang. The gorges are separated from each other by stretches of somewhat broader flow, and each is made of up several segments. Each has its own name, history, legends, and dangers, now mostly in the past (see Chapters 3 and 8).

Power navigation through the Three Gorges into Szechwan was not attempted until the last years of the nineteenth century, and was accompanied by innumerable accidents, frustrations, tragi-comic imbroglios, and insulted sensibilities on the part of Chinese who feared damage to their livelihoods and retribution from offended river spirits. Although the first passage was made in 1899, it was not until a decade later that river craft had become powerful enough to make the passage on their own steam alone—and even then they were not always able to do so. Scheduled runs began soon after but were limited to the most favorable seasons only, when the water was neither impossibly high and fast nor so low as to expose rocks and shoals. Most of the traffic continued in the traditional manner. Since 1949, the present government has done much to improve navigation through the Three Gorges by blasting or dredging away obstructions and by installing more elaborate beacon and buoy systems than those of the early twentieth century.

Just below Hsi-ling Gorge lies the small city of I-ch'ang, the first river port beyond the gorges. This is the site of the huge Yangtze River low dam (Gezhouba), presently in the last phase of construction. It is designed to serve several purposes: partial regulation of water level both above and below the dam, navigation, and hydroelectric power generation. The larger of the two navigation locks is nearly 1,000 feet long—as large as the locks on the Panama Canal—and accomplishes water level changes of up to seventy feet in about thirty minutes.

The Middle River

Once the Long River reaches central China below I-ch'ang it has room to spread out in more leisurely fashion, as though relaxing after the rigors of the gorges. Once again, tributaries begin to join it, just as the Ohio and the Missouri join the Mississippi. These are important river systems as well, and because they enter the Long River from both the north and the south, they form a transportation and human migration network in use from the remote past to the present.

Classical Chinese civilization carried by soldiers, officials, and land-hungry peasants spread from the north into central China and thence into south and southwest China by these riverine and lowland routes. In this migration of power and population—not yet even today quite complete in the southwestern provinces of Kweichow and Yunnan—indigenous non-Chinese peoples were killed, driven out, absorbed, or pushed into remote and marginal terrain where enclaves still exist, the counterpart in China of the conquest of North America by the white man at the expense of native populations. At the southern headwaters of the two major north-flowing tributaries, canals and portages were used for many centuries to cross the

Lingnan divide and enter the river systems that ultimately converge on Canton.

Flowing into the Long River from the south, the two most important of these tributary systems are the Hsiang River, whose basin forms the core of Hunan province (Mao Tse-tung's native province), and the Kan River farther east, draining the province of Kiangsi. Near the mouths of the Hsiang and Kan, where they prepare to join the Long River, are two of the largest lakes in China, two of the myriad lakes and marshlands of central China formed by the action of the Long River below the gorges. These lakes—Tung-t'ing, fed by the Hsiang and several other large tributaries, and P'o-yang, at the mouth of the Kan—give names to the two provinces of central China: *Hunan* (South of the Lakes) and *Hupei* (North of the Lakes).

Tung-t'ing, P'o-yang, and the other lakes of the region form a natural, though only partially effective, mechanism for control of flooding and water level in the Long River. As a result of the spring runoff and summer rains, the lakes fill up, covering reedy marshes and swamps and providing deep enough water for large craft. In autumn and winter, when the river is low, water flows out of the lakes and back into the Long River, the lakes gradually recede, and marshlands appear once again. Insects, freshwater clams and mussels, fish and birds of all kinds thrive in the periodic rise and fall of the lakes, a rich ecological cycle that now may be threatened by the damming of the river.

Unfortunately, these large lakes—and especially Lake Tung-t'ing—have been shrinking rapidly in both size and depth over the past century or so. Part of this infilling is natural, the gradual silting up of low-lying basins through the action of the Long River. But the rate at which silt is accumulating has been greatly accelerated by the side effects of diking strategies. These strategies have helped somewhat with flood control, but they have also greatly increased the inflow of silt, while simultaneously reducing the natural flushing capacity of the lake-and-river system. The other major force reducing the size of the lake is agricultural encroachment—land reclamation and polder fields intruding ever farther on what was once part of the lake. Over the past century, almost 1.3 million acres of farmland have been created out of Lake Tung-t'ing in this way, and the lake is now, at many seasons, little more than a collection of inland estuaries.

This natural flood-control mechanism has long given its clue to man, always ready to alter nature in what he deems to be his own interests. Dikes have been in use for centuries, particularly on the left bank. The dikes served well enough during normal years, but failed in times of unusually high water, causing great loss of life and destruction of farmland. The present government has lengthened, reinforced, and elevated these dikes. It has also straightened out many of the bends in the river, shortening its course by about fifty miles and easing its flow somewhat. But the largest project is the Ching-chiang diversion basin along the south shore of the river, put into initial operation in the early 1950s. This system, which compensates in part for the shrinking of Lake Tung-t'ing, depends on a diversion dike that can be opened during high water in order to drain off a portion of the flow, thus creating a temporary man-made lake. In this way, the rise of water level in the main channel can be slowed and the pressure against the dike system reduced. Since the area is required for flood control only at infrequent intervals, peasants are strongly tempted to colonize the fertile bottomland for agricultural use—though of course they do so at their own peril.

When nearly unprecedented high water poured through the gorges in 1954, this work paid off. Even so, the population of Hankow, central China's most important city, was mobilized in huge sandbag brigades. For forty-eight hours the issue was in doubt. Then the last and highest crest passed, and Hankow was saved. Upstream and down, the flood did great human and property damage, but much less than that brought on by the disaster of 1931, when the river crested six feet lower than in 1954, but all along the river the dikes failed. Vast tracts of land in Hupei were submerged, and for two weeks in the streets of Hankow, boats were the only way of getting around. An estimated 140,000 persons were drowned in the flood waters, and another 3,000,000 rendered homeless.

And so the Long River makes its way to Hankow, at an elevation of 75 feet above sea level and 640 miles inland. From here to the ocean, the slope of the river averages about an inch and a half per mile—an enormous contrast to the Yangtze's persona as the River of Golden Sand, where in some places the fall is hundreds of feet per mile. At Hankow, the Long River receives its largest northern tributary, the Han River. Millennia before present-day Wuhan was founded, this was already an area of crucial strategic significance. The Han River gave its name, 2,200 years ago, to the first long-lived dynasty of China's imperial history, the Han dynasty (206 B.C.-A.D. 220), whose power and glory—and whose legacy to subsequent history—rivals that of the contemporaneous Roman Empire in the West.

Hankow means "mouth of the Han." It is the largest and youngest of the three cities situated at this confluence, and together they make up the most important metropolis in the central reaches of the Long River. The three cities—Hankow, Hanyang, and Wuchang—are collectively called Wuhan, a portmanteau place name somewhat like Texarkana. As a center of commerce and industry, Hankow began to overshadow its older siblings in the early nineteenth century, and it has continued to do so ever since, despite having been nearly razed during the T'ai-p'ing Rebellion (1850–1864) and seriously damaged at the time of the 1911 Revolution, when the last imperial dynasty was overthrown. One of Hankow's great virtues is that oceangoing vessels as large as 10,000 tons can steam directly up the Yangtze, to the very heart of central China, where other major tributaries serve as avenues to collect products for export or to distribute imports. This nodality does much to explain Hankow's importance.

The Lower River and the Delta

Below Wuhan, the Long River continues its stately march to the sea, resembling in some ways the Mississippi between St. Louis and the Gulf of Mexico. But as Mark Twain described the Mississippi, its broad, apparently calm surface hides many treacherous shoals, bars, and snags. So it is with the Yangtze, for it is in the area around Nanking that the Long River was traditionally called by that name. Once the Yangtze passes the Kan River and Lake P'o-yang, the East China Plain is so flat that the river receives no important tributaries. It needs none, for its slow pace and its volume of water broaden it so that in some seasons a person cannot see from one shore to the other. Marco Polo, back home in Italy, was ridiculed when he claimed a river more than ten miles broad, but for the summer months near the estuary, his estimate was quite accurate.

There is one exception, not a tributary in the natural sense, but the man-made Grand Canal. As a feat of engineering and human labor, it surpasses even the Great Wall. Canal building in this region had begun before the birth of Christ or the full incorporation of this region into classical Chinese civilization. By the sixth century, the fertile lower Yangtze region was far outstripping north China in agricultural production, especially in rice, that most productive of grains. There was, however, no efficient way to carry its surpluses to the north, where the capital and the dominant centers of political and military power were still located. At the outset of the second great period of imperial unification—the Sui and T'ang dynasties of the sixth to tenth centuries—canals were linked up and greatly extended northward, across the Yangtze, all the way to north China. Another major extension was made by the Mongols in the 1280s, to bring the Grand Canal to the vicinity of Peking. At its greatest extent, it ran for 1,115 miles, from Hangchow to Peking; today about 700 miles of the Grand Canal are in active use and other sections are being put back in service (see Chapter 6).

Like the lower reaches of all great rivers, most of the land near the mouth of the Yangtze was built up by the river itself, in a never-ending, still-continuing process. To the layman, the measures of water and sediment discharged by the river each year are so large as to be unintelligible. Easier to understand is that every seventy years the delta is built another mile into the sea. Ch'ung-ming Island, in the mouth of the river, was a mere sandbar when first mentioned in the historical records, in about A.D. 600. By 1200, it was an island large enough to support a permanent population. Today, it comprises 300 square miles, and a population of nearly two million. The Long River not only builds the land, but discolors the sea. Sailors have always known when they were approaching this great estuary by the muddy color of the water seeping seaward up to seventy-five miles.

The last area through which the Long River flows is the delta region, which in a somewhat expansive sense comprises approximately the triangle bounded by a line from Hangchow to Nanking, the river itself, and the sea. This region is also called *Chiang-nan* (South of the River), a term that connotes the much greater development and prosperity of this southern region than the area north of the Yangtze. In almost every way—agriculture, traditional crafts and now modern industries, culture, sophistication—the Chiang-nan has been a key area for many centuries. It is a rich, low-lying alluvial plain, with many lakes and a few low hills, almost as much water as land. Virtually all cities and towns are connected by a dense network of streams and canals; from Shanghai, one can go in any inland direction for at least a hundred miles by water.

Shanghai

The ocean port served by and serving the entire Yangtze River system is Shanghai. Shanghai was only a third-rate fishing and trading port until the mid-nineteenth century, but with the coming of the West, the opening of the so-called "treaty ports," and China's increasing involvement in global trading patterns, Shanghai rapidly grew to become the most important economic city in China. Shanghai is a triumph of strategic location over local disadvantages that might reasonably have disqualified it as a major port. It sits on the west bank of the Whangpoo River, the last tributary entering the Long River before it debouches into the sea. It is a trivial tributary by comparison with the rivers upstream, and it snakes its way narrowly northward to join the main flow a few miles behind Ch'ung-ming Island. Constant dredging is necessary to get oceangoing ships across the bars at Fairy Flats, near the mouth of the Yangtze, and into the Whangpoo. Once inbound ships make the left turn that will take them upriver to Shanghai, there is very little maneuvering room. Ships anchor, moor, or come alongside wharves on both sides of the river all the way from Woosung, at the Whangpoo-Yangtze junction, to Shanghai itself.

Yet the disadvantages of this unfavorable port arrangement are far outweighed by Shanghai's access to the entire Yangtze Valley. By the late nineteenth century, Shanghai was already preeminent as a trading city and as the largest center of foreign investment and residence in China. It had far surpassed Canton, where the old China trade had been concentrated prior to 1850. Even the development of British Hong Kong, which helped to stimulate the economy of the region, did not enable Canton to keep up with Shanghai's meteoric growth.

With the turn of the twentieth century, Shanghai added modern industry to its other activities. As in most industrializing nations, light industry—

and especially textiles and food processing—were among the first to spring up. Cotton and silk were both highly developed handicraft industries, with conveniently available sources of supply, and it was relatively easy to supply both the raw materials and the cheap labor, large numbers of young women and children among them, necessary to get factories up and running. The largest and best capitalized of these industries were owned by the British and the Japanese, with Chinese industrialists competing under a number of crippling disadvantages, but somehow surviving and making money. In time, heavy industry—shipyards, iron and steel, manufacturing—were added to commerce and light industry. Shanghai was also a major Asian banking center, a major center of financial speculation, currency exchange operations, and get-rich-quick schemes of all kinds. By the 1930s, fully one-half of all foreign investment in China was concentrated at Shanghai, and nearly half of all foreigners resident in China lived in Shanghai, in the foreign-run International Settlement or French Concession.

For many Chinese, Shanghai was a magnet drawing them in, even as they found much of what Shanghai stood for repugnant, cruel, and humiliating. This was the Shanghai where, along the waterfront Bund in the International Settlement, were posted signs barring "dogs and Chinese" from using the park facilities. But this was also the Shanghai where revolutionaries, a price on their heads, could put themselves beyond the reach of Chinese law and find haven in the very enclaves ruled by foreign imperialism. Sun Yat-sen often took refuge in the foreign settlements, and the Chinese Communist Party was founded in the French Concession in 1921. Meanwhile, most of the waterfront, the opium business, prostitution, and gambling were run by Mafia-type outfits like the Green Gang, headed by Tu Yueh-sheng, known to some as "Big Ears Tu." Like the Mafia, the Green Gang was a brotherhood, a ruthless quasi-family that had its nineteenth-century origins among displaced transport workers on the Grand Canal in the chronically poverty-stricken and disaster-prone areas north of the Yangtze River.

Missionaries, educators, and reformers of all kinds joined traders, industrialists, adventurers, and fast-buck operators. The very wealthy and down-and-outers, the flotsam of the world, could be found in Shanghai, along with White Russian refugees and stateless Jews. Altruism and culture thrived alongside the most apparent greed and materialism. In America, Shanghai became a watchword for the exotic and the sinister, and everyone knew what it meant to be "shanghaied." It was "Sin City," where anything goes. No one ever caught the kaleidoscopic character of pre-revolutionary Shanghai better than Edgar Snow in his autobiography, *Journey to the Beginning*, describing his first impressions of Shanghai after his arrival in China, a young journalist fresh out of the University of Missouri:

Western business men who lived there when I arrived in 1928 acted as if the Settlement were real and would last forever. In their euphoria they felt that they were the continent and the four hundred million Chinese beyond were a kind of suburb put there by God for trading purposes. And yet it was a fascinating old Sodom and Gomorrah, at that, while it lasted!

At first I too mistook Shanghai for China. The bizarre contrasts of very old and very new, the sublime ugliness of the place, its kind of polyglot glamour, and its frank money-is-all vulgarity held me in puzzled wonder. . . .

The streets of downtown Shanghai likewise seemed a continuous freak circus at first, unbelievably *alive* with all manner of people performing almost every physical and social function in public: yelling, gesturing, always acting, crushing throngs spilling through every kind of traffic, precariously amidst old cars and new ones and between coolies racing wildly to compete for ricksha fares, gingerly past "honey-carts" filled with excrement dragged down Bubbling Well Road, sardonically past perfumed, exquisitely gowned, mid-thigh-exposed Chinese ladies, jestingly past the Herculean bare-backed coolie trundling his taxi-wheel-barrow load of six giggling servant girls en route to home or work, carefully before singing peddlers bearing portable kitchens ready with delicious noodles on the spot, lovingly under gold-lettered shops overflowing with fine silks and brocades, dead-panning past village women staring wide-eyed at frightening Indian policemen, gravely past gambling mah-jongg ivories clicking and jai alai and pari-mutuel betting, slyly through streets hung with the heavy-sweet acrid smell of opium, sniffingly past southern restaurants and brightly-lighted sing-song houses, indifferently past scrubbed, aloof young Englishmen in their Austins popping off to cricket on the Race Course, snickeringly around elderly white gentlemen in carriages with their wives or Russian mistresses out for the cool air along the Bund, and hastily past sailors looking for beer and women—from noisy dawn to plangent night the endless hawking and spitting, the baby's urine stream on the curb, the amah's scolding, the high falsetto of opera at Wing On Gardens where a dozen plays went on at once and hotel rooms next door filled up with plump virgins procured for wealthy merchants in from the provinces for business and debauch, the wail of dance bands moaning for slender be-jewelled Chinese taxi dancers, the whine of innumerable beggars and their naked unwashed infants, the glamor of the Whangpoo with its white fleets of foreign warships, its shaggy freighters, its fan-sailed junks, its thousand lantern-lit sampans darting fireflies on the moon-silvered water filled with deadly pollution.

Shanghai!

After 1949, all this changed. As Snow predicted, "Shanghai had waxed fat and corrupt and was soon to pay a dismaying price for the past its Western heirs had forgotton. History always collects, and the Chinese had waited a hundred years." No more foreign settlements or foreign warships; no more Green Gang; no more "wealthy merchants in from the provinces for business and debauch." Within a few short years, Shanghai apparently became one of the most orderly and least notorious cities in the world (was there, or is there now, a little more going on than meets the eye?). Despite its dramatic changes in outward appearance, however, Shanghai has remained China's most important economic and industrial center, and a major political force as well. The same forces that made Shanghai a great city after 1850 continue to make it a great city more than a century later.

Yet without the Yangtze, Shanghai would not exist as we have known it in either its prerevolutionary or postrevolutionary incarnation. On the other hand, long before Shanghai became an important city, the Yangtze was an important river. From the perspective of Shanghai, it is difficult to bring to mind the glaciers and snows of the lofty plateau on which the great river has its source, and down which we have just journeyed so quickly. We now return to the Yangtze to look more closely at that spectacular region called The Three Gorges, a region from which one can look upward toward the young and turbulent river, or downward toward the ancient, placid stretches and the sea.

3

THE THREE GORGES

For as long as Chinese memory reaches, the Three Gorges have inspired awe and captured imagination. We do not know when man first made his way through this spectacular and terrifying channel, but its passage was a recognized fact by the middle of the Han dynasty, at about the time of Christ. In either direction, the Three Gorges are the highest adventure the Long River affords to travelers—and, until recently, the most dangerous and laborious obstacle to commerce and transport, whose practitioners wanted no adventure and were often indifferent to scenery. The ravines above I-pin, where the River of Golden Sand plummets off the Tibet-Chinghai Plateau, must be even more breathtaking, but as we have seen, this part of the river is virtually impassable. And surely the Three Gorges are enough for anyone who must traverse them on the ordinary business of the world.

Origin and Structure

The natural history of the Three Gorges appears not yet to have been definitively written, although work involved with the gorge dams—the nearly finished Gezhouba, and the Three Gorges Dam, which is still in the planning stage—must have required intensive geological investigation. What follows, therefore, is a nonspecialist stratum overlaid upon the uncertain foundation of earlier geological surveys.

Observant travelers as well as geologists and geographers have long noted two remarkable phenomena associated with the Three Gorges. The first is that through this stretch the Long River flows almost due east. Through the Gorges there are only a few bends in the river, and these are usually offset by bends in the other direction, so that the overall flow retains its pronounced linearity. Moreover, north and south of the Three Gorges, other rivers have this same linearity: the Han River to the north and the Ch'ing River to the south are almost exactly parallel to this stretch of the Long River.

The second unusual phenomenon is that nearly all the higher mountain and ridge summits near the Three Gorges, however jagged they may be, have almost identical elevations of about 3,000 feet. Furthermore, it is the more resistant limestone formations that reach this altitude; all the sandstone formations are lower, which strongly suggests differential erosion and weathering of a landscape originally at a more or less uniform elevation. These formations seem to be older than the Mesozoic Era (i.e., more than 250 million years).

Such phenomena suggest a drainage not only confined *between* channeling mountain chains, but erosion *across* transverse formations which would otherwise block or divert a river's flow. This crosscutting phenomenon may have been associated with drainage across a *peneplane*, a broad area of gentle slopes, itself produced by even earlier weathering and erosion of landforms which lay on top of deeper folded formations. As rivers established themselves on this peneplane, they eroded their way down and into or through the underlying formations. That the Han and the Ch'ing rivers share this east-west linearity with the Long River strongly suggests a shared pattern of river formation.

This same explanation applies to tributaries in the gorge region. The most important of these is the north bank Ta-ning River, which flows nearly due south before its confluence near the town of Wu-shan, at about the middle of the gorges. Despite its difference in course, the Ta-ning is so similar in structure to the Long River that its scenery is often called "the small three gorges"—small only in the sense that the river is smaller, not that the mountains are less lofty, the cliffs less sheer. George Barbour, one of the principal geological explorers of China, in his own 1935 geological study, quotes a 1907 survey:

> The course of the Taningho [Ta-ning] is nearly at right angles to the structure of the region. . . . It is evident that the course of the Taningho, across very pronounced folds and in spite of very marked differences among the rocks, is not one which could have been acquired under existing conditions of relief. The stream could only have originated upon a surface not far below the summits of the present mountains and on a slope which sufficed to give every advantage to brooks that flowed southward.

Barbour reasons in like vein about the Long River: "We are therefore forced to the conclusion that the present general course of the river is a later development than the folding of the margins of the [Szechwan] basin."

The other debatable issue is whether or not the Long River always flowed in its present direction, that is, from west to east. In the 1930s, Barbour and J.S. Lee (Li Ssu-kuang)—perhaps China's most eminent geologist—disagreed. Where Barbour thought it had always flowed eastward, Lee's hypothesis was more complex. He argued that about 250 million years ago, when the Szechwan Basin was part of a large inland sea, one elongated bay stretched eastward into what is now the gorge area. At this time, Lee argued, there may have been two rivers, one flowing westward into the Szechwan Sea, the other eastward along something like the present middle and lower course of the Long River. Eventually, according to Lee, the sources of the two rivers joined together to form a single eastward-flowing river. A recent Chinese source skirts the issue:

> In western Hupei the ancient Long River began gradually to take shape and actively to extend its source back toward the Szechwan basin . . . [and it] now connected up with the Szechwan drainage system. Since the topography was now higher in the west than in the east, a mighty rolling river was formed—the Long River as we know it today.

If originally there were two rivers with nearby headwaters but flowing in opposite directions, a watershed would be required, and in fact the remains of such a divide may still exist. This is the Huang-ling anticline, an elliptical formation of very ancient rock—pre-Cambrian, a billion or more years old—which straddles the Long River just a little upstream from I-ch'ang, in Hsi-ling Gorge. In geologically more recent times, erosion has removed whatever originally overlay this ridge of granite and quartzite, and the river has cut down through it to its present channel. In doing so, it has exposed numerous unstable layers of shale and other material which from time to time collapse in huge landslides into the river.

In passing through the gorges, one needs no geological knowledge to see that some places are narrower, more precipitous, and more turbulent than others, but even the observant traveler would be hard put to identify the precise starting and ending points of the principal segments into which the Chinese have traditionally divided the river. In the eighth century, the famous poet Li Po described a fast downstream trip through the gorges:

> Dawn gone from White King, all misty-hued,
> Down river to Chiang-ling, a thousand li a day.
> From both banks monkeys' screeching sounds;
> Behind our boat, already, myriad folded ranges.

Figure 3-1 shows the Three Gorges: from the upstream end down, they are Ch'ü-t'ang Gorge, Wu (or Witches) Gorge, and Hsi-ling Gorge. For all their apparent arbitrariness in a river passage so endlessly and consistently spectacular that the mind is eventually benumbed, these names do mean something. One often hears that Ch'ü-t'ang has the sheerest cliffs and the swiftest current, Witches Gorge the most spectacular peaks and the worst whirlpools, and Hsi-ling the most dangerous rapids and shoals. From a structural point of view, the gorges constitute V-shaped valleys, while the stretches between them are broader U-shaped valleys.

Each of the gorges, indeed each locale along the river, has impressed upon centuries of boatmen and travelers its peculiar difficulties, its historical memories, even the real or imagined similarity of rock formations to other things. The Chinese have a penchant for saying that *this* resembles *that*, but even so, to liken an irregular but otherwise unremarkable outcropping to animal entrails—"Horse-lungs Ox-liver Gorge"—seems to be stretching things pretty far.

Ch'ü-t'ang Gorge

The first of the gorges, Ch'ü-t'ang, is also the shortest, only five miles long. It begins just below Pai-ti ch'eng, the White King City of Li Po's poem. As one approaches White King City from a distance, there seems no opening ahead, only a cliff-girt fjord. As one draws abreast of the little town, however,

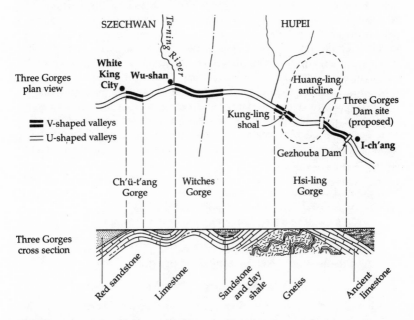

FIGURE 3-1. Top: the Three Gorges, showing location of the three principal gorges (Ch'ü-t'ang Gorge, Witches Gorge, Hsi-ling Gorge). Bottom: cross section of the Three Gorges, showing alignment of anticlines and synclines.

the awesome K'uei Gate comes into view, requiring a right turn in order to enter the gorge itself. Nearly sheer cliffs frame this gate, where the river is a mere 350 feet wide, the narrowest point anywhere after the river leaves the mountains of the far west. In full spate, the current sometimes reaches fifteen knots, but more typically six or seven knots. Near the entrance to Ch'ü-t'ang Gorge was the dangerous Yen-yü rock (now blasted away), the visible size of which depended on water level. With centuries of experience watching Yen-yü, boatmen sang a long advisory doggerel that began,

> When Yen-yü's an elephant, upstream you shan't
> When Yen-yü's a horse, don't downstream course.

Along the cliffs on the northern or left bank, one can see cut into the rock face the recessed towpath along which gangs of trackers hauled heavily loaded junks—the boat and its cargo might be as much as 120 tons— upstream against this fierce current. On the south side—one has to be alert in order to see them, they pass so quickly—are Meng Liang's Ladder and Windbox (or Bellows) Gorge. The former is an upward zigzag line of square holes cut into the cliff, as sockets into which timbers were inserted horizontally as rungs to climb upon. The most prominent legend—a false legend— tells of the patient valor of General Meng Liang and his troops, trapped in Windbox Gorge, and how they cut a laddered staircase to the top of the cliff, thus surprising and defeating their complacent foes. Unfortunately for the legend, the sockets run only about halfway up the cliff. More likely and less heroically, the holes were cut in order to get at valuable herbs growing on the cliff. Windbox or Bellows Gorge takes its name from crevices high above the river into which large cypress coffins were once placed vertically, creating an appearance that from below resembled the segments of a bellows. Hence the otherwise incomprehensible lines from Meng Chiao's surrealistic eighth century poem:

> Above the gorges, one thread of sky:
> Cascades in the gorges twine a thousand cords.
> Overhead, the slant of splintered sunlight, moonlight:
> Beneath, cliffs curb the waves' wild heave. . . .
> Trees lock their roots in rotted coffins
> And the twisted skeletons hang tilted upright.

Witches Gorge (Wu-hsia)

Below Ch'ü-t'ang, the river widens out for a time before entering *Wu-hsia* (Witches Gorge) just below the small town of Wu-shan, in a small estuary valley where the Ta-ning enters the Long River. Cornell Plant describes the twenty-five miles of Witches Gorge:

The river winds round the base of precipitous cliffs, which rise almost perpendicular in places to a thousand feet and more in height, and are backed here and there by lofty and fantastic peaks—walls of solid rock, with strata crumpled like paper, and set at various angles by great faults. In many parts, where the strata run horizontally, these rocky wall-like sides are benched with terraces, the lower terraces being fluted along their faces by thousands of pot holes, bored vertically right down the water surface of the cliff to low water level, resembling somewhat the great pipes of an organ.

These "lofty and fantastic peaks" characterize Witches Gorge, in contrast to the massive rounded crests in Ch'ü-t'ang and the talus piles and rapids of Hsi-ling. Because its steep walls and spirelike peaks block the sun during much of every day—even in the absence of the swirling clouds which so often swathe the higher elevations and overhang the river—Witches Gorge is the most somber and foreboding of the Three Gorges. Here, to a degree even more pronounced than in the other two gorges, the wind blows in only two directions: upriver or downriver. Needless to say, upbound boatmen always prayed—and sometimes waited—for a following wind.

Visibility permitting, river veterans can call out the names of six peaks on the north bank of the river and six on the south: Ascending Dragon, Wise Man Springs, Pure Altar, Congregated Immortals, etc. The most famous of these—a glimpse of it augurs safe passage and good luck—is the storied Goddess Peak (*Shen-nü feng*), which takes its name from a smallish rock formation that from the river nearly a thousand feet below resembles the standing figure of a robed woman, bent slightly forward as in sorrow or in benediction. In a land where stories—historical, legendary, or frankly fantastic—cluster about much more ordinary phenomena, one may well imagine the elaborate myths surrounding this supernatural woman. One of these myths tells how she and her eleven sisters, only slightly less beautiful and able than she, came to earth to help Great Yü the flood-tamer drain the Chinese earth and make it habitable for ordinary humans, how the eleven sisters became eleven peaks of Witches Gorge, and how she herself remained in petrified but otherwise human form as a sentinel on the twelfth peak to help rivermen safely through this still dangerous passage.

Hsi-ling Gorge

Hsi-ling, the third and longest of the gorges (almost thirty miles), is impressive enough in its own right but scenically it is overshadowed by its companions. Traditionally it was the most feared of all. While each gorge had its peculiar perils, Hsi-ling was notorious for its shoals and rapids, formed by periodic landslides as the river cut through the shaly and

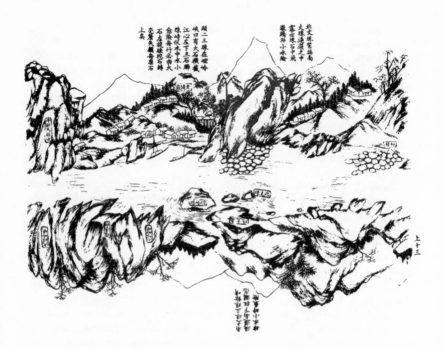

A view of K'ung-ling Rapids from a 19th-century Chinese illustration.

unstable layers of the Huang-ling anticline. Not far into Hsi-ling, one encountered *Hsin-t'an*, or "New Rapids," which took its name from slides in the sixteenth century that created this hazard. Three successive rapids, Head Rapid, First Rapid, and Second Rapid, covering a mile and a half of the river, were so difficult for large upbound junks during low water that they were often compelled to off-load and portage their cargos while the boats themselves were towed through by extra gangs of trackers—perhaps a hundred or more joining the thirty or forty regular trackers embarked on the junk itself—taken on from a couple of local villages, the mainstays of which were income earned by tracking and by salvage of flotsam from wrecks. Head Rapids was by far the worst of the three.

Downbound, New Rapids was as dangerous as it was arduous in the other direction. At its worst during the winter low-water season, the current ran at 13 to 14 knots (15 mph) across a total fall—until the channel was improved in the 1950s—of nearly twenty feet. In order to maintain steerage, junks had to exceed the velocity of the current by rowing—otherwise they were simply drifting out of control in the current—so that they entered the rapids at perhaps 16 or 17 knots. If they missed the proper openings to the rapids, they were almost certain to suffer damage, perhaps destruction. In New Rapids as elsewhere, accounts tell of junks virtually exploding in collision with rocks, and teak beams, planking, and cargo flying in all directions.

During the 1950s, New Rapids was dredged out and the name was changed to "Green Rapids" (*Ch'ing-t'an*). Landslides into the river still continue, however. In September 1896, a slide estimated at 700 by 400 yards fell out of the north bank to form New Dragon Rapids, which for some months nearly blocked the river. In 1984, another large section of the north bank near "Yellow Ox" (*Huang-niu*) also gave way.

At about the midpoint of the Hsi-ling Gorge lay the worst of all the Long River's rapids, the feared K'ung-ling Shoal. Once again, Cornell Plant describes the scene and offers advice:

> An immense mass of black rock, some 50 feet high at low level, sticks up right in mid-stream, which, surrounded by a number of smaller ones, during low level, renders the passage on the one hand [along the south bank] impassable, leaving only the other which is studded with submerged rocks, the channel between them being very narrow, crooked and dangerous. There are local Chinese who pilot boats up and down these Narrows during low level season. . . . Their services should always be engaged, especially when on the downward passage; an error of judgment in making the narrow fairway between the submerged Pearl Rocks means destruction.

In addition to K'ung-ling itself, junks had to avoid Pearl, Second Pearl, and Third Pearl, and also Monk's Rock, Chicken-wings, and the seductively named but deadly Come-to-Me Rock. In the illustrations on pages 34, 36, and 37 we see three representations of K'ung-ling Shoal: the first from a Chinese source of about 1890, a two-perspective rendition as though one were looking left and right from a boat on the river itself, with commentary above the horizons; the second from Plant's shipmaster's guide, published in 1920; and the third a sketch from Barbour's geological survey.

Which channel, north or south, to take through K'ung-ling depended on the water level. Indeed, from Chungking on down through the Three Gorges to I-ch'ang, water level determined the degree of danger in any particular stretch, and, at extremes of high and low water, whether or not the river was navigable at all. Summer is the high-water season, with the highest levels usually achieved in July or August, and winter is the low-water season. Low water is much more dangerous than high water, excepting flood stage, because it exposes the worst hazards the river can present.

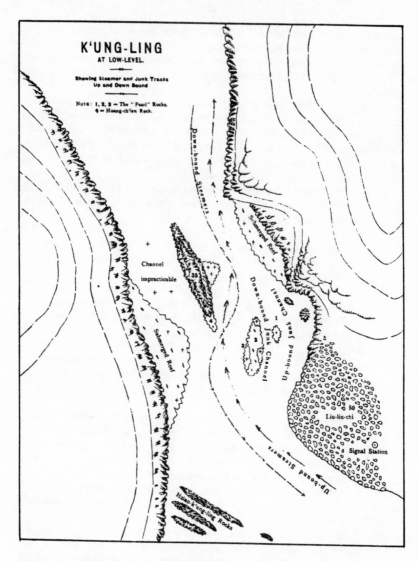

A view of K'ung-ling Rapids from Cornell Plant's pilotage guide in the 1920s.

The flow through the gorges, with its peculiar and often menacing whirl-pools, eddies, and crosscurrents, is influenced not only by water level; also significant is the widely varying water depth in the Three Gorges—from rapids breaking the surface to more than 350 feet. This variation comes from the underlying ridges and troughs (anticlines and synclines) across which the river runs, as though it were running *across* the rows on a sheet of corrugated roofing. When this variation is added to the difference of 200 feet from low water to high in the most constricted channels, one begins to have some sense of the hydraulic effects that may be created. Barbour describes some of them:

> Anyone acquainted with the river is familiar with the striking alterations in character which the currents undergo as the water level changes. . . . Besides the running and stationary whirlpools, "boiling" water, and other hydraulic features, there are peculiarities in the behaviour of silt and gravel banks that merit attention. . . . This may lead to a sudden wash-out of the silt which virtually forms a moving body of quicksand so dangerous that boats tie up to the bank when "the sands are on the move."

Paradoxically, the force of the main current sometimes produces eddies along the bank that flow in the opposite direction—upstream—for consid-

A sketch of K'ung-ling Rapids accompanying George Barbour's geological survey in the 1930s.

Fish inscribed on White Crane Ridge, near the town of Fu-ling. The eyes of the fish were used as reference points for recording low-water levels. The earliest such fish were carved in the 8th century.

erable distances at velocities of two or three knots. This can produce the very peculiar sight of two junks headed in opposite directions, each borne by its own favoring current.

Marking Water Levels

If the river was so mercurial, it was important that boatmen know what water levels lay ahead. Markings above mean water level were easy enough to paint or inscribe, and such markings are often seen just upstream or downstream from critical passages. In addition, beautifully written calligraphic inscriptions which had been cut into prominent rocks or cliff faces in order to memorialize historical sites, famous personages, or scenic beauty can also be used as references by noting water levels on the Chinese characters of the inscription.

Low water was harder to mark, since obviously it could only be done when the water was low, and very low water occurred only about once a decade, in the late winter. The most remarkable of the low-water hydrologic stations on the Long River was located at Fuling, about a third of the distance downstream between Chungking and the gorges. Here, on a gently sloping sandstone bar called "White Crane Ridge," representations of fish were carved into the rock at various periods to serve as reference markers, the most recent dating from 1685—two carp facing upstream, one with a lotus sprig in its mouth. The eyes of the fish were the zero point. Associated with the fourteen presently visible fish are 163 inscriptions, totaling in excess of 30,000 Chinese characters, many of which contain valuable information quite apart from water level observations, which typically took the form, "Water level is below the fish x feet. Date."

A tenth-century historical text reports that in A.D. 763, in the middle of the T'ang dynasty, unusually low water at White Crane Ridge exposed a carved fish, which the local inhabitants took as the harbinger of a good harvest. This fish, cut into the rock at some unknown earlier date, no longer exists, but its mention testifies to the development of regular navigation in the upper Long River, which is the only reason why low water observations would be wanted, since low water is a peril only to shipping, and does not threaten onshore activities as high water may. All up and down the Long River between Chungking and I-ch'ang and on major tributaries are water-level markers dating from the thousand years between the early years of the Sung dynasty (tenth century) and the end of the nineteenth century. The large number of high-water marking stations above the Three Gorges suggests that flooding may well have been more common in Szechwan than farther downstream. In the Three Gorges themselves, only in Hsi-ling are there many such markers, a fact that we can now understand: The rapids and shoals characteristic of Hsi-ling Gorge require more attention to water level than is the case in the other two, and hydrologic data would also be useful farther downstream, where the breadth of the river and the very low terrain makes such markers harder to establish and maintain.

We will be returning to the Three Gorges, as to the rest of the Long River, when we look more closely at migration, navigation, commerce, and history—in short at the flow of people, products, and human experience along this great artery.

PART II

SOCIAL TIME

A HISTORICAL AND REGIONAL RECONNAISSANCE

Time

The poet Tu Fu, writing at a time of devastating rebellion and dynastic crisis 1,200 years ago, set the following lines to paper:

> The state is shattered;
> Mountains and rivers remain.

Chinese through the ages have often contrasted man's ephemeral efforts with the seeming permanence of nature. It is a land the Chinese have known from time immemorial. Most evidence points to the conclusion that indigenous human evolution eventually produced Chinese culture and the Chinese people as we know them in historical times. Other peoples and other influences drifted in during paleolithic or neolithic times, outside influences continued throughout historical time, and aboriginal non-Chinese cultures also played their part. But what we call the Chinese people and Chinese culture seem to have developed in the area we call China. Thus the whole of Chinese civilization has been enacted on this single vast geographical stage. Even very early in their history, the Chinese were conscious of having occupied this land from time out of mind. A greater contrast with Americans, migrants to "the new world," could hardly be imagined.

A glance at a world map will show that until the age of modern communications, China was relatively remote from other centers of high culture, unlike the situation in the classical Mediterranean world, where quite different cultures were in constant contact and conflict with one another. To the east lay the trackless expanse of the Pacific; to the north, the steppes and deserts of Mongolia, giving way to Siberia. The nearly impenetrable Tibetan Plateau blocked access from the west, while the jungles and mountains of the southwest cut off that avenue. Only in the northwest was there a narrow corridor out of China, which then divided to follow the string of oases along the foot of either the northern T'ien-shan or southern K'un-lun mountains, thence over the Pamir Mountains to the Middle East and finally to Europe. These routes came to be known collectively as the Silk Road, across which this precious fabric was caravanned to the Roman Empire. This was also the path along which Buddhism was carried from India to China, beginning in the first century of our era. More than a thousand years later, Marco Polo made the same journey on his way to the court of the Mongol emperor, Kubla Khan. It was this northwestern corridor, not the seacoast, that the Chinese traditionally considered their front door.

Although China was by no means totally isolated from outside influences, Chinese civilization tended to develop—and was so perceived by the Chinese—indigenously, rather than out of interaction with other equally developed cultures elsewhere. As the Chinese looked about themselves, at the nomadic people to the north, at Korea, Japan, and Vietnam, they were convinced that China was the Middle Kingdom: superior, self-sufficient, the giver of civilization and its highest values. This conviction was neither surprising nor altogether unreasonable.

Like the white races in North America, the Chinese spread out over a continent, assimilating, driving out, or killing most of the peoples who stood in their way. But the Chinese conquest of China began in a past so distant that it is only now being reconstructed with the help of an archaeological explosion rivaling that of the Mediterranean world which began about a century ago.

Within this single vast geographical stage, layers of remembered time lie like geological strata on the land. There is hardly anyplace in China that does not carry deep historical associations, remains of some sort, memories. Our conception of Western civilization involves the idea of movement, and to retrace our heritage, we travel to Egypt, Greece and Rome, the Holy Land, Italy, France, England. We remember the brutalities of the slave trade, and Black Americans seek their roots in Africa. For the Chinese, it all happened here.

It was once thought that "Chinese culture" had its origins in a nuclear area in north China and spread out from there. More specifically, we believed that a distinctive cluster of traits developed among neolithic inhabitants of the Wei River Valley, in the vicinity of the modern city of Sian, and farther east on the North China Plain. These traits included settled, intensive agriculture, domestication of animals, the high development of ceramic and later bronze technology, strong kinship systems with the beginnings of ancestor worship, elaborate burial customs, and religious practices relying heavily on shamanism and divination. The culmination of these traits was to be found in the Shang "dynasty," roughly 1500–1000 B.C., of which the two most familiar artifacts are its magnificent bronzes and the "oracle bones," shoulder blades of animals and the carapaces of tortoises used for divination, upon which were incised the earliest examples of the Chinese written language.

According to the nuclear-area theory, these traits were spread by conquest, assimilation, migration, and simple diffusion or imitation. In this way, early Chinese culture gradually spread and became conscious of its differences from other cultural constellations, especially those based on the herding of animals. Meanwhile, of course, these traits were interacting with those of the peoples being encountered, gradually evolving toward those features we recognize as historic China.

The great archaelogical explosion of recent decades is showing this theory to be badly flawed. Indeed, so much new and striking material—comparable in importance to that discovered at Troy, Mycenae, Knossos—is coming to light in such pell-mell fashion that no one can fully comprehend it, let alone yet fashion a new and definitive explanation of Chinese origins. Nevertheless, some things seem clear.

Instead of a single core area of distinctively proto-Chinese culture, we now perceive a rich and untidy complexity. We begin to appreciate how much the early evolution of Chinese civilization was an amalgam of various and disparate elements from different regions of what we would now call China. It appears that there were many centers, each with some distinctive traits but sharing many other characteristics. Rather than the expansion of a single core, though the Wei River Valley and the North China Plain may have predominated, it was the growing together and the interaction of these several nuclei that shaped the development of early China.

This concept is important to our story of the Long River, because it changes our notion of what was central and what was peripheral. In the valleys and plains of central China, along the Long River, were several important centers of early civilization. From these centers came, for example, rice and silk, two products that we think of as inseparable from Chinese culture. If their stories had been recorded, inhabitants of the culture areas known as Ch'u (in the middle Yangtze, below the Gorges) and Wu (centered in the Yangtze delta region) might have claimed that *they* represented the finest flowering of a new civilization.

There is an irony here. The Chinese who produced China's earliest coherent written records during the first millenium B.C. themselves affirmed with pride their belief that they, the men of the Wei Valley and the North China Plain, members of the culture complex they called "Hua," alone represented high culture. All the rest were, they believed, barbarians, and very early a whole range of cultural stereotypes grew up. Thus, our twentieth-century acceptance of the core area theory has rested in part on the notions of men who lived 2,500 years ago. For these men of Hua, Ch'u and Wu were southern frontier regions toward which they felt a strong mixture of distaste, fear, and attraction. Some of these images, mingled with and overlaid by others, have persisted to the present.

Edward Schafer tells the story of a Hua nobleman, Ssu-ma Niu, exiled in 481 B.C. for some offense to the Yangtze delta region—the south was a frequent place of exile for outcast northerners—among people generically called "Man" who probably spoke tongues related to Thai or to Burmese and Tibetan:

> Doubtless Ssu-ma Niu endured some agony of spirit as he left his friends in the north to take up his life among the unknown strangers of the southeast. To him, as a Hua man, the Middle Kingdom was a beacon of civilization to the benighted heathen who inhabited the shadowy realms of both the north and the south. . . . The haughty minds of the early Hua men also envisioned the savage rice cultivators of the subtropical valleys as reptilian, slithering nastily on the dark southern frontier. A book already old in Ssu-ma Niu's time characterized the inhabitants of the central Yangtze basin:

> > How they writhed, the Man in Ching,
> > Playing the rival to our great domain!

Yet, at the same time, "it was a richly diversified landscape into which Ssu-ma Niu rode, very different from the monotonous yellow plains of the old country. . . . Strangely and fearfully attractive to him, this youthful land would become a realm of romance for his descendants, the home of rainbow goddesses, ecstatic priestesses and lotus-gathering girls." And the ancient book conceded that the southerners were "rivals to our great domain."

One often encounters this strange and fearful attraction. In the Analects, Confucius sounds like a modern parent inveighing against rock and roll: "Beware the songs of Ch'u, for they are licentious." And the greatest historian of early China, Ssu-ma Ch'ien, characterized the region, three centuries after Ssu-ma Niu's exile, as follows:

> A large territory, sparsely populated, where people eat rice and drink fish soup; where land is tilled with fire and hoed with water; where people collect fruits and shellfish for food; where people enjoy self-sufficiency without commerce. The place is fertile and suffers no famine or hunger. Hence the people are lazy and poor and do not bother to accumulate wealth.

In this southerly direction, there was no environmental boundary to stop the slow seepage of the Chinese and their ways of life. The lowlands and river basins were well-suited to intensive agriculture and to the development of towns and cities, and along these routes the Chinese gradually advanced. It comes as a surprise to realize that in the far southwestern provinces of Kweichow and Yunnan, this process is not yet quite finished, as the Han people continue to fill in what land is left, and the boundary between China to the north and Vietnam, Laos, Thailand, and Burma to the south is thus more an accident of recent political history than a geographical reality. (The term "Han" refers to ethnically Chinese people, as distinct from the non-Chinese minorities, of which there are more than fifty in China. The term derives from the name of the first long-lived Chinese dynasty, which extended from about 206 B.C. to A.D. 220. Today, Han people comprise about 95 percent of the total Chinese population.)

It is otherwise in the north. North China is dry enough to make intensive agriculture precarious. Farther north, toward Manchuria, Mongolia, and Central Asia, rainfall becomes increasingly scanty, growing seasons shorter. Finally, agriculture of any sort becomes impossible, except in oases at the feet of mountain ranges, and human life can be supported only by seasonal movement of animal herds across steppe grasslands.

Sheep (with some goats also) were the animals most frequently herded; camels were bred for caravanning, and large numbers of horses were raised to be ridden in work and war. Cattle were less often raised, because they could not easily be driven over long distances. As elsewhere in the world, the nomadic cycles were well-established seasonal movements along known routes, not unsystematic searches for water and pasture.

The Mongol herder and the Chinese peasant on the inner Asian frontier thus correspond to the cattle rancher and the sodbusting farmer on the western American frontier, each playing out its version of a perennial struggle between open spaces and parceled land. But the herder and the farmer—when they were not fighting—also depended upon one another. The Mongol herder needed the manufactures and the luxuries of the south, which his own mobility and lack of resources made impossible to produce. Grain was also needed to supplement meat, milk, and cheese in the diet. Conversely, the Chinese depended on the pastoralists for most of their horses, mules, and other draft animals. Wool, leather, and felt were other products that moved south. So, sometimes, did fighting skills and the tactics of mounted war.

Thus, along the inner Asian frontier of China lies a transitional zone across which Chinese ways become increasingly difficult and ultimately impossible to maintain. This frontier zone was historically—and remains today—the ragged edge of Chinese culture and society. Today, within this ill-defined zone, peoples are hodge-podged together—Chinese, Tibetans, Mongols, Uighurs, Salars, Kazakhs, and others—with all their linguistic and cultural diversity.

Viewed from this environmental perspective, the Great Wall—completed in the third century B.C. by the founder of the first unified imperial regime in Chinese history, the Ch'in dynasty, from which the very name China derives—can be seen as an attempt to impose a clear-cut and defensible boundary between what was inside and what was outside of China. In other words, the first emperor of Ch'in sought to overcome through an act of human will and enormous cruel investments of human labor the natural ambiguity of a transitional zone.

Beyond the Great Wall, beyond this frontier zone, Chinese political and military power could reach—if it were strong enough—but Chinese populations could not migrate there and still remain Chinese. Conversely, when Chinese outposts were weakly held, fierce mounted raiders could gallop south to prey on the farmers and rich cities of China proper. If the Chinese were unable to expel them, they might stay to exploit, perhaps even to rule, rather than simply loot and depart.

In contrast to the ever-expanding southern frontier, where much sporadic violence occurred but whence came no threats to Chinese rule in the larger sense, the northern frontier was always unstable, and there was always the dangerous possibility that nomadic peoples might form powerful leagues or coalitions. Such comings-together had often happened, and could take place with great rapidity, given a charismatic leader and the right circumstances along the frontier and in the Chinese heartland. The ebb and flow of power across the inner Asian frontier is one of the great dramatic themes of Chinese history—indeed, of world history.

Although we think of China as having been a unified realm from early times to the present, this is a distorted view, at least from a political perspective. For long periods of time, China was fragmented and partly or wholly under the rule of aliens from beyond the Great Wall. Even during the more powerful and unified of Chinese dynasties, control over the border marches was often shaky or worse.

A look at the accompanying chronology reveals that after nearly 500 years of the early empire (the brief but definitive Ch'in dynasty, followed by 400 years of the Han and a short-lived successor), there followed almost four centuries of fragmentation, when the north was lost in a welter of barbarian regimes, and a succession of genteel but not very powerful Chinese states held on in the lower Yangtze Valley.

The decline and fall of the Han bears an eerie similarity to the roughly contemporaneous decline and fall of Rome—a similarity so striking that Arnold Toynbee used it as evidence for a general (but fatally flawed) theory of the rise and fall of civilizations. Both Rome and China saw the influx of powerful and ruthless northern barbarians; the fall of Rome and of the Han dynasty seemed to herald the end of civilization as previously known; and these two collapses were not only political and military but also religious

HISTORICAL PERIODS

	Dynasties	Disunity	Unity	

B.C. / A.D.			
1200	SHANG		ANCIENT CHINA
1100	1122(?)		
1000			
900			
800			
700	CHOU		FEUDAL ERA
600			
500			
400			
300	CH'IN		
221	(Unification)		
206			EARLY EMPIRE
100			
0	HAN		
100			
200	222		
300	"SIX DYNASTIES" PERIOD		"NORTHERN AND SOUTHERN STATES"
400			
500	SUI		
589	(Unification of second empire)		
618			
700	T'ANG		MIDDLE EMPIRE
800			
900	907		
1000	No. Sung		
1100	1127 — SUNG		
1200	So. Sung		LATE EMPIRE
1279	YUAN (Mongols)		
1368			
1500	MING		
1600			
1644			
1700	CH'ING (Manchus)		
1800			
1900	1912 REPUBLIC		
1949	PEOPLES REPUBLIC		

Principal periods and dynasties. The sidelines indicate periods of unified rule and periods of disunity.

and moral crises. Rome was Christianized, China turned to Buddhism. In attenuated and altered ways, Byzantium maintained the traditions of the Roman Empire; the southern dynasties performed a somewhat similar function in China.

Unlike Europe, where the Holy Roman Empire was but a faint echo of Rome's glory, China's medieval period was one of the most powerful and resplendent eras of her history. Once again a short unifying dynasty (the Sui) was followed by a powerful and long-lived inheritor—the T'ang. In many ways, the T'ang was even more glorious an era than the Han had been, but after roughly two centuries, its lustre was rapidly dimming. By the end of the T'ang, the frontier marches were virtually independent, and the succeeding Sung dynasty was never able to solve its border problems. In the twelfth century, frontier defenses collapsed. North China fell once again into the hands of barbarians, this time from the region we today call Manchuria, and once again a refugee Chinese regime—the Southern Sung—was driven south to the lower Yangtze, the lands of Ch'u and Wu, where it made its "temporary" capital in the lovely city of Hangchow.

After the Southern Sung—the late empire—there were interregna but never again a long period of disunity. Ironically, however, this unity was twice imposed by non-Chinese peoples from beyond the Wall: the Mongols of Genghis and Kubla Khan, to whose court came Marco Polo; and then the last dynasty, and in some ways the culmination of the imperial process, the Manchu Ch'ing dynasty, which occupied the Dragon Throne from 1644 until 1911, when—in one of history's greatest not-with-a-bang anticlimaxes—the abdication of a six-year-old boy emperor ended not only that dynasty but all dynasties, and more than 2,000 years of imperial history came to an end. These two alien dynasties—the Yuan (1279–1368) and the Ch'ing (1644–1911)—were the only two periods of foreign rule over *all* of China.

This very brief chronological survey introduces the names of the principal dynastic periods, and provides a reference chart, since I will be moving back and forth in time through most of the essays in this book. Periods of disunity also influence the story directly, since it was under the impact of barbarian onslaughts that Chinese influence was pushed into the Yangtze Valley more rapidly and forcibly than would otherwise have been the case. Indeed, during the three and a half centuries between the Han and the T'ang, refugee populations and exile dynasties so developed the lower basins of the Long River that by the time of the Sui-T'ang unification this region had replaced the North China Plain as the economic center, the grain basket, of China. A similar developmental pulsation took place again during the Southern Sung dynasty—approximately A.D. 1100 to 1300—when the north was lost to the Chin, before both were overwhelmed by the Mongol hordes of Genghis Khan and his grandson, Kubla.

Space

If historical time is marked by the rise and fall of dynasties, historical space is shaped by the large regions into which China is more or less naturally divided by mountains, rivers, and other geographical realities. We saw some of the beginnings of this regionalism in the exile of Ssu-ma Niu to the exotic and menacing lands of the lower Long River, then the southern frontier. By the time of the T'ang dynasty (the Middle Empire) the southern frontier had receded to the Yun-Kwei and Lingnan regions, and most of the Yangtze Valley was well into the process of domestication to Chinese population and Chinese ways. By the late empire, particularly the two last dynasties—the Ming and the Ch'ing, covering together five and a half centuries—one could discern with some clarity eight large regions. Each of these regions, larger than all but the largest of our states, of course contained many distinctive smaller regions within it, but was nevertheless oriented toward a regional "core" more heavily populated, more prosperous, and more developed in general than the increasingly peripheral areas around it. In most regions, the cores were related to river systems. In these river basins and valleys one finds plains and bottom lands more extensive and fertile than anywhere in the uplands or mountains of the surrounding terrain. The rivers bring abundant and dependable water for irrigation and other human uses, though floods may threaten and sometimes devastate.

In many areas, and certainly throughout the Long River and its tributary systems, rivers offer cheaper and more convenient transport than any other mode. Indeed, as we shall see in the next chapter, these river systems were major migration routes along which the Chinese people spread and in whose valleys they settled. It is thus no accident that China's largest cities have always been located in the regional cores, mostly near important rivers—as is the case, of course, in many other societies.

The regions differ greatly among themselves, in almost every way—climate, resource endowment, size, population, prosperity. *Chiang-nan* (South of the River), that rich, varied, and lovely lower Yangtze region containing Hangchow and Suchow, is no more similar to the Yun-Kwei plateau of the far southwest than the Mississippi delta is similar to Arizona and New Mexico. Because the regions are characterized by complex economies of their own, their cycles of prosperity or decline may differ from those of other regions. But the three very large macroregions making up the basin of the Long River, among the most important in all China, are strung together more closely than any others because of the river that flows through them.

One might reasonably suppose that China's provincial boundaries would follow the natural geographic realities defining these macroregions. To some extent they do, but the fit is too imperfect to permit simple correspondence, just as is the case with state boundaries in the U.S. Chinese provinces are as much the result of administrative convenience, political accident, horse-trading, and local tradition as are the states of the United States. Furthermore, the macroregions are too large to be governed by single administrative units—the eight macroregions cover the area of eighteen provinces. It is not unusual therefore to find provincial boundaries crosscutting or subdividing natural geographic zones.

Major cities are, however, almost always important administrative centers, with lesser cities and towns playing their roles as regional or county seats. Occasionally here too there are misfits, where a smaller and economically less important city occupies a higher place in the administrative scheme of things (or vice versa), but this is less common in China than in the United States, where many states have deliberately chosen a capital that is not economically the most important city, to prevent that city from also having dominant political power, e.g. Albany vs. New York, Springfield vs. Chicago, etc. When this happens, as it does only rarely in China (e.g., Chengtu vs. Chungking in Szechwan province), it is because of accidents of geography and history, not because of deliberate policy.

We can envision, then, the patterning of space in late imperial China from two perspectives, understanding that the two overlap and interact in important ways. The first is the natural pattern imposed by geography, resources, trade, and the accumulated effects of myriad daily or seasonal decisions of millions of people over long stretches of time. This pattern seems to grow from the bottom up, following a natural common sense and manifested in actual behavior. The second is a top-down administrative and political pattern, self-consciously imposed, in which each locale occupies a discrete place.

Influences growing out of one system permeate the other, but by no means always harmoniously. As we shall see, for example, in Chapter 11, when we consider important development projects that have profound economic and regional consequences and are at the same time controversial political and administrative issues—especially the stupendous Three Gorges Dam and plans to divert Yangtze River water hundreds of miles to the North China Plain, to Tientsin and Peking—regional and provincial interests come into conflict as often as they cooperate.

5

MIGRATION AND SETTLEMENT: PEOPLE ON THE MOVE, PEOPLE AT REST

China generates paradox. The Chinese are renowned for their attachment to place, their deep identification with native soil. And yet whenever one looks at Chinese history one finds people everywhere on the move. Migration is part of this movement, the permanent transfer of people from one region to another, sometimes pushed out of their original homeland by overpopulation, poverty, disaster, or war, and sometimes attracted to new lands by real or presumed opportunities for betterment of their lives.

But migrants were not the only travelers across the Chinese landscape. Merchants big and small set forth on business trips; Buddhist monks and devout layfolk made pilgrimages or sought centers of learning; scholars aspiring to prestigious careers in the imperial civil service headed for provincial capitals or Peking to take the most fiendishly demanding examinations ever devised. Officials took up their posts across the far-flung realm, and some were exiled for real or alleged offenses to the most remote and dangerous corners of the empire; corvee labor gangs were sent to work on canals or defensive walls; boatmen and transport coolies moved the goods of the empire; one might even spot a rare travel buff exploring his world out of curiosity or scholarly interest. There were foreign traders, Japanese and Korean monks who had come to learn from Chinese Buddhist masters, ambassadors and their retinues, entertainers, bandits, fugitives. In wartime, armies were on the march. Rebel hordes, angry and desperate peasants headed by ambitious or megalomaniac leaders with their own dynastic dreams, followed the same routes as migrants, merchants, and scholars. In the mid-1960s, during the Cultural Revolution, urban youth went on an orgy of hitherto prohibited travel, sanctioned by Mao Tse-tung's revolutionary dictum to "exchange revolutionary experience"; later, beginning in 1969, some fourteen million of these urban youth were sent—whether they wanted to go or not—to the countryside to "learn from the peasants."

Routes

Before the era of modern roads and railways, rivers (and later canals) were everywhere major avenues of continental travel. In China, as we have already seen, river basins were also most favorable to settlement and agricultural development; as a result, they became the heartlands of the regions through which they flowed. In short, rivers both transported people and were the destinations of those who came first and could occupy the fertile bottom lands. Later arrivals pushed their way up tributaries; still later migrants, usually desperately poor, could find space only in the remote highlands, scratching out a living through precarious agriculture, lumbering, mining, banditry, and rebellion.

But unlike roads, which at least in principle can be built wherever needed, rivers are where they are. Although the Chinese did not always accept this verdict of nature—vide the Grand Canal—the fundamental fact is that the major river systems of China flow from west to east: the Yellow River in the north, the Yangtze in the center, and the West River system in south China, with its confluence near Canton. Yet the expansion of the Chinese people took a southerly as well as a horizontal, east-west direction, and in this southerly movement, the many tributaries of the Yangtze River system played a major role.

In late January A.D. 809, a man named Li Ao departed with family (including his pregnant wife), baggage, and servants from the eastern capital, Loyang, on a tributary of the Yellow River. Li Ao is best known to history as a scholar, philosopher, and poet, but like so many of the educated elite throughout Chinese history, he was also an official of the imperial government, having succeeded in those difficult civil service examinations that were the most prestigious route to such service. Li Ao was leaving to take up an official post in the far south, in present-day Kwangsi province on the Vietnamese border. In T'ang times this was the southern frontier, and northerners viewed it as their ancestors had once viewed the now better settled and familiar Yangtze Valley, as a lush and sensuous but half-civilized and dangerous land.

From Loyang, Li and his retinue followed the Grand Canal—called at this time the Pien Canal—eastward, then southward into the ambit of the Yangtze Valley. In mid-March, he reached Yangchow, that wealthy and colorful trading center where the Grand Canal joins the north bank of the Yangtze River. Li Ao's itinerary from Loyang to Yangchow followed the easternmost of several routes out of north China into the Yangtze watershed.

Although Li Ao followed the Grand Canal, his approximate route could also be accomplished overland, since the North China Plain gradually gives way southward to level or gently rolling terrain, with no pronounced barriers to passage. The principal obstacles to easy movement were lakes and marshes which expanded or contracted with the season or according to periodic fluctuations of rainfall. Most of these marshes were the product of the Huai River and its tributaries, which lay about halfway between the Yellow and the Yangtze rivers. The Huai is a most unusual river, since during most of its history it had no clear outlet to the sea, either draining into Hung-tse Lake (Big Marsh Lake) and other swampy lakes or finding an indeterminate route to the sea. Sometimes, indeed, these waters drained southward into the Yangtze River.

As these routes neared the Yangtze, they split into an inverted Y, the eastern branch continuing on into the delta and beyond, toward present-day Soochow and Hangchow. The western branch led southwestward, whence the traveler could either head upriver or continue—as Li Ao did—his southward journey.

Like the Low Countries in Europe, this area provided no natural defenses, and these easy routes connecting the most productive plains of north and central China were much fought over throughout Chinese history. "This is a place over which north and south must fight," said one commentator, sounding a familiar warning. "If we hold it, we can advance to capture Shantung, but if the enemy seizes it, we can lose everything south of the Huai between morning and evening."

The second route, farther to the west, led from the old capital districts around present-day Sian (Ch'ang-an in T'ang times) or Loyang over the rugged Ch'in-ling divide into the upper waters of the Han River. From Sian, it was about ninety difficult miles, up and over a 7,000-foot pass, some of it on a plank road stuck into cliff walls. No wonder there were more than sixty rest stations along the North Gallery Road. The routes from Ch'ang-an and Loyang joined at the important river-junction city of Hsiang-yang. From that point, it was an easy journey down the Han River to its junction with the Long River at the Wuhan cities. Not far upstream and downstream from Wuhan are the two major tributaries flowing into the Long River from the south, the Hsiang and the Kan rivers, which are the two major routes to the south. We shall soon return to these two important rivers.

The third and most westerly route from north China into the Long River's watershed was the most difficult of all—which should not surprise us when we recall how elevations increase and terrain becomes ever more rugged the farther west one goes. This route depended on a terribly difficult road over steep mountain ranges into the enclosed Szechwan Basin. In what sounds like poetic hyperbole but was not, the T'ang poet Li Po wrote of this road:

> Eheu! How dangerous, how high!
> It would be easier to climb to Heaven
> Than walk the Szechwan Road
> . . . they made sky-ladders and hanging bridges—

Above, high beacons of rock that turn back the chariot of the sun,
Below, whirling eddies that meet the clashing torrent and turn it
away

Li Po's "sky-ladders" are gallery or trestle roads, found along the most
precipitous parts of this route—fully one-third of its 270-mile length—and
on other difficult passages, such as the one just described above. A millenium
after Li Po, in the 1650s, they were described by the Frenchman Louis
Lecomte:

> . . . upon the side of some Mountains which are perpendicular
> and have no shelving they have fixed large beams into them,
> upon which beams they have made a sort of Balcony without
> rails, which reaches thro' several Mountains in that fashion; those
> who are not used to these sort of Galeries, travel over them in a
> great deal of pain, afraid of some ill accident or other.

Once he came down off the sky-ladders into northern Szechwan, Li Po
had much easier going on the road system or the many navigable rivers of
that province, draining south toward Chengtu, Chungking, or the Long
River itself. These roads illustrate how closely the Chinese integrated their
road and river systems, and how access to riverine routes justified even the
most arduous overland links.

All-Rivers Weir (Tu-chiang Yen)

As Li Po approached the "Damask City" of Chengtu, the greatest city of
western China until the recent development of Chungking, he passed by
the most remarkable irrigation system in world history prior to the modern
age. If he visited the site, as he very likely did, he may have seen a stone
statue of a certain Li Ping standing in one of its main channels.

This was the irrigation system that made, and still makes today, the
Chengtu plain the most fertile area in all China. The system is called *Tu-
chiang Yen* (All-Rivers Weir), and it was designed and put into operation in
the third century B.C. It has been in continuous use ever since, for over 2,200
years. Joseph Needham comments that this "irrigation system made it possible for an area of some 40 by 50 miles to support a population of about five
million people, most of them engaged in farming, and free from the dangers
of drought and floods. It can be compared only with the ancient works of
the Nile."

The layout of All-Rivers Weir is attributed to Li Ping, who also began
work on the project, later to be finished by his son, Li the Younger. Almost
nothing of a personal nature is reliably known of Li Ping, except that he was
sent by the state of Ch'in to govern Szechwan a couple of decades before

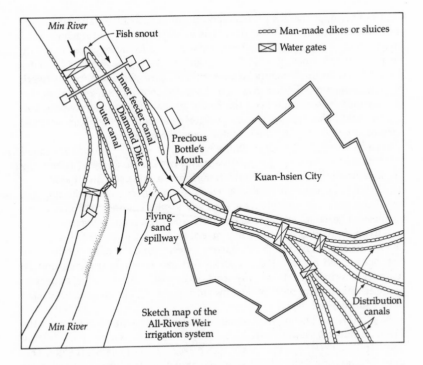

Min River

Fish snout

Inner feeder canal

Diamond Dike

Outer canal

oooo Man-made dikes or sluices

Water gates

Precious Bottle's Mouth

Kuan-hsien City

Flying-sand spillway

Distribution canals

Min River

Sketch map of the All-Rivers Weir irrigation system

FIGURE 5-1. Plan of All-Rivers Weir (Tu-chiang Yen), showing major design features.

the Ch'in unification of China under the first emperor. This was not the only major engineering work he undertook during his stay in Szechwan, but this project alone is sufficient witness to Li Ping's genius.

The location he chose for Tu-chiang Yen lies about thirty-five miles north-west of Chengtu, in a beautiful setting where the heavily forested Greenwall Mountains (*Ch'ing-ch'eng Shan*) rise abruptly, almost without foothills, from the gently sloping plain. The topynym reflects its importance: *Kuan-hsien*— "Irrigation County." Natural beauty was not, however, the reason Li Ping chose this spot in about 240 B.C. Here the Min River debouches from the mountains onto the plain, before flowing southward toward its junction with the Long River at I-pin, picking up other large tributaries on its way. So impressive is the Min River that, as we have seen, most Chinese once thought it, rather than the River of Golden Sand, was the true headstream of the Long River. Like other rivers in this region, the volume of water in the Min varies greatly with the season, from summer's floods to winter's low water.

Li Ping's problem was how to regulate the flow of water to the fertile

Chengtu Plain, so that the proper amount would be available all year round, regardless of the flow in the river. His solution, one requiring both bold imagination and a sophisticated understanding of hydrology, was to divide the river into an inner channel and an outer channel (see Figure 5-1). Water diverted into the inner channel would enter an intricate, fan-shaped network of increasingly subdivided irrigation channels, an artery supplying smaller and smaller vessels until even the finest capillaries might receive the life-giving fluid. The outer channel—the original bed of the river—carried surplus water, bypassing the irrigated regions altogether.

As a first step, Li Ping divided the waters by a wedge-shaped jetty called "Fish Snout" (*Yü-tsui*) at the upstream end of "Diamond Dike" (*Chin-kang t'i*), a crescent-shaped islet in midstream, much reinforced with stone embankments. To make this solution work, however, one has to assure that about the same amount of water enters the inner channel year round, regardless of seasonal changes in the river. Li Ping's boldly elegant solution was to slice a vertical gateway in a steep, rocky cliff near the lower end of Diamond Dike. It is through this narrow gateway that the waters of the inner channel are led off into the network of irrigation canals crisscrossing the plain. Appropriately named "Precious Bottle's Mouth" (*Pao-p'ing k'ou*), this opening admits 60 percent of the flow during low water, but only 40 percent or less during high water.

Nor is this all. During high water, the surplus flow that cannot enter the Precious Bottle's Mouth is shunted back to the outer channel via "Flying Sand Spillway" (*Fei-sha Yen*), at the downstream end of Diamond Dike. This periodic shunting action flushes out accumulated sand and silt, preventing

Perspective view of All-Rivers Weir, from a contemporary Chinese tourism brochure.

it from eventually clogging Precious Bottle's Mouth. Finally, after the waters of the inner channel pass through the Precious Bottle's Mouth into the irrigation network, a complex system of weirs, sluices, and watergates regulates its subsequent distribution, so each part of the system receives its due share.

Li Ping left a simple but crucial injunction to his descendants, in the form of an inscription cut in a stone cliff overlooking his engineering masterpiece: "Dig deep the channels, keep low the embankments." With this advice Li Ping was stressing the importance of keeping the channels clear and condemning the thought that higher dikes could compensate for inadequate dredging. For the most part, this advice has been faithfully followed. It is astonishing to realize that through all the vicissitudes of Chinese history, Tu-chiang Yen was almost continuously maintained—sometimes better or less well, but maintained nevertheless.

Since the present government came to power in 1949, refinements have been added and irrigated acreage has been considerably enlarged, but the fundamental design of the system has remained unchanged since Li Ping's day. And then, in 1974, one of the gangs assigned to "dig deep the channel" discovered a stone statue of Li Ping, 9.5 feet high, lying in the bed of the inner channel. Inscriptions indicate that the statue was emplaced in A.D. 168, about four hundred years after Li Ping's death. The statue did double duty: to memorialize the creator of Tu-chiang Yen, and to act as a water-level gauge.

Routes to the Deep South and the Miracle Canal (Ling Ch'ü)

Sixty years after Li Po's acrophobic lament and a thousand miles farther east, Li Ao and his family were resting for a few days in bustling and prosperous Yangchow. In mid-March A.D. 809, they set out via one of the two major routes to the south. From Yangchow, they traveled up the Long River past Nanking, as far as Lake P'o-yang, the more easterly of the two great lakes of central China. This lake is formed by the confluence of the Kan River with the Long River, a lake that expands and recedes with the seasons, a rich ecological zone upon which centuries of peasants have gradually encroached to reclaim fertile rice fields from the surrounding marshes.

Across this lake sailed Li Ao and his family, thence proceeding upriver to the headwaters of the Kan, across a low pass named after the Great Yü, the legendary flood-tamer and mythic culture hero, marking the divide that separates the Yangtze drainage system from that flowing south toward Canton. South of the pass, with his new daughter—his wife had given birth on May 6, six weeks earlier—the group entered the North River, which they followed south to reach Canton on July 25, six months after their departure from Loyang. Almost the entire journey had been made by water.

The other major route south, even more important than the one Li Ao took, lies farther west. Superficially it resembles the Kan River route, in that it follows a major river with a very large and seasonally variable lake at its mouth. But both the lake (Tung-t'ing, once China's largest) and the river (the Hsiang) are larger and more extensively navigable than their more easterly counterparts. The Hsiang also flows through richer agricultural regions, a region known as "the land of fish and rice."

An astonishing feat of engineering lies near the headwaters of the Hsiang River: the world's earliest contour transport canal, that is, one which follows land contours of the same or nearly the same elevation as a way through higher terrain which would otherwise block passage. This is the Ling-ch'ü—the aptly named Miracle Canal—which connects the north-flowing Hsiang with the south-flowing Kwei River, thus linking the two watersheds and enabling continuous riverine communication from north China all the way to Canton. The project was conceived and executed during the first imperial dynasty, the Ch'in, in the late third century B.C., with elaborations and improvements in later dynasties. This means it was almost exactly contemporary with All-Rivers Weir, half a continent to the northwest.

The reputed architect of the Miracle Canal was Shih Lu—of whom, like Li Ping, we know nothing else—who was ordered by the first emperor of Ch'in to open a conquest route to the south. Historical records tell us that two centuries later the waterway was improved, again to serve strategic needs associated with military operations as far-ranging as modern Vietnam. After a period of neglect, it was further dredged and improved during the T'ang period, when simple one-gate flash locks were first introduced. By the twelfth century (Sung dynasty), a whole series of conventional two-gate locks (pound locks) had been installed. Despite the original military purpose of the canal, its day-to-day use as a transport artery was its main importance, and for this purpose, it could in T'ang times accommodate barges of up to 35 tons capacity. This and the more easterly route followed by Li Ao were avenues not only for staples but for all the special products and exotica of the south as well—hardwoods, aromatics, copper and tin, cinnabar, "opulence of teeth, hides, feathers, furs; profits in fish, salt, clams, cockles."

As early as 200 B.C., the Miracle Canal was, as Joseph Needham has noted, a key link in "a single trunk waterway extending from the 40th to the 22nd parallel of latitude, that is to say a distance of some 1,250 miles in a direct line." Although the Miracle Canal fell into decay during certain periods, it seems always to have been put back into service. Like All-Rivers Weir, it has thus been in almost continuous service for more than 2,000 years. Today, however, with the main trunk railway between Hankow and Canton following the same route, the Miracle Canal carries no cargo but finds a more limited utility as an irrigation system for the surrounding area.

The otherwise anonymous Shih Lu devised an elegant plan for crossing the watershed, one that demonstrates the same broad repertoire of land surveying and engineering skills employed by Li Ping (see Figure 5-2). Boats were worked up the Hsiang to the man-made Northern Channel, created as an easier alternative to the natural channel. Where the Northern Channel and the natural river reunite in a widened pool, the waters are divided by a wedge-shaped jetty—again the same principle as All-Rivers Weir—to flow into both the Northern Channel and the Southern Channel, the latter being the passage to the Li River and thence southward. Overflow water is guided back into the Hsiang's original channel below the divide via spillways behind the wedge-shaped jetty and along the Southern Channel.

The Southern Channel is guided through the small town of Hsing-an and onward for about three miles along a contour-level route, the channel faced with dressed stone. It then joins a headwaters tributary of the Li River, only a few meters lower in elevation than the head of the canal. Here the Li River has also been improved—"semi-canalized"—for another seventeen miles. Not far below the Miracle Canal lies the fabled beauty spot of Kweilin, with its karst formations thrust up from a lush and fertile plain. Well into the twentieth century, Kweilin was the provincial capital of Kwangsi province, in part because of its location near the Miracle Canal.

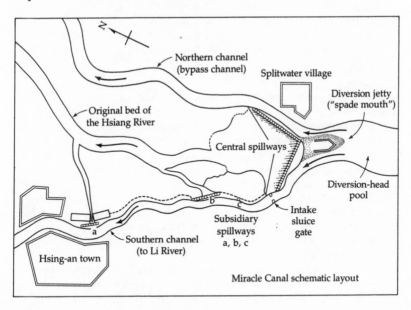

FIGURE 5-2. Plan of Miracle Canal (Ling-ch'ü).

Migration

The Kan and the Hsiang were the major routes southward, but they were not the only ones. Indeed, nearly all of the southern tributaries of the Long River were used to penetrate the low-lying hinterlands through which they flowed. This expansion was then followed by infilling or internal colonization that took place over the centuries at the expense of aboriginal peoples; yet even today this process is not complete. Groups of these peoples still survive—Miao, Yao, Lolo, Yi, and others—some in substantial numbers. In the far southwestern provinces of Yunnan and Kweichow, remote areas away from rail lines and major cities are even today not yet very deeply sinicized.

Motives for migration reduce themselves to the forces pushing people out of their present location and the attractions pulling them elsewhere. In China, the pull operated more or less continuously, the push more spasmodically. As the scholar Herold Weins wrote,

> No doubt the psychological appeal of the southern rice regions has had its influence in effecting a continuous migration southward. Since the earliest days the south has been regarded as a granary for the north, and in this manner, the north early became a parasite on the south. First the grain of Szechwan was drawn upon to support northern political and military power. This became especially significant after the construction of the Grand Canal.

Conquest and pacification also played a major role, as armies opened new lands for settlers to follow behind, or as soldiers settled permanently where they were demobilized. Many towns and villages on the expanding southern frontier are named "fort," "camp," "garrison," "peace," "settled," etc.

The greatest "push" forces came from major invasions of northern people, forcing mass migrations southward. The earliest such breakthrough took place after the collapse of the first long period of imperial unity, the Ch'in-Han Era of more than 400 years (ca. 200 B.C.-A.D. 200). As we have already remarked, this collapse and the subsequent breakthrough of northern barbarians was the Chinese equivalent of the fall of the Roman Empire and the sack of Rome by the Visigoths in A.D. 410, a profound crisis at once military, political, moral, and psychological.

The next great breakthrough came in the eleventh and twelfth centuries, when north China was threatened by the Khitan people (the Liao dynasty, centered in eastern Inner Mongolia and western Manchuria) and then lost to the Jurchen tribes—ancestors, probably, of the Manchus who ruled China in the last of the imperial dynasties. The rulers of the Sung dynasty made a fatal error in seeking the help of the more distant Jurchen to attack their nearer enemies, the Khitan. The Jurchen, happy to oblige, not only demolished the Liao dynasty on China's outer frontier, but then marched—or rather, rode—straight into north China, driving the Sung Court and a huge refugee populace to the south, where a "temporary" capital was established in Hangchow. In north China, the Jurchen established a Chinese-type dynasty called Chin (Gold), but they were unable to unify all of China under their sway.

Another large conquest migration accompanied the Mongol invasion of China in the second half of the thirteenth century. Although Genghis Khan (A.D. 1167–1227) did not himself live to see the subjugation of Sung China under the Mongol Yuan dynasty—of which his grandson, Kubla Khan, was the best-known emperor (Great Khan, A.D. 1260–1294, reigned over all of China after A.D. 1279)—he laid the foundation of the greatest territorial empire in history. Sung China, by reputation among the less militarily powerful of the major dynasties, was nevertheless the most difficult of all the enemies the Mongols faced from Eastern Europe to the Pacific—partly because in the lakes, rivers, and marshes of the Yangtze Basin their horses and their tactics of high-speed mounted warfare were almost useless. The principal path of invasion followed one of the routes we have already described: over the Ch'in-ling Mountains and down the Han River.

Chinese resistance was symbolized by the seige of Hsiang-yang, which controlled the middle Han River and hence secured access to the middle and lower Yangtze. It took the Mongols five years to capture the city and end Chinese resistance. Both sides used enormous catapults, some requiring a hundred men to operate, and both sides also employed gunpowder though not with decisive effect.

One more conquest dynasty was yet to come. This was the last of the imperial dynasties, the Ch'ing, which exercised its sway from 1644 into our own twentieth century, until 1911. These conquerors of China were Manchu people whose ancestors had been hunters in the forests of Manchuria, rather than mounted, nomadic peoples like the Mongols. In their triumph over the Chinese Ming dynasty (1368–1644), they emulated many of the features of Chinese rule, and for the most part they were accepted as culturally legitimate, despite being ethnically alien to China.

The Ch'ing conquest and subsequent rule illustrates another type of migration in China, one in which opposite ends of the Yangtze Valley were key locales. Thus far, we have discussed what might be called "expansive" and "consolidative" migrations, the former referring to the outward movement of large numbers of Chinese into territory they had not previously settled, rather resembling the westward expansion of the white race across the North American continent. Consolidative migration fills in the spaces left behind expansive migration.

A third sort of movement, recurrent throughout Chinese history but particularly visible during the Ch'ing dynasty, can be termed "replacement" migration. In this case, a settled population is so decimated by famine, disease, war, or rebellion—or some combination of these—that serious underpopulation results: few are left to cultivate the fields, while cities are ravaged and largely deserted. Into this partial vacuum come new populations, replacing the dead and often surpassing earlier population levels. The history of Szechwan province demonstrates both consolidative and replacement migration.

Today, Szechwan is China's most populous province, consisting of about 110,000,000 people. If Szechwan were an independent nation, it would possess the seventh largest population in the world, exceeded only by the rest of China, India, the USSR, the USA, Brazil, and Japan. Since early times, Szechwan has always been a part of China proper, yet even late into China's imperial history, the Szechwan Basin and the upper Yangtze region were only lightly inhabited. About A.D. 1640, with the Ming dynasty about to fall and the Manchu conquest about to roll over China, Szechwan contained perhaps five million people.

For the next forty years, warfare became a way of life in Szechwan. First came the depredations of a murderous invading warlord, then the ruthless Manchu armies determined to crush all resistance. By about A.D. 1680, the province was finally "pacified," but only about two million survived; one is reminded of Tacitus's sad comment on the Roman conquest of Britain, "They make desolation, which they call peace." The richest areas of the regional core were worst affected, and whole cities were turned into ghost towns.

During the following three centuries, Szechwan came to be populated far beyond its previous highs by steady immigration from other parts of China (as well as from natural increase): 9 million in 1750, 27 million in 1850, and 64 million in 1980.

About three centuries also elapsed between the landing on Plymouth Rock in 1620 and the addition of Arizona, the forty-eighth state, in 1912. During these three hundred years, voluntary immigrants from Europe (along with involuntary immigrants from Africa and semi-voluntary immigrants from Asia) extended their sway across the North American continent. The Chinese, too, spread out across a continent. But their expansion took thousands of years, not hundreds, and was accomplished by people originating in those lands, not by long-distance immigrants. Throughout Chinese history, movement has continued, sometimes facilitated and sometimes obstructed by the natural pattern of major rivers and their tributaries. In all this movement, the Yangtze River system has played a central role.

THE GRAND CANAL

Canals and walls, like *yin* and *yang*, are correlative opposites. The canal, yin-like, is dug into the earth and is filled with water; the wall rises boldly yang-like, open to sun and sky. Walls were meant to defend against outsiders, to stop movement, to divide within from without. Canals, on the other hand, are made to move things and to link one region with another. The predominant direction of the Great Wall is east-west; that of the Grand Canal, north-south.

In China, both canal- and wall-building began very early, sometime in the first millenium B.C., and both were recurrently undertaken throughout Chinese history. Each culminated in a massive accomplishment, one the Great Wall, the other the Grand Canal, that built on earlier foundations. Each was also the product of a powerful but short-lived dynasty that exhausted itself in conquest and public works and in imposing a unity it unintentionally bequeathed to its usurping successor. The Great Wall, completed by the Ch'in dynasty in the third century B.C., could not save that violent and spectacularly authoritarian regime from its own excesses and defects, but it subsequently did much to protect the Han and to help achieve a pax Sinica of nearly four centuries.

The Grand Canal was not completed and put into operation until nearly eight centuries later. After 350 years of disunity and a welter of barbarian regimes in North China, the Sui dynasty managed in A.D. 589 to impose unified Chinese rule once again—although in the blood of the ruling Yang clan were admixtures from vigorous northern tribes. The Sui emperor Yang-ti completed the Grand Canal, much as the first emperor of Ch'in had completed the Great Wall, as part of his grandiose program of war and construction.

During the three and a half centuries following the collapse of the Han dynasty, the basin of the Long River witnessed many changes. As we have seen, the barbarian breakthrough of the early fourth century caused initial panic, sustained violence, and an ongoing southern migration of Chinese elites and ordinary folk into the three large regions strung out along the Yangtze and its major tributaries: (1) the upper river, centered on the Szechwan Basin; (2) the middle river around the modern provinces of Hunan and Hupei, particularly the regions drained by the Han, Hsiang, and Kan rivers; and (3) the lower Yangtze, from about Nanking eastward to the sea.

The Szechwan Basin was fertile and productive, but because of its isolated geographic location it served better as a refuge, a haven in exile, than as a base from which to play a strategically central role in empire-wide struggles for supremacy. The middle Yangtze *was* strategically important and had great economic potential, but it was not yet "the land of fish and rice" that it later became. Of the broad lowlands near the Long River and its major tributaries, many were marshy and unhealthful; only after centuries of human effort did this area come fully into its own during the last two imperial dynasties. Even so, its remoter areas were still—and to a degree are still today—a kind of interior frontier, on the fringes of state and society and containing only partially assimilated minority peoples.

The Lower Yangtze: Grain Basket of China

By the sixth century A.D. the lower Yangtze region, favored by fertile land and a benign climate, had already undergone much settlement and agricultural development. Settlement had been greatly accelerated by the barbarian invasions farther north, and it was in this region that a succession of six Chinese dynasties sought to keep alive the guttering candle of tradition and legitimacy they claimed to have inherited from the Han and their immediate predecessors. Although they professed a longing to return to their homeland in the north, in fact they gradually adapted to life in the lower Yangtze and in the hinterlands under Chinese control, and at the same time they increasingly domesticated the Yangtze Valley. The outer frontier was now beyond the Miracle Canal and south of the Lingnan divide that separated the Yangtze watershed from that of the West River.

As the Sui rulers surveyed their newly unified domain, they knew that north China, their own bailiwick and the region in which they planned to establish their capital, was no longer the grain basket of the empire. Over the centuries since the Han, the economic center of gravity had gradually but definitively shifted southward to the Yangtze Basin, and particularly to the lower Yangtze. The early advantages of the north—a large population, effective irrigation and drainage works, and the relative ease of cultivating loess-lands and the North China Plain—had by now been lost. This was partly the result of war and migration, which devastated the north and decimated its population. But it was inevitable sooner or later in any case, because of the abundant rainfall, longer growing season, and fertile soil resources of the Yangtze Valley. Once sufficient labor was available to spread and intensify rice culture, to reclaim ever-growing acreage from marsh or rivers' edges, to engineer and emplace the terraces that turned hillsides into level land, there could be no question that the lower Yangtze region would become China's key economic area. It has remained that ever since, adding commercial to agricultural development, and, finally, industrial capacity. In the nineteenth and twentieth centuries, Shanghai came to represent this many-sided primacy, but in the sixth century, only farming and fishing villages existed in the region.

There was therefore a growing gap between political power and economic resources, the former remaining in the north and the latter centered in the lower Yangtze. Two solutions seemed possible: either move the capital south or move the grain north. Neither the the Sui nor, with two brief exceptions, any of its successors up to the present day gave serious consideration to a voluntary move south. This location was partly a matter of tradition; both the Ch'in and Han, the very paradigms of unified rule, had had their capitals in the north, in the vicinity of present-day Sian, or farther east, near modern Loyang.

But there were also practical reasons for the Sui and its successors to stay in the north. Their own base of power lay in the north, and it would have been folly to cut their roots and move into unfamiliar regions. At least equally important, the most serious threats to their rule came always from across the inner Asian frontier to the north.

Locating the capital in the Yangtze Basin would place it too far from the frontier to exercise effective command, or even to supervise the large armies stationed along the Great Wall. Left to themselves in an ambiguous area between agricultural China and the pastoral steppe, these commanders of the marches were all too likely to feel growing uncertainty in their loyalty to the throne; and too likely to build their own regional power bases, to reach understandings with their ostensible enemies, and perhaps even challenge imperial power itself. This was, in fact, precisely how the Yang clan built their power and established the Sui dynasty. Like conquerors throughout history, they knew how they had come to power and they were at pains to prevent history from repeating itself, this time with themselves in the victim's role. Unfortunately for the Sui rulers, history did repeat itself and in less than thirty years. Just as the Ch'in bequeathed unity to the Han, so the Sui bequeathed its efforts to the T'ang.

So the solution was to move grain north by canal, a plan breathtaking in its essential simplicity, its boldness, and its ruthlessness in mobilizing human labor. The ruthlessness stands out all the more boldly because the Grand Canal was not the only massive undertaking of the Sui rulers. They rebuilt the Great Wall, as if in memory of their Ch'in predecessors, and they sent great expeditions of conquest beyond the frontiers into Vietnam, into Central

Asia, and through southern Manchuria into Korea. The most far-flung of these conquests failed, but that did not reduce their cost. The Sui also attempted an ideological unification, seeking to become the arbiters of a religious and intellectual arena in which Confucianism, Taoism, and Buddhism were all accorded a legitimate place.

The "Old" Grand Canal—Northwest to Loyang and Kaifeng

Like many simple notions, the notion of the Grand Canal was exceptionally difficult of execution. There was nothing new about canals per se. Irrigation canals were probably dug in neolithic times, as suggested by archaeological evidence and by the Book of Songs, one of China's most ancient books (eighth century B.C.): "The waters of the Piao pool northward flow, flooding the rice fields." From irrigation to transport was a natural step, but one which also required some understanding of rafts, barges, and boats. This step, too, was taken very early, so that when the Sui rulers conceived the Grand Canal, they were already familiar with long-distance transport canals.

All these efforts, early and late, took advantage of three fortunate geographical conditions. First, the terrain reaching from the lower course of the Long River across the Huai River system to the Yellow River was virtually flat: over the nearly 400 miles between these two great rivers, there exists a net rise from south to north of only about 100 feet, almost all of it in the approaches to the Yellow River. Second, the Huai River system drained gradually from west to east, thus providing a source of water for the canal. Third, the alluvial nature of the soil made it relatively easy to excavate.

The Yellow and Huai river systems had created these conditions in the course of many millennia, conditions that made these two rivers among the most unstable in the world, constantly shifting their channels. The peculiar feature of the Yellow River, that across much of the North China Plain its bed lies *above* the level of the surrounding terrain, made periodic changes of course inevitable, as we have seen in Chapter 1, and will see again.

The earliest transport canal in Chinese history, dating from the sixth century B.C., may have been a 260-mile link known as the Wild Goose Canal between the Yellow River and tributaries of the Huai River system. If so, it was also the earliest segment of the system that later became the Grand Canal, but its existence has been called into question: its origin is not clearly documented and no physical traces of it have been found.

Evidence abounds, however, for the Han-kou (Han Ditch), which first connected the Huai River with the Yangtze near modern Yang-chou in the fourth century B.C.; and it was probably at about the same time that a canal was pushed south of the Yangtze, past Lake T'ai toward modern Soochow and Hangchow. Remains of these latter two canals have been found on the ground as well as in written sources.

In the centuries that followed, these canals were elaborated to serve regional interests, often of a military nature. They were used during the early empire (Ch'in-Han), but a unified waterway from south to north was not conceived, probably because the lower Yangtze region was not yet sufficiently developed to warrant such a massive undertaking. During the period of division following the fall of the Han, the southern (Chinese) dynasties further developed the canal system of the Yangtze delta, but most canals north of the river fell into disrepair; the northern dynasties lacked capacity and probably interest, and the southern dynasties saw such canals as increasing their own vulnerability.

All this changed with the accession of the Sui. Now China was unified once again, and the products of the south were crucial to the consolidation and exercise of power. Between the years A.D. 600 and 610, some two to three million laborers were mobilized to create the "Great Transport River," as the Grand Canal is still known to the Chinese, in the route it followed for nearly 700 years. The principal segments of the canal were the following, some of them utilizing the forerunners described above (see Figure 6-1):

(1) The South-of-the-River Canal (ca. 215 mi.), which connected the principal regions of the Chiang-nan—those centered on Soochow and Hangchow—with the southern bank of the Yangtze. This segment met the river at Chenchiang, opposite Yangchow on the northern bank.

(2) The Shanyang Cut (ca. 200 mi.), from Yangchow in a route parallel to the old Han-kou but somewhat to the west, through a chain of lakes into the Huai River system.

(3) The Pien Canal (ca. 500 mi.), up the Pien River, a tributary to the Huai, then cross-country to a point on the Yellow River near its confluence with the Lo River, on which was located the capital of Loyang. Because the Pien Canal segment was the longest segment of the canal north of the Yangtze, it often gave its name generically to the entire passage between Loyang and the Yangtze River.

(4) The Yung-Chi Canal (ca. 500 mi.), from the Yellow River near Loyang along a northeastern course to the vicinity of present-day Peking—in Sui and T'ang times a militarily important frontier region but not yet as politically significant as it later became. As with other segments, its surveyors sought to follow the most nearly level terrain and to use existing rivers, either as part of its own channel or as a water source. Contemporary documents tell us that over a million peasants were mobilized for three years and that for the first time women were also dragooned into the work force, males having been used up by the combined demands of agriculture, war, and corvee labor.

The Yung-Chi Canal, completed in A.D. 605, was in several respects quite

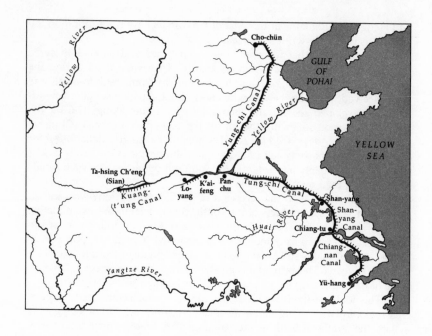

FIGURE 6-1. Grand Canal ca. A.D. 600–1300 (also known as Pien Canal), linking capitals at Kaifeng and Loyang with the lower Yangtze region.

unlike the other segments of the Grand Canal. First, it was a completely new undertaking by the Sui rulers, unlike the other segments, each of which had earlier precedents. Second, it was designed to radiate political and military power outward from the capital districts, rather than to transport economic resources inward to the capital area; as such, the Yung-Chi Canal was not only one element of a frontier defense system but also part of the abortive Sui effort to conquer southern Manchuria and northern Korea. Third—and not least—it was only periodically successful, mostly because of difficulties in supplying or regulating adequate amounts of water for dependable transport. During the winter months, of course, it was useless because of low water and ice.

The Grand Canal of the Sui dynasty, then, covered a total of about 1,400 miles, or nearly 1,000 miles if the Yung-Chi stretch is set aside. This was essentially the route that it followed from the seventh century to the thirteenth century, that is, through the T'ang and Sung dynasties, up to the Mongol conquest in A.D. 1268.

The T'ang moved their capital back to the old Ch'in and Han site, west-

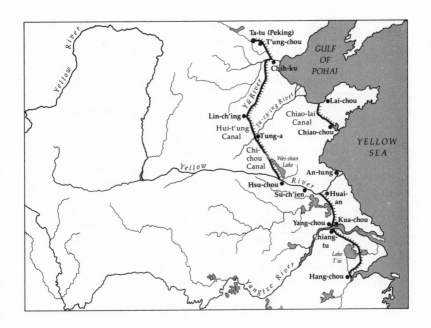

FIGURE 6-2. Grand Canal ca. A.D. 1300–1800, running northward to Peking. Note change in course of Yellow River.

ward to Ch'ang-an (modern Sian), beyond the Yellow River's right-angle bend and choke point, Three-gates Gorge (*San-men hsia*), necessitating re-habilitation of the difficult Han dynasty portage-and-waterway called the Kuang-t'ung Canal. But the T'ang also maintained a secondary capital in Loyang, thus somewhat alleviating the need to send such massive supplies so far west. It was from Loyang, we recall, that Li Ao, the philosopher-poet of the T'ang period, began his journey to the deep south. In the tenth century, the Sung dynasty, concerned about the supply problem, moved the capital eastward once again, this time to modern Kaifeng, a little farther east than Loyang.

The "New" Grand Canal—North to Peking

With the Mongol conquest and the establishment of the Yuan dynasty in A.D. 1280, Peking became for the first time the capital of the Chinese Empire. This frontier region now became the political center of the entire realm, a centrality it has retained to this day. The conquest, however, rendered ob-solete the Pien Canal, which had served capitals located on or near the

Yellow River. Now the Grand Canal would have to be rerouted almost straight north from the Shanyang Cut, rather than following the Pien Canal toward the northwest.

This work, performed between A.D. 1290 and 1300, was both facilitated and obstructed by a major change—nearly 45 degrees—in the course of the Yellow River that had taken place a century before, in 1194. The Yellow River now flowed southeastward into the Huai River system, rather than north-eastward to empty into the Gulf of Pohai north of the Shantung Peninsula. This new course continued for 700 years, until 1855, when the Yellow River once more returned to its northern channel.

The new southerly route of the Yellow River greatly enlarged the lakes and marshes along the Shanyang Cut and silted all outlets of the Huai River. Before long, this silting also raised the water levels sufficiently so that the flow of the combined Yellow River-Huai River waters now flowed southward in the Grand Canal, toward the Yangtze. Northbound transport now had to oppose a slow-moving current, and serious flooding was common. On the other hand, the canal could now follow the Yellow River upstream for about 200 miles to Hsü-chow, before striking north across Shantung province to Lin-ch'ing. The four segments north of the Yellow River are summarized below, from south to north (see Figure 6-2). These northerly segments were the most difficult sections of the Grand Canal to build, to maintain, and to administer.

(1) The Hsü-chow to Tung-a segment, about 350 miles in length (the Chi-chou Canal), from the new Yellow River channel at Hsü-chow to the junction with the old Yellow River channel at Tung-a, in which a smaller, less turbid river now flowed, the *Ta-ch'ing*, or "Big Clear River." The difficulties here were first, crossing the westward spurs of the Shantung hills, and second, a gain in elevation of nearly 100 feet to the bed of the old Yellow River.

(2) A short section, from Tung-a to Lin-ch'ing (the Hui-t'ung Canal), of about 70 miles. At Lin-ch'ing, the canal once again entered a natural water-way, that of the north-flowing Wei River. The principal problem was the rather rapid descent from the summit of the old Yellow River bed, a problem whose solution required constant and ingenious efforts to assure adequate supplies of water to the canal and also to install locks, ultimately numbering more than thirty, to enable boats to pass safely through in either direction. Water was supplied by a number of reservoirs on upstream rivers, controlled by watergates and sluiceways, a plan first conceived by Kubla Khan's engineers and further elaborated during the Ming and Ch'ing dynasties. Nevertheless, during part of the Yuan and occasionally thereafter, this segment was covered by portage rather than by water.

(3) From Lin-ch'ing to the vicinity of modern Tientsin (the *Yü-ho*, or "Imperial River," sometimes also known as the Southern Canal), a distance of about 240 miles. From Lin-ch'ing on, the canal followed the Wei River on

the alignment of the ancient Yung-Chi Canal of the Sui period, but considerable improvement of the river channel was necessary.

(4) Finally, up the canalized Pai River to T'ung-chow and thence to the capital via the T'ung-hui Canal, about ninety miles in all. This final stretch was a difficult one also, because of a net change in elevation of nearly one hundred feet between Tientsin and Peking. Locks and slipways (many assisted by capstans which pulled boats up and over rampways) were required here as well. During much of the Ming period, however, the T'ung-hui Canal was abandoned in favor of overland transport; it is said that willow trees were planted on both sides of the road to provide shade to the carters, and wells were dug every couple of miles to slake the thirst of men and draft animals.

This, in bare outline, was the Grand Canal in its two major incarnations, first by the Sui, T'ang, and Sung; and second by the Yuan, Ming, and Ch'ing. In its later incarnation, this remarkable engineering achievement stretched for just over 1,000 miles, from Hangchow in the south to Peking in the north, about the same as the straight-line distance from Miami to New York. By contrast, this country's famous Erie Canal, built between 1818 and 1825, covered a distance of 350 miles between the Hudson River and Lake Erie; the Erie Canal, however, had a lift of 570 feet, several times as great as that of the Grand Canal, despite the latter's much greater length.

The Grand Canal in Operation

Observers often marveled at the Grand Canal, as well they might. Marco Polo, consistently enthusiastic about the accomplishments of the Chinese people and his imperial host-employer, remarked:

> Kayn-gui [probably Chen-chiang] is a small town . . . where annually is collected a large quantity of corn and rice, the greatest part of which is conveyed from thence to the city of Kanbalu [Peking] for the supply of the establishment of the Emperor. This place is in the line of communication with the province of Cathay [north China] by means of rivers, lakes, and a wide and deep canal which the Great Khan has caused to be dug, in order to pass from one river to the other . . . without making any part of the voyage by sea. . . . On its sides, likewise, are constructed strong and wide embankment roads, upon which the travelling by land also is rendered perfectly convenient.

Impressive amounts of cargo were shipped northward—for the Grand Canal was after all a one-way transport system, with very little cargo headed south—on both the Pien Canal and the later Grand Canal. During the T'ang, an annual average of ca. 130,000 tons was not unusual. These shipments over the Pien Canal nearly trebled during the Northern Sung dynasty, a figure reached and then exceeded by the Ming, over the longer Grand Canal route to Peking. Once the system had reached maturity, the total fluctuated from about 150,000 tons during the 1420s to a high of 450,000 tons in 1431. In 1420, a particularly bad year, only 45,000 tons reached the capital, but a more typical figure was 350,000 tons.

These grain cargos, supplemented with salt, some luxury goods, and (legally or illegally) private goods of the transport workers were loaded onto boats like those shown in the illustration on page 75, taken from the famous Northern Sung handscroll, "Ascending the River on the Spring Festival." Transport boats carried from fifteen to twenty-five tons of cargo and required a crew of ten or a dozen men, who towed, poled, or rowed the boat, sometimes assisted by wind or, occasionally, draft animals. The boats were grouped into convoys and proceeded in stages with periodic changes of crew and sometimes reloading onto different boats. Rarely did one crew or one boat carry the grain all the way from first loading to ultimate destination. A good day's progress along the level and open sections of the canal might be about ten to fifteen miles, at perhaps two miles per hour, but much less over difficult passages and places where locks or capstan pullovers had to be negotiated. Leaky boats, bad weather, low water, damaged locks, broken dikes, or other canal conditions might require laying up for days or weeks.

Shipments were organized on a seasonal basis, spring and fall, to take advantage of the two harvests per year in the grain-supplying regions of the Yangtze River. These were also the seasons in which transport was most feasible, avoiding the low water (and ice) of the winter dry season and the worst of flood dangers during the summer rains. In an effort to assure regular deliveries, granaries were constructed along the way from which grain could be shipped as needed; remnants have been found of a huge Sui granary, with a capacity of over 30 million bushels, at the junction of the Lo and Yellow rivers. During the Ming period, about 3,000 boats were assigned to transport the tribute grain.

Rice and other grains were supplied by quotas assigned to various regions, mainly those of the lower Yangtze and its immediate hinterland. In the levying of "tribute" grain, an overage of 50 to 80 percent above the nominal quota was collected to allow for "shrinkage" along the way, so that the amount actually collected was much larger than recorded shipments. In addition, local administrations were responsible for moving the grain to collection points, whence it entered the Grand Canal or connecting waterways.

The entire operation, impressive though it most certainly was, was also complex, fragile, and easily subject to disruption or destruction. It was also inordinately expensive; in the early nineteenth century, the Ch'ing authorities may have been spending 15 million ounces of silver, nearly a

quarter of their total annual income, for this purpose alone. The grain tribute system required a massive and complex support system to keep the
canals and locks in order and to repair damage due to natural or human
accident; to see that the boats were built and manned; to requisition, organize, and train the labor for these tasks, and to provide food and shel-
ter; to construct granaries along the way; to protect shipments against pe-
culation, theft, and piracy; to administer the entire operation and to give
careful accounting at each stage. The historical records are a doleful litany
of the difficulties attendant on getting the tribute grain from the Yangtze
Valley to China's capital.

So great were the difficulties that the Yuan sought to use a maritime route
as an alternative. The sea route had many advantages, and the Yuan had not
succeeded in reliably solving the many engineering difficulties of the northern part of the Grand Canal, Marco Polo's testimony notwithstanding. But
maritime transport was enormously risky and losses to storms, adverse
currents, and endemic piracy were consistently high. The ships were often

Two cargo boats under way, and a passenger boat moored alongshore. The boat on the left is
being propelled by an offset stern sweep and steered by a bow sweep, each operated by six
men. The boat on the right is being towed by five men. Masts were designed to be lowered
easily to pass under the many bridges along the canal and raised to sail before the wind or (as
here) to provide a secure fastening for the tow rope high enough to pass over other boats or
obstructions on the bank. From a famous handscroll, "Ascending the River on Ch'ing-ming
Day," by Chuang Tse-tuan, late 11th century.

unseaworthy and the crews badly trained, since experienced seamen went to great lengths to avoid such dangerous and unrewarding expeditions. In an effort to reduce the distance and the danger of the voyage, the Yuan attempted to cut a canal across the neck of the Shantung Peninsula, the Chiao-Lai Canal, but this effort never bore fruit. A little later, the early Ming rulers were so successful in working out many of the problems attending the inland route that in 1411 they gave up their experiments with maritime shipment. The *Ming History* states:

> Transport over the sea was beset with dangers. Every year boats were suddenly destroyed and men drowned. The authorities had to meet time-limits in making good the losses. They afflicted the people with numerous levies and the boats were not solidly built. It was reckoned that one sea-going vessel needed a crew of 100 men and could carry 1,000 piculs [ca. 60 tons], from which its costs may be seen. A river craft which carries 200 piculs [ca. 13 tons] needs 10 men. . . . One can compare the profit and loss on this basis.

What the *Ming History* and other official sources do not make clear is that the Grand Canal had also become a morass of vested interests. The bureaucracy in charge, one of the three great superintendencies (along with the Yellow River Conservancy and the Salt Administration), had become a Byzantine maze of corruption, patronage, and theft, harder to clean out than the silt that continually clogged the canal. The sea route—to which there might be, of course, legitimate objections—challenged these vested interests, and was thus strenuously opposed.

The Ch'ing dynasty continued the pattern of the Ming, with its accomplishments, corruptions, inefficiencies, and vested interests all mixed together. By the early nineteenth century, the system was headed for crisis, partly because corruption and patronage had gotten completely out of hand, and partly because the bed of the Yellow River was now dangerously high, despite all the dredging, sluicing, and diversions that had been undertaken. The two conditions were not unrelated: contemporary estimates suggest that by 1800 only about 10 percent of the 6 million ounces of silver allocated annually for Grand Canal water conservancy was spent legitimately; all the rest lined the pockets of officials and hangers-on.

In 1850, the T'ai-p'ing Rebellion erupted, the most destructive in Chinese history (see Chapter 9). This massive upheaval, which lasted fourteen years and cost perhaps 20,000,000 lives, devastated central China and nearly overthrew the Ch'ing dynasty. A year later, in 1851, serious floods on the Yellow River damaged the middle course of the Grand Canal, and these floods were followed by equally serious inundations during the next couple of years. The challenge of the Taiping and yet another rebellion, the Nien, this one centered near the flooded areas in the Huai River region, meant that the dynasty had scant resources of time, energy, and manpower to deal with acts of nature and neglect.

Finally, in 1855, the Yellow River broke through catastrophically, flooding enormous tracts of land, and eventually returning to the northerly course it had occupied before 1194. These related events—maladministration, rebellion, natural disaster—combined to destroy or render useless the Grand Canal north of the Shanyang Cut.

Furthermore, it was now possible to use the sea route; modern ships and the coming of steam greatly reduced the risk and increased the capacity of maritime transport, and the fearsome pirates who had once preyed on ocean shipping were now largely swept from the seas. By the 1920s, trunk railways carried freight and passengers from north China to Shanghai or Hankow. Thus for a century, until after the accession of the present government in 1949, the Grand Canal fell into the most dilapidated condition, with only a few segments—South-of-the-River and parts of the Shanyang Cut—still serving local traffic.

The Yellow River continued in its northern course until 1938, when Chiang Kai-shek deliberately blew up the dikes in order to flood the North China Plain and hold up the advance of the Japanese invaders. The plan slowed the Japanese only temporarily, but it inundated nearly 3 million acres, caused an estimated 500,000 deaths, and produced 6 million refugees. The Yellow River was returned to its northern course once again in 1946, in a large project overseen by the American engineer Oliver J. Todd, called by *Time* magazine "the man from Palo Alto." Todd, famous for his flood control works in China and also for his imperious temperament, was sometimes called (behind his back) "Todd Almighty."

Ecological Impact and Social Distress

The environment and the human geography of northern Kiangsu/Ahwei and southern Shantung has been profoundly and adversely affected by the Grand Canal, both through its existence and in the changes wrought by the instability of the Yellow River. From its beginnings during the Sui and T'ang dynasties, the Grand Canal interrupted and backed up the natural eastward drainage of the Huai River system, depriving a seventy-five- to one-hundred-mile-wide band along the coast of normal ground water, with the result that this otherwise fertile soil has long been heavily saline, and only marginally productive. The chain of lakes and marshes just to the west of the Grand Canal—Kao-yu, Hung-tse, and Wei-shan—are all wholly or largely the creation of the Grand Canal, as can clearly be seen in the satellite photograph on page 78. As this area silted up, a process much accelerated after the Yellow River's A.D. 1194 change of course, the elevation west of the canal

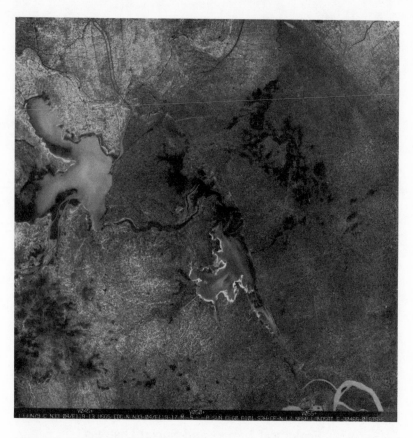

Satellite photograph of the Grand Canal just north of the Yangtze River, a small part of which appears at the bottom of the picture. Note how the Grand Canal forms a kind of dam along the east side of Lake Kao-yu; Lake Hung-tse drains into it from the northwest.

gradually increased, requiring more attention to dikes and sluices on the east side of the Grand Canal. When these dikes gave way, as they sometimes did even in "normal" times, the canal was disrupted and large tracts to the east were flooded. One can hardly imagine the devastation that followed the periodic irruptions of the Yellow River.

In romanticized form, these conditions passed from oral storytelling into folklore and finally to literature. The great picaresque novel, *Tales of the Marshlands* (best known to English readers in Pearl Buck's translation, *All Men Are Brothers*), tells of a band of good and fearless men made outlaw by a corrupt and rapacious society who took refuge in precisely these regions.

Marshlands and mountains were the Chinese equivalent of Sherwood Forest, havens not only for primitive rebels and ordinary bandits in traditional times, but also in modern times as revolutionary bases for the Chinese Communist Party during their search for power in the 1930s and 1940s.

The hard reality was a large area of chronic hunger and frequent disaster. The people of this region have long been known for the poverty and hardship they were forced to endure, conditions unusual even in the traditional Chinese scheme of things.

> Pitiful Huai people—victims of flood.
> Temples awash, ancestral graves submerged,
> Houses like fish in a stewpot . . .
> Good fortune brings dense green shoots,
> Then all at once the fields become white waves.
> Aiya, why is the river god so ruthless?
> Though you raise your head and cry unto heaven,
> Heaven answers not.

Despite the poem, these folk were more often despised for their backwardness than pitied for their poverty, attitudes that survive into the present. They were (and are) called *chiang-pei jen* (north-of-the-river people), a term whose literal translation hides a derisive contempt reminiscent of dust-bowl "Okie." After the terrible floods and revolts of the 1850s and 1860s, conditions worsened, since even the uncertain and harsh livelihoods associated with the Grand Canal were no longer available. It is therefore not surprising that a major source of labor for Shanghai, just as Shanghai was booming in the late nineteenth and early twentieth century, came from this region—coolies, ricksha men, young girls to work in the textile mills or to be forced into cheap prostitution—all the dirty, physically demanding, and demeaning work for which the *chiang-pei jen* were thought particularly suited. It is little wonder that this area was plagued with violence and unrest.

Banditry was a survival strategy, often a part-time employment for poor peasants who could not make a living off the land, as predators sought to wrest what they could from those who had something to take. Local elites—pretty shabby elites mostly, with the exception of a few wealthy landlords-cum-moneylenders—organized the local peasantry into myriad protective groups, like the Red Spears, to ward off the predators. But the difference between predators and protectors was always hazy and uncertain. To the extent that predators were successful they had something to protect; to the extent that protectors commanded the power to hold their turf, they might be tempted to use that power at the expense of others.

The powerful Green Gang, modern Shanghai equivalent of the Mafia—which also had its origins in a harsh, poverty-stricken land and spread from there—had its twentieth-century beginnings in the Huai area around the Grand Canal as one of these bands. Coolie and transport workers carried it to the city where it took independent root, first as a protective association to help the new migrants but soon expanding to control much of the waterfront, the opium trade, prostitution, and indentured recruitment of young girls from the home area to Shanghai factory work under terrible conditions. The Green Gang also provided the muscle necessary to enforce and expand its jurisdiction, and to do favors for patrons who could benefit it—most spectacularly in April 1927, when its boss, Tu Yueh-sheng (alias Big Ears Tu), following the urging of Chiang Kai-shek, unloosed a white terror against the Chinese communists, labor leaders, student radicals, and leftists in general, a bloody campaign euphemistically called "party purification."

Since 1949, sporadic efforts have been made to rehabilitate the Grand Canal. In recent years these efforts have increased and become more systematic, particularly along the middle and northern stretches, which were most severely affected by the events of the last 150 years. In part, this restoration serves transport needs, though tribute grain is no longer the overwhelmingly dominant cargo. More important is the long-range intention to use the Grand Canal as an aqueduct to ship the waters of the Yangtze to the thirsty north: instead of shipping the grain watered by the Yangtze, the Chinese now plan to transport the water itself. In Chapter 11, we shall have more to say about this astonishing concept, the "Southern Waters North Project."

7

MERCHANTS, COMMERCE, AND PRODUCTS ON THE MOVE

Marco Polo traveled widely during his long stay in China, and during the early 1290s found himself in the lower Yangtze region. A merchant himself, he was astonished by the volume and variety of commerce he saw everywhere about him, and he understood the importance of the Long River as the central artery of a vast economic area.

> A great number of cities and large towns are situated on its banks, and more than two hundred, with sixteen provinces, partake of the advantages of its navigation, by which the transport of merchandise is [carried on] to an extent that might appear incredible to those who have not had an opportunity of witnessing it.

By the time of his travels, China was indeed a highly commercialized society. Marco Polo often ranked it ahead of his native Venice, a ranking all the more striking because of China's size and fundamentally agrarian economy. And nowhere in China was the transport and exchange of goods more highly developed than within the watershed of the Long River; even the mercantile southern provinces centered on Canton, with its splendid access to overseas trade networks reaching the Philippines, Southeast Asia, and beyond, were no rival in the aggregate amount of commerce passing to and fro.

Merchants and Mercantile Activity in China

As in other cultures, the origins of barter, trade, and commerce in China emerged from prehistoric times; precious materials borne from afar—jade from central Asia and cowry shells from the Indian Ocean—have been found in neolithic graves. But Chinese social philosophies, as they developed during the centuries before the first imperial unification in the Ch'in-Han period, disparaged both mercantile activity and merchants. Confucianism, Taoism,

Legalism, and Mohism all viewed the merchant as a parasite or worse, one who made a profit at others' expense without himself producing anything of value. The orthodox Confucian social order placed the scholar-official at the top, the agriculturalist second, the artisan third, and the merchant both last and least. Legalists emphasized only two legitimate occupations—agriculture and war. Mohists deplored all forms of display and all consumption beyond that necessary to survival, rather like unbending and ostentatiously frugal Puritans. Contemplative and mystical Taoists, like Chuang-tzu, ridiculed scholars, merchants, and dour Mohists altogether. All of them considered the pursuit of "profit" unworthy of comparison with higher and more moral concerns and probably also detrimental to the social order.

Reality, of course, was quite different. Commercial activity ran the gamut from itinerant peddlars to enormously wealthy and powerful merchants whose influence added force to the persistent Confucian bias against merchants and mercantile activity. Their concern was further heightened because quite early in China's history one's position in the social order was no longer determined by birth. Pedigree was tremendously important, but, unlike aristocratic and feudal societies, one could in theory and even sometimes in practice move from one social stratum to another. Wealth was influential, like wealth anywhere, but in China mercantile wealth was not legally protected and mercantile activity always carried some stigma. Merchants were often vulnerable to "squeeze" by officials, and a defiant merchant could easily be bankrupted or simply ordered out of business, his goods and properties confiscated. The fact that both officials and merchants centered their activities in cities large and small meant that merchants had no urban arena of their own in which autonomously to develop their own values and institutions, to become, that is, a genuine bourgeoisie.

The Chinese situation differed from the European in this regard. In Europe, the feudal barons were rooted on large domains in the countryside, and for this reason, although they also disparaged merchants and commercial activities, European towns and cities tended to grow outside their immediate purview and control. With the rise of monarchical power and the emergence of nation-states, city merchants often financed kings in their struggles with the feudal aristocracy. In return, kings granted to these cities charters that enlarged the arena and legitimacy of commercial activity.

Another important difference was that in medieval Europe birth determined status; it was not ordinarily possible for a commoner to enter the nobility. In China, merchants—or merchants' descendants—could aspire to acceptance as scholar-officials by assuming the hallmarks of such status: ownership of land, classical education, preparation for the civil service examination, patronage of literati arts, etc. This meant that in China merchants were more likely to adapt themselves to the existing order than to conceive a risky and ultimately revolutionary alternative. This internal flexibility *within* the Chinese system was one important key to its *overall* stability and continuity.

Throughout the early and middle dynasties—roughly through the T'ang (until about A.D. 1000)—the state sought with varying success to impose restrictive regulation upon commercial activity. It also milked such activity via regular and irregular levies. In the magnificent and meticulously planned T'ang capital of Ch'ang-an (at modern Sian), certain quarters of the city were assigned to commercial activity, with all merchants engaged in a particular trade (*hang*) grouped together in the same ward. Wards were walled, with gates locked at night. Such grouping, a common Chinese practice then and later, together with merchants' sense of vulnerability, led quite early to the formation of common-trade guilds for mutual support, protection, and responsibility. Guilds in China were defensive with respect to political authority, not vehicles for the development of an alternate vision of society.

Efforts of the state and of the gentry-literati elites who staffed the bureaucracy to regulate, control, and tap the resources of commerce were never entirely successful, and they became progressively less successful as commercial activity burgeoned in the late T'ang and, especially, in the Sung period. The few centuries centered on A.D. 1000 were a period of remarkable growth and development in virtually all aspects of Chinese life—economic, social, political, technological, cultural, philosophic.

Although this period did not match the muscular feats of military conquest of the Ch'in-Han (220 B.C.-A.D. 220) and Sui-T'ang (A.D. 589-906), and was hence considered an era of relative weakness, in every other realm it was a vibrantly creative time. Many pages would be required simply to list the many new developments that took place during this period, all the way from the invention of printing and its widespread use, paper money, greatly improved agricultural and transport technologies, a new synthesis of Confucianism and Buddhism that remained orthodox for a thousand years, and many others.

Following this "medieval economic revolution," Chinese society, as Elvin puts it,

> was much more productive, commercialized, monetized, urbanized, literate, and numerate than it had been before. It was also much larger in numbers. The population rose from a maximum in the times of greatest prosperity of perhaps 60 to 70 million to possibly 140 million at the height of the Sung, and then, after a decline in the 14th century, to an eventual premodern maximum of 430 million by 1850.

The China that took shape after about A.D. 1000 is the "traditional" China that most readily comes to mind, the China of the last imperial dynasties, which led into the great changes of this century.

One consequence of the medieval economic revolution was that the state finally eased or abandoned most of its efforts to regulate and oversee commercial activity directly, but it did continue to derive income from commerce, not from taxes in the ordinary sense because such activity was viewed as outside the normal pale, but rather from "unofficial" levies—a kind of state-sanctioned extortion. Since the distinction between the public treasury and the private interests of officials was often vague, many officials ran their offices and enriched themselves from a formally unacknowledged but universally understood relationship with merchants. Moreover, officials not infrequently used merchants as conduits for investment of funds which, as scholar-officials, they had neither the knowledge nor the inclination to handle themselves.

In return, merchants obtained a measure of informal influence and protection as an alternative to the formal recognition and protection denied them by conventional social usage. A fortunate and successful few might even use official connections to become agents of the state, an appointment that virtually assured opportunities to amass great wealth, however vulnerable that wealth might be in the long run. The most spectacular of these state licensees were the salt merchants, merchant princes whom we shall consider below.

This symbiosis grew increasingly close during the later dynasties, following the medieval economic revolution. Although the formal Confucian distinction was maintained between the prestigious career of scholarship and official service on the one hand and profit-oriented commerce on the other, in real life the lines were blurred and overlapping. A given lineage, perhaps even a given extended family, might well include both merchants and aspirants to the civil service examinations, the arduous route through which a talented or lucky few scaled the ladder of prestige and power.

Meanwhile, through the years, merchants grew in number and specialization. Nowhere was this commercialization, this varied mercantile activity, more extensively and intensely developed than along the Yangtze River and its many tributaries, as Marco Polo enthusiastically testified over and over again. The core areas of this trade, linked like three pearls on the connecting strand of the Long River, were the Szechwan Basin, central China, and the lower Yangtze (Chiang-nan) region that in modern times has come to center on Shanghai. Until the explosive growth of Shanghai, which began about 1850, domestic trade during the latter dynasties was most highly advanced from the eastern end of the Three Gorges to Yangchow, where the Grand Canal crosses the Long River, and in the Chiang-nan, that rich and fertile delta triangle which contained Nanking, Hangchow, and Soochow.

Particularly was this so in the large middle-Yangtze region centered on

Hankow, fed by major tributaries both north and south. Hankow was a particularly important commercial hub, one that shaped the trading patterns of almost all the major commodities of the region. It was also a center for domestic trade in more than 350 different products, of which the most important were "the big eight": grain, salt, tea, vegetable oils, medicinal herbs, hides and furs, cotton, and mixed goods from Fukien and Canton. Also prominently traded were beans, hemp, sugar, wax, timber, bamboo, and coal.

Where the commerce of the early empire had been mainly in luxury goods for a small elite—excepting salt, iron, and grain shipments to the north— trading patterns now affected millions of ordinary lives as well. The social structure had filled out at all levels, not only through sheer population growth, but also through considerable social mobility. In particular, middle and upper gentry strata could now afford amenities previously unavailable—partly because they had more money, but partly also because larger and more efficient production had brought prices down. Tea, cotton, silk, porcelains, lacquer, vegetable oils, printed books, liquor, and myriad other products were widely and actively traded.

Merchant networks arose to handle this trade. These networks came to have a number of similar features, regardless of the product being traded. Most products were identified with a particular place or region. Even such apparently generic products as tea or silk were traded as particular varieties from identifiable producing regions. This specialization included also the knowledge and skills necessary to both the production and distribution of the particular product. These skills, no less than the product itself, were a community resource. Human skills, like commodities, respond to the law of supply and demand, so when these skills were needed elsewhere or were in surplus at home, their possessors went where they thought they could make a better living.

Merchants also tended to come from places associated with these products or services, and many of them traveled extensively and remained away from home for a long time, but always with the intent and expectation of returning home. The sadness of long separation, a burden on the merchant and his family, was already lamented in the eighth century by the poet Li Po, who spoke for a young wife, lonely for her husband who had gone on a trading expedition to the San-pa region of Szechwan, beyond the Three Gorges:

When I was sixteen, you journeyed off.
The surge in Ch'ü-t'ang Gorge piles against Yen-yü Rock.
Gorges now impassable in the rains of May
Are empty save for monkeys wailing against the sky.
Someday, when you leave San-pa,
Please write a letter beforehand,

For though I cannot walk very far,
I will come to meet you at Long-wind Sandbar.

In the major trading cities all along the Yangtze (and elsewhere, too, of course), associations of these sojourning merchants and artisans began to grow up, conveniently organized either by common origin or by common trade. Since both products (or services) and those who traded (or provided) them often came from the same place, these associations commonly had *both* characteristics—such as silk merchants from Wu-hsi, bankers from Ningpo, legal specialists from Shao-hsing, tung oil dealers from Ch'ang-te, and so forth. The sojourners, grouped by the natural affinities of place and trade, bought land and built impressive lodge halls; both the lodges and the associations housed in them were called *hui-kuan* (assembly halls) or *t'ung-hsiang hui* (native-place associations). These *hui-kuan*, under whatever name, were numerous and often powerful. While not every trade had a guildhouse, many did, and many were exceedingly elaborate, testifying at once to the wealth, power, and prestige of the merchants of that trade and/or region.

The illustration of the guildhall below is accompanied by vivid and detailed description of the activities carried on by the guild. At almost exactly the same moment (1887) but in an entirely different city, Archibald Little (see Chapter 10), described the Shansi Guild in Chungking, hundreds of miles

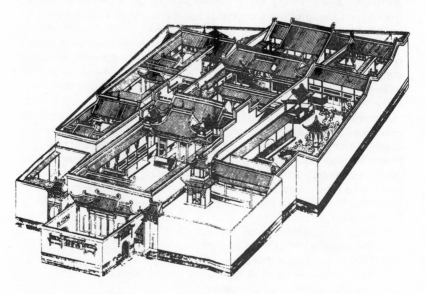

The Shansi-Shensi guildhall compound in Hankow, about 1890.

upriver: "On this day I visited the Shansi Guildhall—a handsome, spacious, highly decorated building, situated just within the wall, and facing the picturesque hills on the opposite bank." Little went on to characterize some guild functions:

> The universal interest with which all public festivities, religious as well as secular, are regarded; the rigid thrift observed in private combined with a magnificent lavishness in public; the settlement of all trade disputes by the guild, and the shunning of all laws and lawyers; the rules laid down by the guilds obeyed unquestioned, and the unwritten etiquette of business no less strictly observed; the liberal subscriptions and legacies given to the guilds, and the way in which these institutions are the first to be called upon in times of calamity and distress. . . .

Hui-kuan and *t'ung-hsiang hui* were home away from home for merchants and sometimes for officials and scholars as well. They provided temporary lodging for those passing through and companionship with regional compatriots who spoke—literally and figuratively—the same language. They were centers of business news and market gossip; their directors provided informal trade supervision and price discipline; their representatives might intercede with officials in the interest of compatriots. In interactions with outsiders, and especially if there was friction or conflict, guild members supported one another and might seek to mobilize the larger community of compatriots. Public demonstrations or violence were not unheard of.

In addition to these practical economic and social functions, guilds also fulfilled important ritual and religious functions, particularly those that ceremonialized home-place deities and the patron saints of that particular line of business. Major festivals were open to all guild fellows, even those who would not be admitted into the lodge on ordinary occasions. Lavish ceremonies and celebrations, with much food and drink, opera performances, parades of figures representing the dieties, burning of incense and presentation of sacrificial offerings—all this both reinforced communal bonds and also increased the prestige of the group both in their own and in others' eyes. Even in death, the guild served its constituency: if one's family or friends could not manage, the lodge saw to embalming, coffining, storage, and transport of the deceased back to his native place for proper burial.

Although guilds were found in all major cities throughout the empire, they were most highly developed where trade was most prosperous and merchants most numerous: in the Yangtze Valley, and particularly in the cities along the river itself. Viewed through lenses of official Confucian disdain, one could not have predicted the richness, vibrancy, and influence of merchants and mercantile activity in late imperial times. One may doubt that such development could have occurred without the favorable geography of the Long River.

Rice

Neolithic peoples who first began the domestication of grasses belonging to the genus *Oryza* were probably unaware of the first-stage "green revolution" they were setting in motion. Today rice is unique among the major grain crops of the world in the calories it provides per unit of cultivated area; only corn is a near competitor. It is also the only major grain grown almost entirely for direct human consumption, as opposed to the much less efficient practices of feeding livestock or of processing into other foodstuffs. Overall figures tell how important and efficient a crop it is. In the 1980s, 40 percent of the world's population, nearly two billion people, depend on rice for at least half their diet, yet rice is grown on only 11 percent of the world's arable land.

Although rice is cultivated and consumed almost everywhere, it has always been overwhelmingly an Asian crop: over 95 percent of the world's rice is grown in East, Southeast, and South Asia. It is no exaggeration to say that the massive populations of China and India, and the high population densities found in, say, Taiwan or Bangladesh, depend on a rice diet. China is the largest producer of all, with over one-third (36 percent) of the world's total; within China, the Yangtze Valley has long been China's most productive grain producer, accounting for nearly three-quarters of the national output (or about 25 percent of the world's total).

The grain trade shaped China as it evolved into modern times; and rice—grown in the Yangtze Valley, transported on its river systems, and shipped north via the Grand Canal to make Peking possible—has been the most important part of that trade. The economic historian, Dwight Perkins, writes:

> Grain more than any other single commodity directly or indirectly determined many of the key features of Chinese commerce, even though it was not itself the largest single commodity in long-distance trade . . . it was grain marketing problems that influenced the size and location of Chinese cities, and these cities in turn set the amount and direction of long-distance internal commerce.

Even so, less than one-tenth of total grain production ever entered long-distance trade. The remainder was consumed by those who grew it or was traded within a narrow radius, to other rural areas or to nearby towns.

The pattern and technology of Chinese rice production, like that of Asia more generally, early assumed distinctive features, many of which have not fundamentally changed. The creation and maintenance of the rice paddy, the intensive cultivation, the investment of enormous amounts of hand labor—all have remained constant from early times. But if the basic technology remained the same, through the centuries the acreage devoted to rice culture expanded to nearly maximum feasible limits, through more extensive and more sophisticated irrigation, through terracing, and through reclamation of polder fields near rivers, lakes, or marshes.

While these processes continued inexorably, another major breakthrough was the increasing use, after about A.D. 1000, of improved strains of rice, either introduced from abroad (probably from modern Cambodia) or developed domestically. These included various strains, some more productive, some more drought or disease or insect resistant, and some that matured more rapidly than older strains. The most important of these was early-ripening rice, which made double-cropping increasingly feasible. In the far south, this meant that one could obtain two rice crops on the same plot in a single year (effectively doubling the acreage); in the Yangtze Valley, a summer rice crop and a crop of winter wheat (planted in the fall, harvested in the spring) were and are common.

In either case, the effective acreage is dramatically increased, as though new farmland had been settled. This was critically important, since new farmland was not easily available; even if it were, building productive paddy fields with adequate supplies of water requires so much labor and other capital that most peasants prefer the more intensive exploitation of existing paddies to construction of new ones. The utilization of improved seed strains continues right up to the present, sparked by work done over the past thirty years at the International Rice Research Institute in the Philippines. This is the contemporary "green revolution" that has helped to make so much of Asia self-sufficient in rice.

Rice culture, as practiced in Asia, proceeds in a sequence of carefully controlled, accurately timed, laborious steps. In the spring, seed is planted very densely in meticulously prepared seed beds. During germination and early growth, the fields are cleared of their earlier crop (for example, wheat or vegetables), plowed, harrowed, leveled, and flooded—turned, that is, into paddies awaiting the rice plants. When the seedlings have grown to a height of about eight inches (three to four weeks), they are carefully uprooted and bound loosely with a piece of straw into handful-sized bunches. The bunches are immediately distributed on flooded paddy fields where transplanter crews await them. With a seedling bunch in one hand, the worker (both men and women do this work) transplants seedling by seedling, thrusting each about three inches deep into the welcoming muck, about eight inches apart. Transplanting several parallel rows at once, the worker moves backward in a straight line. When one bunch is gone, another is conveniently at hand, with the process repeated over and over until all paddies are transplanted.

插秧
晨雨麥秋潤午風
夏涼溪南與溪北
歌揮新秧拋擲不停
左右無亂行我教
插秧惠伊勞民莫忘

Transplanting rice, from an early 18th-century source. The poem in the upper right reads:

"Transplanting Rice Shoots"
Dawn rains fatten autumn grains,
A midday breeze cools the trees.
South of the brook and north of it too
Everywhere songs of shoots planted anew.
Thrusting and throwing, hands ever-going,
Left and right, rows never askew.
I'll teach the use of the transplanting tool,
Saving labor, the people will never forget.

Once the rice is transplanted, it grows in the flooded paddy, drawing air through its leaves and deriving nourishment from algae and minerals present in the water. The waterlogged soil, therefore, is primarily an anchor for the roots rather than a source of nourishment for the plant. Unlike dry-field agriculture, therefore, the paddy can be used over and over without loss of productivity. During the growing season, the plants are weeded and fertilized. In some areas, weeding is done standing upright, with the toes and a weeding stick; elsewhere, in an all-fours position, straddling a row of plants. Traditionally, application of fertilizer relied heavily on a liquified mix of nightsoil and compost; now chemical fertilizers, pesticides, and herbicides have been added. It is crucially important that during this growth phase the water level remain nearly constant. Although rice can be adapted to a wide range of conditions and water depths, once it is in place it is damaged by fluctuating conditions.

As the rice approaches maturity (approximately 100 days after transplanting), the plants' heads nod with their loads of grain. At this time, the fields are drained and allowed to dry out, and it is from dry fields that the rice is harvested by hand sickles. Cutting and threshing require care because, unlike wheat and other grains, mature grains of rice are only very loosely held in the stalk and may easily "shatter"—fall out and be lost. This is why threshing is done in the fields near where the rice plants were cut, by portable threshers driven by foot-treadle. The unmilled rice ("paddy") is then carried to drying grounds of bare, hard-pounded earth (more recently concrete). There it is spread out and repeatedly raked in order to reduce its moisture content, an important step to prevent rotting or germination in storage. Finally, the milling process removes the husks and polishes the grains of rice. Traditional farm practices, without modern inputs, were capable of producing just under one ton per acre.

Nothing could contrast with this laborious cycle, sometimes called the "four stoops" (stoop to plant, to transplant, to cultivate, to harvest) more than the California practice of sowing rice from airplanes, without transplanting, and harvesting by machine. Through use of best seeds and heavy applications of fertilizer, herbicides, and pesticides, yields per acre in the U.S. are slightly higher than in China (1.6 tons per acre vs. 1.3 tons per acre); highest of all is Japan (1.85 tons per acre).

Salt

"A man would not be unwell if he abstained for an entire year from either the sweet or sour or bitter or hot [flavors]; but deprive him of salt for a fortnight, and he will be too weak to tie up a chicken. . . ." This seventeenth-century commentator may have exaggerated a little, but he was pointing to the necessity of dietary salt. In fact, this necessity arose with the shift from a predominantly meat diet, which contains adequate salt, to a cereal or vegetable diet—and hence with the shift from a primitive hunting-gathering economy to agriculture. Thus in most parts of the world, the production and use of salt is not only of great antiquity but of great religious and symbolic importance as well. In addition to salt's dietary importance, it was also essential to many traditional techniques of food preservation and to a wide range of pre-modern material technologies (for example, leather, enamel, and preparation of other chemicals). Nevertheless, in China, with its large population and heavy reliance on a grain diet, food uses took the major part of salt production.

Salt was the bulk commodity most widely traded throughout all parts of China, from early times onward. The salt trade was also a major source of revenue for the state, also from early times, due to two favorable circumstances: first, because everyone needed salt, large amounts were required on a regular basis; and second, because production was limited to areas along the coast and a few inland locales, the first stages of distribution could, presumably, be fully controlled.

This combination of volume, aggregate value, and possibility of control appealed to Chinese rulers as early as the seventh century B.C., 400 years before the first unification of China. Although Confucian scholars repeatedly expressed their distaste for official involvement in such commerce ("If a country possesses a wealth of fertile land and yet its people are underfed, the reason is that merchants and artisans have prospered while agriculture has been neglected"), the state persistently sought to derive income from salt, usually with considerable success. Despite serious abuses of all sorts—unauthorized production, corruption, smuggling, theft—salt was a major source of revenue right up to the twentieth century, by which time its income had been encrusted with commitments to everything from repayment of foreign loans to support of the imperial stud. In some periods, revenues were raised through direct taxation on the sale of salt by what amounted to a state-run enterprise.

More common, particularly in the later dynasties, was an indirect system of government licenses purchased by private salt producers and private salt merchants, in return for which they were permitted to make, transport, and sell salt on their own account within designated monopoly districts, paying additional sums according to the amount shipped, the whole process ostensibly overseen and kept honest by a very large official bureaucracy. These licensed "prime contractors"—about thirty merchants in charge of production and thirty others in charge of distribution—then sold shipments of salt wholesale to perhaps two hundred authorized subdealers, who were themselves men of substance, and so on down the ladder to the individual peddler and the ultimate consumer. By the time salt reached the cash-poor peasant family, it was expensive; indeed, soy sauce was invented as a way of making salt go farther, by dissolving it in liquid rather than adding it directly to food.

Salt in China comes from three sources: sea water, by solar evaporation or boiling; brine obtained from wells, by boiling; and dry salt lakes in the interior (mining of rock salt was insignificant). The first is overwhelmingly the most important of these, while the last has had only local significance;

the brine wells in Szechwan province are of especial interest. Salt is evaporated in suitable districts along the China coast from Manchuria to Canton, but once again the most productive areas were those in Central China, the Liang-huai factories north and south of the Huai River along the coast of Kiangsu province with access to the superb distribution system available in the immediate vicinity of the factories and throughout the Yangtze Valley. In the Liang-huai district, both solar evaporation and evaporation by boiling were employed; in the latter case, extensive coastal reed plains were included as a part of the factory, as a fuel source. A schematic depiction of a typical solar-evaporation saltworks is shown below.

From these yards the salt was packed and shipped in bulk along the network of canals leading westward into the Grand Canal, most of it going south to Yangchow, the great emporium at the junction of the Grand Canal and the Yangtze. It was thence transshipped throughout its monopoly district—the Yangtze Valley, from the Chiang-nan to the Three Gorges, north

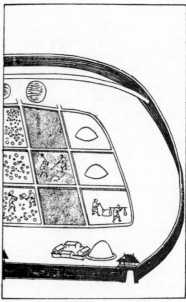

Producing salt by solar evaporation of sea water. Note the walls and gates to prevent theft. On the left, salt pans are being prepared and flooded with sea water, which will be led in increasing salt concentration through successive pans until all water has evaporated; on the right, the salt is being pulverized, swept, and prepared for shipment. (From the 1637 encyclopedia of technology, *T'ien-kung k'ai-wu*.)

along the Han River, and south along the several major tributaries to the watershed north of Canton. Hankow, at the junction of the Han and the Yangtze and close to the mouths of the various southern tributaries, was the principal breakdown and distribution point for the very large bulk shipments moving upstream from Yangchow. In the seventeenth century the Lianghuai district supplied in excess of 300,000 tons of salt annually.

If one of the foundations of Yangchow's prosperity was the grain tribute trade, surely the other was salt. Here were the businesses and residences of the great salt merchants of Yangchow. They were not, however, natives of that city. With few exceptions, they came from two widely separated regions in which business skills had developed to a high degree—in part because soils were poor and other resources were lacking—and through which an intensively ingrown network of fellow-locals, clansmen, and protégés grew up. The first of these was the rather small district of Hui-chou in the Appalachia-like hill country of Anhwei province south of the Yangtze; the second was a hard-scrabble northern frontier region comprised of the adjoining provinces of Shansi and Shensi, where government-licensed merchants had gotten a start through grain transport to the armies operating along the Great Wall. Both Hui-chou and Shansi natives were active in many businesses, for example the premodern banking system, which was dominated by Shansi factions. Little wonder that the Shansi-Shensi *hui-kuan* in Hankow was so elaborate and opulent.

During the Ming and Ch'ing dynasties (A.D. 1368–1644), these salt merchants were the wealthiest merchant princes in the empire and they sought in a variety of expensive ways to indulge their tastes. The Chinese scholar Ho Ping-ti describes how at the more genteel end of the spectrum, some merchants sought vicarious prestige "by patronizing scholars and poets or by cultivating the expensive hobbies of bibliophiles and art connoisseurs." But the so-called "salt fools" indulged the obsessions of the nouveaux riches everywhere, as a late eighteenth-century source testifies, with wonder and dismay:

> Formerly, the salt merchants of Yang-chou vied with one another in extravagance. . . . There was a lover of orchids, who planted orchids everywhere from the gate to the inner studios. There was one who erected wooden nude female statues in front of his inner halls, all mechanically controlled, so as to tease and surprise his guests. . . . There was one who loved beautiful things. From his gate-keepers to kitchen-maids only good-looking young persons were selected. On the other hand, there was one who was fond of ugly things. . . . There was yet another who liked big things. He designed for himself a huge bronze urinal container five or six feet tall. Every night he climbed up to relieve himself.

While the whole Yangtze Valley east of the Three Gorges was supplied with salt from the Liang-huai district, Szechwan produced its own salt in an industry of great antiquity and technological sophistication. Salt in Szechwan is the result of its geological history. As we have seen, prior to the collision between Indian and Asian crustal plates, Szechwan was submerged by a great primordial ocean. As the land uplifted, Szechwan became an inland sea, then finally took on the mountain-girt basin character it has possessed throughout historic times. This process, dating from Triassic times 250 million years ago, produced large underground brine or solid salt deposits and, from the dense vegetation of many millions of years, large pockets of natural gas and extensive beds of coal.

The underground deposits lie at various depths, though a few brine pools can be found on the surface. We do not know when this salt was first exploited, but the earliest wells are claimed for the third century B.C. and attributed to Li Ping, the engineering genius who conceived All-Rivers Weir above Chengtu (see above, Chapter 5). In early times, these wells must have been quite shallow, but within a few hundred years records indicate dozens of deep wells in the most productive regions. The brine obtained from these wells was evaporated by boiling, with wood (or charcoal) from the abundant forests as the principal fuel. At a later date, coal was also used for this purpose. In a few fortunate locations, even shallow wells brought in natural gas as well as brine. This enabled the brine to be boiled with gas carried by bamboo pipes.

Striking evidence of this early activity was discovered in the early 1950s in the form of two tomb tiles, dating from the Eastern Han (A.D. 25–220), bearing reliefs depicting a scaffolded well with workers drawing up brine and what appear to be bamboo pipes leading to evaporating pans. This process later became very much more developed, particularly around the appropriately named town of Tzu-liu Ching (Self-flowing Wells), as depicted in the illustration on page 96.

At its height, perhaps two thousand gas or brine wells were operating in the Tzu-liu Ching area, some with both brine and natural gas in the same well. An eighteenth-century writer, Li Jung, described the patience and labor required to drill wells that sometimes reached a depth of 3,000 feet:

> To drill a well, an opening is dug at the surface three feet in diameter and nine feet in circumference. First, stone rings shaped like mortars, but open at the bottom are prepared. For the first hundred feet or so, these rings are fitted in the well one above the other. . . . This is done to keep the fresh water out. Then a board for a lever is installed above the well and to this a bamboo rope is attached with an iron drill tied to the other end. Some ten people take turns in treading it. . . .

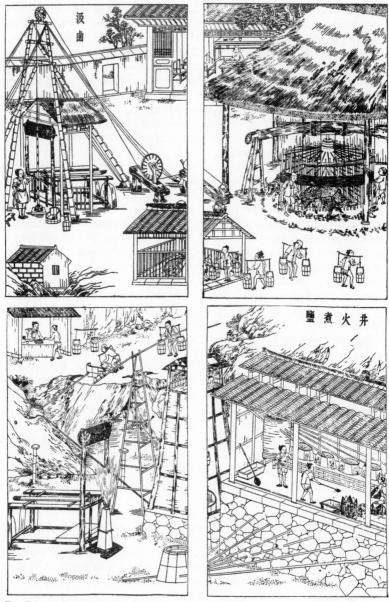

Top: Brine well with winch and windlass. Bottom: Gas-fired evaporation works. (Also from *T'ien-kung k'ai-wu*, 1637.)

One day's labor may drill more than a foot, 7 to 8 inches, or 4 to 5 inches. Sometimes it may take several days to drill one inch. When brine is reached it is called "success." Usually it takes 4 or 5 to some 10 years to reach the stage of "success." . . . If, at a depth of 3000 feet, the amount of brine is still insufficient, the well is abandoned.

Li Jung was describing a churn drill, which operates by up-and-down motion, although twisting the woven bamboo cable imparted some rotation from stroke to stroke. The drill was operated by a kind of teeter-totter, on one end of which crews of six to ten men jumped rhythmically on and off at the same time, thus causing the drill head to rise and fall about six or eight inches. The drill head was periodically drawn up for replacement and to permit the removal of debris in the hole. On unhappy occasions when the cable broke, it might take six months to crush the old drill head and remove it piecemeal. Brine, usually at high salt concentrations, was drawn up by long buckets attached to a windlass, as shown at the top of Figure 9, then taken by shoulder pole or bamboo pipe to the evaporators.

The salt thus obtained was licensed to supply Szechwan and two other provinces in the southwest (Kweichow and Yunnan), but it was often smuggled downriver through the gorges to compete illegally with sea salt from the Liang-huai works along the coast. Except for remote mountainous areas, almost all bulk salt was transported by boat on the intricate river systems both above and below the Three Gorges.

Silk

Not long after the time of Christ, the straitlaced Roman philosopher-orator Seneca voiced a frequently heard denunciation: "I see silken clothes, if one can call them clothes at all, that in no degree afford protection either to the body or the modesty of the wearer, and clad in which no woman could honestly swear she is not naked." If salt was China's premier domestic product, silk was China's first international trade commodity. This remarkable textile gave its name not only to the route (the Silk Road) across which it was traded to the Near East and the Mediterranean but also to the Latin name for China (*Seres* or *Serica*). Silk was an ideal product for long-distance trade: high in value but low in bulk and weight, and not subject to deterioration in transit.

Silk is produced from the pupal cocoon of any of several varieties of moths, but above all the domesticated species, *Bombyx mori*, which feeds on mulberry leaves. There is no doubt of its antiquity in China, nor of the fact that China was both the earliest to develop this remarkable technology and the source of its eventual diffusion to other lands. The domestication of the silkworm from wild varieties probably began in north China—a cocoon has been found in a neolithic site dated about 2500 B.C., and abundant evidence comes from the Bronze Age Shang-Yin period about a millennium later—but the most important centers of silk production quite early moved to the Yangtze Valley, probably because its moderate climate was more conducive than the colder and increasingly arid north to maintaining the temperatures required by the silkworms as well as to the cultivation of the mulberry bushes upon which they depend. From about 500 B.C. onward, Szechwan and the lower Yangtze, especially the Chiang-nan, became and remained the principal centers of silk production and processing (eventually a southern center, around Canton, also became important). Examples surviving from these early centuries attest to an astonishing sophistication in production, dyeing, and weaving—hence the early development of loom technology as well.

Before the time of Christ, high quality silk fabrics had made their way westward in sufficient quantities to motivate some of Alexander the Great's campaigns and then, as we have seen, to become the subject of denunciation in Rome for their extravagance and for their sheerness. Large amounts of silk fabric were periodically exported to the rough nomadic peoples living north of China, as part of the price paid for peace along the Great Wall. From China, the technique spread to Korea in the fourth century and thence on to Japan. India probably learned the technology at about the same time. Finally, around A.D. 550, *Bombyx mori* eggs were smuggled into the Byzantine Empire in hollow canes carried by certain Indian monks who had lived for a long time in the Central Asian oasis city-states on the Silk Road. But the mere possession of eggs did not assure the successful development of sericulture.

The finest natural fibre known to man, silk requires the most complex and precisely controlled production sequence of any textile. The diameter of the filament is less than a thousandth of an inch, and from a single high-grade cocoon, 800 to 1200 yards of unbroken filament can be reeled (individual fibres of high-grade cotton are about the same diameter, but long-staple cotton is less than two inches long, requiring the spinning of many fibres together to make yarn or thread). Silk possesses other unique qualities. It has a tensile strength approaching that of iron wire of comparable diameter; it is elastic, capable of stretching 20 percent of its length without breaking or deforming; it absorbs moisture readily and as a consequence takes dye evenly and uniformly and resists fading; it has excellent insulating properties.

The hatching of worms from eggs must be timed to coincide with the first leafing of mulberry plants, usually about mid-April. It is critically important that all the worms hatch at the same time, so that subsequent stages occur simultaneously; if this is not done, cocoons will be spun and moths emerge at different times, thus ruining most cocoons. Damaged cocoons cannot be reeled, and are good only for silk floss or spun silk. The eggs are tiny, but the worms grow rapidly and—particularly late in their growth—they eat voraciously. One ounce contains about 35,000 eggs, which will in turn produce about 600 pounds of mature worms. During their lifetime, these worms will consume two and a half tons of mulberry leaves.

The growth process typically takes about thirty-five days, during which time the worms molt four times, resting briefly ("sleeping," the Chinese say) before recovering their appetites. The mature worm signals readiness to spin its cocoon by raising and moving its head. Workers, who have been carefully attending each moment of the process, controlling temperature, laying out fresh leaves, etc., now move the worms to specially prepared straw trusses, and the worm begins to spin its cocoon by ejecting a viscous fluid from two spinneret glands. Upon exposure to air, this fluid immediately hardens to form a single filament. Two other glands coat the filament with the gummy resin, sericin. Forming the cocoon takes about three days, after which eight to ten days elapse before the insect is ready to escape. The chrysalis moistens (and stains) one end of the cocoon, cuts or pushes the filaments aside and emerges after a three-day effort. Mating occurs within a week, with the female laying 500 to 750 eggs, after which both sexes quickly die; seventy female moths are required to replace the 35,000 eggs (one ounce) with which we began this account.

Meanwhile, cocoons not reserved for egg production must be harvested during the week of dormancy after spinning is complete and before the chrysalis begins to escape. These must now be treated with boiling water, steam, or dry heat to kill the chrysalis and prepare the silk for reeling. Our one ounce of eggs, transformed into 140 pounds of cocoon (not all of which are suitable for reeling) now yields twelve pounds of reeled raw silk. The process of silk production, from the hatching of worms up to the delivery of cocoons, has changed very little over the centuries, as a visit to the silk districts of China or Japan today will confirm. Although thermostatically controlled breeding rooms, better disease control, etc., have improved productivity, the life cycle of the worm and the growth pattern of the mulberry bush set rigid limits on the technology that can be imposed on the process.

Beyond this point, reeling, dyeing, and weaving of silk—evolved from household or workshop enterprise—are well-suited to the division of labor and to economies of scale, i.e., to industrial production. It is in these phases of the process that the rivers and canals of the Chiang-nan and of Szechwan play a role, in the movement of cocoons to the reeling mills, of reeled silk to the dyeing and weaving sheds, and finally in the transport of the finished fabrics through the Yangtze system to their ultimate markets in China and abroad. In this sense, the "hinterland" of the Yangtze—the reach of its influence—had intercontinental scope.

Silk has always been an elite product, amounting to less than 1 percent of cotton and 3 percent of wool production in the twentieth century. In world trade, it reached its peak in about 1920, when its major use was for women's silk hosiery—perhaps the only mass use of silk in its history. Thereafter, artificial fibres—rayon, nylon, orlon, etc.—were developed and replaced silk in many of its previous uses. Although silk technology was developed in China, by the mid-1930s Japan was the dominant Asian and world producer, partly because of aggressive adoption of the best production methods, especially quality control, and partly because Chinese production was seriously disrupted by unrest, revolution, and Japanese invasion.

Tea

Like silk, tea has become virtually a synonym for China. Also like silk, tea culture—plant, drinking practices, paraphernalia—spread from China to other parts of Asia: to Vietnam, Korea, and to obsessive ritualization in Japan. Huge tea plantations in Ceylon and India, established under British auspices in the 1840s and later, were by the end of the century seriously challenging the demand for Chinese teas. Within China, tea was, of course, a major item of internal trade, in much wider use than silk from about the seventh century on. Even so, poorer elements of the population often had to settle for boiled water, sometimes euphemistically called "plain tea." Tea growers, shippers, brokers, and merchants were highly organized. Their guildhalls in the major trading centers were perhaps not quite so opulent as those of the big salt merchants but they were nevertheless very impressive; and successful tea merchants, like their colleagues in other trades, often tended to diversify their commercial activities. Once again, the provinces up and down the Yangtze Valley produce the best teas and the largest crops, although Kwangtung (Canton's province), Fukien just to the north, and Taiwan all grow excellent tea.

Tea—the name comes from the Chinese term as rendered in Fukien (Amoy) dialect, *t'e*, pronounced "tay" (Mandarin *ch'a*)—is made from the leaves of certain species of bush belonging to the genus Camellia, a native of Asia. It adapts to a fairly wide variety of natural conditions from tropical to temperate, if winters are not too cold and if it receives considerable rainfall during the growing season. Tea is customarily grown in the well-drained soils of hill country where the air is fresher and where it does not compete for land with rice or other vegetable crops, but where there is also an abundant source of labor. Seedlings are planted out at one year, and produce commercially usable leaf from age three to eight. During this time, they are kept carefully pruned to maximize development of new leaves and shoots—the "flush"—which emerge throughout the growing season, permitting four crops to be picked each year, in April, May, July, and August or September. The first crop is the most highly prized, with each picking less valuable than the one before. An experienced tea plucker can take about 30,000 shoots a day, which will produce nine or ten pounds of tea.

The process of turning freshly picked leaves into finished tea, complicated in the details of different varieties and qualities, is simple in its essentials. Green teas and black teas (which the Chinese call "red teas") come from the same plants, differing only in the method of processing. In making green (unfermented) tea, fresh-picked leaves are first allowed to wither briefly, then heated for several minutes in order to prevent fermentation and retain some green color. They are next carefully rolled, twisted, and squeezed (originally by hand, now by machine) so as to break down the leaf cells to express some of their enzymes and juices. Then comes firing, in broad wok-shaped pans above a wood fire (now electricity), while being constantly hand-stirred by the worker. The green tea is now ready for sorting, blending, packing, and shipping. Black teas are rolled more strenuously than green immediately after withering, without the short first heating. This expresses more of the juices and permits fermentation to occur before firing dries the leaf.

Depending on treatment, quality, and variety, tea may end up as pieces, tight shreds, or even powder. It may be packed loose, in pads, or in hard

"The Evolution of Tea." The painting depicts the entire economic cycle of the tea trade, from cultivation in the hills to the loading of chests certified with "chops" onto lighters for transfer to clipper ships. Note the foreigners doing business at the wharf. By an unknown Chinese artist (mid-19th century, in "western style").

bricks for trade with Tibet and Mongolia. Chinese teas are at least as numerous as French wines—one source claims about 1500 growths and 2000 possible blends—and tea connoisseurship is as developed in China as is the wine palate in France. Tea names—pekoe, hyson, souchong, oolong, bohea, gunpowder, imperial—have a romantically exotic sound in Western ears, enhanced by widespread uncertainty as to what kind of tea, precisely, is being named.

Although tea is mentioned as a medicinal in ancient Chinese sources, it did not become a beverage of widespread use until about the seventh century—rather late on the Chinese scale of things. Some claim that it was promoted by Buddhist monks as an alternative to alcoholic beverages, and it is true that much of the lore and ceremony of tea in the Sino-Japanese culture area is associated with Buddhism. In any case tea was thereafter inseparable from Chinese life, including an elaborate lore, knowledge of which was a symbol of status and polite attainment. One knew the best waters to use, how to boil the water and how long to steep the tea, which brewing and serving implements to use in what setting, and the specialized argot of tea. The teahouse was a traditional center for social and business contacts.

Thus when Europeans began arriving in Chinese ports in the sixteenth century, they found a highly developed tea culture flourishing throughout the empire and indeed the entire East Asian region. Chinese teas began to show up in England in the mid-seventeenth century, as evidenced by a newspaper advertisement in 1658: "That Excellent and by all Physitians approved China drink, called by the Chineans *Tcha* . . . is sold at the Sultaness Head Cophee House in Sweetings Rent, by the Royal Exchange." A couple of years later, Samuel Pepys wrote in his diary, "I did send for a cup of *tee* (a China drink) of which I had never drank before." With the vigorous promotion of the British East India Company, which had a monopoly on the trade until 1834, it soon caught on. Curiously, England had been well on the way to becoming a nation of coffee drinkers—as seen in the popularity of coffee houses in the sixteenth and seventeenth centuries—before tea replaced coffee. Meanwhile, in the American colonies, an initial preference for tea gave way to coffee, particularly after the Boston Tea Party. Tea imports to England tell the story.

1705	800,000 lbs
1721	1,000,000 lbs
1766	6,000,000 lbs
1840	37,000,000 lbs
1860	81,000,000 lbs
1875	127,555,000 lbs

Until the late eighteenth century, the value of these tea shipments was not offset by any product for which Great Britain could find a ready market in China. Woolens had a limited market in hot and humid Canton, to which port trade was restricted; the result was, for England, a worrisome and growing trade deficit, and for China a handsome inflow of silver. This deficit was made up following the discovery that opium would sell briskly in China, where it had long been known as a medicinal and anaesthetic. By this time, however, it was becoming, in today's parlance, a "recreational" drug, thought at first to offer benign release from fatigue, worry, and stress, an escape into "pipe dreams." Indeed, China's experience then with opium provides many parallels with America's experience now with cocaine.

By 1800, the value of opium imports was growing even faster than the value of tea exports. When the Chinese government outlawed the import of opium in the 1790s, the British East India Company complied with the ban. Instead, it grew and processed opium on large plantations in India and sold these increasingly potent forms of the drug to private traders, called "country merchants," who took the risk of getting the opium to China and selling it to Chinese smugglers, receiving large amounts of silver in return. This silver they turned over to East India Company representatives in Canton or Macao, in return for certificates of deposit in London banks. Proud and upstanding business houses—Jardine-Matheson and Butterfield and Swire among them—were founded on fortunes made as country traders of opium. Meanwhile, the company now had more than enough silver to pay for the season's teas.

By the 1830s, the company was exporting annually to China something like 30,000 chests of opium (ca. 165 lbs per chest), the sale of which in China netted a profit of something like £1.5 million per year over and above *all* purchases (tea and all other products)—not counting the profit made at the producing end in India from the sale of opium to the country traders. Peter Ward Fay describes the trade with rueful admiration:

> What a marvelous interlocking system it was—and at the bottom of it, opium! Its sale at Calcutta contributed significantly to the revenue of the Government of India. Its sale at Lintin [a small island near Hong Kong] financed the purchase of England's teas, while at the same time making it easier for returning English nabobs and the Government of India to get Indian rupees home. In England . . . Whitehall depended upon the tea duty for a considerable part of its revenue. How convenient the drug was, how indispensable even—but at the same time how dangerous to the future tranquillity of the China trade.

These and other grievances led eventually to the First Anglo-Chinese War

GREAT RACE

OF THE

TEA SHIPS,

WITH THE FIRST

NEW SEASON'S TEAS.

PRICE OF TEAS REDUCED.

THE "Taeping," "Ariel," "Fiery Cross," and "Serica" have arrived, with others in close pursuit, with something like FORTY-FIVE MILLION POUNDS OF NEW TEA on board—half a year's consumption for the United Kingdom. This enormous weight coming suddenly into the London Docks, Shippers are compelled to submit to MUCH LOWER PRICES, in order to make sales.

We are thus enabled to make a Reduction of FOURPENCE in the pound.

4/0 down to · · 3/8
3/8 „ · · 3/4
3/4 „ · · 3/0

And so on downwards.

We may add the above Ships have brought a few lots of must unusual fine quality.

Reduction takes place on Friday the 21st inst.

155, OXFORD STREET;
57, STRETFORD ROAD; and
171, STRETFORD ROAD—
"Great Northern."
} **BURGON & CO.,**
TEA MERCHANTS.

Handbill advertising arrival of new teas. The amount of tea claimed is incorrect; it should be 4.5 million pounds.

(1840–42)—better known as the first "Opium War"—and to a century of Chinese humiliation under the structure of "the unequal treaties," imposed then and later. One major consequence of these coerced agreements was the opening of five "treaty ports"—later to increase to more than thirty— of which the most important was Shanghai, then a modest coastal town but soon to grow into China's greatest city. Within twenty years, most of the export tea trade had abandoned Canton, which had owed its importance as much to imperial decision as to natural economic advantage. By the 1880s, after the awful disruption of the Taiping Rebellion, even Hankow exported more tea to foreign countries than did Canton, all of it through foreign firms which tapped into Chinese trading networks through Chinese agents called *compradores* (literally "buyers," from the Portugese, but later connoting "agents of the foreigners," something close to "traitors").

During these same years, with the ponderous and decrepit British East India Company now defunct, the combination of free trade and tea led to the evolution of the clipper ships, the finest and fastest long-distance sailing vessels ever built. Although the first clipper ships were designed in the United States, their main purpose was to get the first teas of the season to England as quickly as possible—one hundred days was an excellent passage—it being believed that delays impaired the flavor of the brew. During a brief heyday in the 1850s and 1860s, their voyage each year from China ports to London excited enormous attention as "the great tea race," a 16,000-mile competition, with the Straits of Sunda, the Cape of Good Hope, and the Azores as marker buoys. Risks and rewards—a pound sterling or more per ton for cargos of about 500 tons—both ran high in the hunt for "The Blue Riband of the Sea," but on the other hand the enormous sail area and the extreme length-to-width ratio made the fastest of the clippers vulnerable in storms.

The most closely contested of all the tea races was that of 1866. Eleven ships left the Pagoda Anchorage at Foochow beginning on May 29. All down the China Sea, across the Indian Ocean, around the Cape of Good Hope, and up the south Atlantic, the leaders—the *Ariel, Taeping, Serica, Fiery Cross,* and *Taitsing*—were never more than a couple of days apart. At dawn on September 5, with a strong following wind, the *Ariel* and the *Taeping* were beam to beam up the English Channel at 15 knots. At Deal, near the mouth of the Thames, the *Ariel* was ten minutes in the lead, but with some unscrupulous maneuvering of tugs and final berthing, the *Taeping* was declared the winner by twenty minutes. The *Serica* came in three hours later on the same tide, with the *Fiery Cross* one day and the *Taitsing* three days behind. After 99 days and 16,000 miles, three ships arrived on the same day, within a few hours of one another.

After this, nothing but anticlimax. Even in their finest moment, the clippers were becoming obsolete in the face of steam vessels and the opening of the Suez Canal in 1869. Surviving clippers hung on for a time in the China trade, and were then relegated to unseemly tasks, like an old thoroughbred racehorse harnessed to a milk wagon, tramping around, hauling timber and the like until they broke up, were lost at sea, or were abandoned as hulks. Only the *Cutty Sark* survived, by sheer fortune, and was fully restored during the 1950s and 1960s as a maritime museum moored at Greenwich.

> The ships so brave and beautiful that never more shall be,
> By the old Pagoda Anchorage when clippers sailed the sea—
> Racing home to London River—
> Crack her on for London River—
> Carry on for London River with her chests of China tea!

Almost hand in hand with the decline of the clippers was the decline of the China export tea trade, as the Indian, Ceylonese, and Java-Sumatra

A cutaway drawing of the *Cutty Sark*, fully loaded with tea chests.

plantations came into production. Quality was high, costs were relatively low, and the voyage to China was now unnecessary. Opium plantations in India were no longer needed in order to pay for China teas—and China was producing plenty of opium of its own. By 1900, China had fallen to fourth place, and in 1930 it was exporting less than one-half the amount of fifty years earlier, despite rapid growth in the world tea trade as a whole. Not until the 1980s did China's tea exports once again approach those of the nineteenth century. Despite this fall from monopoly to insignificance, China remained the world's largest tea producer, returning to patterns of trade centered on the Yangtze River as they had existed before the coming of the Europeans.

Tung Oil

If tea and silk are full of history and romance, familiar to all and identified with China, tung oil is a blue-collar product few have ever heard of. But tung oil resembles these more aristocratic products because its properties, like theirs, are unmatched by any other natural substance and because it was produced almost nowhere else. Although used in China for millennia, it did not attract international attention until the late nineteenth and early twentieth centuries. The tung oil trade grew spectacularly in both volume and unit price between 1918 and 1937, with about 70 percent of the product shipped to the United States. In 1937, the first year of the Sino-Japanese War, over 20,000,000 gallons were exported (at about $1.40 per gallon), making it China's most valuable single trade product. In just a few years, tung oil had soared past tea, cotton yarn, metals, eggs and egg products, skins and furs, and raw silk. War devastated this trade and U.S. chemical industries, impelled to invent alternatives for many products now unavailable, developed petroleum-based substitutes to take the place of tung oil in most uses. In this, too, tung oil resembles silk, which also fell victim to the chemical industry's rayon and nylon.

Tung oil is classified as a "drying oil," by which is meant that when exposed to air it oxidizes readily, forming a tough, hard, waterproof film. Tung oil can be applied alone as a waterproofing varnish, and this is one of its main uses in China. The Chinese also use tung oil for preparing caulking materials (*chunam*), dressing leather, waterproofing paper, making soap, treating skin afflictions, and producing lampblack for solid inksticks.

But perhaps its most important function is (or was) in the manufacture of paint. Reduced to its barest essentials, paint has two principal components: the pigment, comprised of extremely fine particles of the coloring agent, and the vehicle, or liquid medium in which the insoluble pigment is carried. A volatile thinner, such as turpentine or mineral spirits, is added to provide the proper consistency for application. When brushed out, the thinners evaporate, leaving a film of pigment bonded in the vehicle, which is also responsible for sticking to the object being painted. For this purpose, tung oil is superior to linseed oil, traditionally the most widely used drying oil in Europe and the United States; tung oil dries faster and produces a harder, more durable film.

Tung oil (sometimes also called wood oil) is obtained from the nut of the tung tree (*Aleurites cordata*), which is native to China. Almost all commercially grown tung trees are found in the central provinces, north and south of the Long River, particularly in Szechwan and Hunan. As the demand grew, more and more trees were planted, particularly on hilly, otherwise unproductive land along the navigable tributaries of the Long River, in order to reduce the cost of overland transport—usually by shoulder pole—which could quickly erode the profits to be made.

Typical tung tree culture involved a cycle of about forty or forty-five years, although practices varied from place to place. Selected slopes were cleared by first removing everything useful for fuel, then burning the rest. Ideally, these hilly areas were located fairly close to agricultural land, since—like tea—tung production was a sideline occupation, for which labor was only periodically needed. After the hillsides were prepared, mixed crops of corn and soybeans were grown for about three years, until the soil was exhausted.

Then one-year-old tung saplings were set out, to produce their first crop in three to five years. Although the tung tree grows very well unattended in barren soil, it requires abundant rainfall; as one may imagine, erosion is a serious problem in tung-growing regions. Tung trees produce for about twenty years, after which they are abandoned or cut for fuel, and the hillside allowed to grow wild for another twenty years or so. The forty-five-year cycle then begins anew.

Three to five oil-bearing nuts, about the size of small Brazil nuts, are held in a globular fruit two inches in diameter; harvest is in September or October, after the main crops are gathered. The fruit is first heated briefly in large pans over a fire and the nuts are removed. Then they are processed like most other Chinese seed-oil crops, with equipment at the same time ingenious and crude—a labor-intensive combination one encounters time and again in China. The nuts are crushed by stone roller turned by bullock, mule, or man, then placed in a wedge press. The wedge press is most commonly made from a large tree trunk or two logs pinned together and laid horizontal, with a wide trough running lengthwise on top and a narrow slot, also lengthwise, on the bottom. The crushed nuts are held in place by a number of iron rings butted up against one end of the trough. Wedges are driven with a sledge, side by side, pushing hardwood disks against the nut mash in the iron rings, expressing the oil, which oozes out between the rings and is collected through the slot at the bottom. The process can be repeated to get a second, smaller pressing, until about 35 percent of the original weight of the nuts has been obtained as oil. The best oil has a light ruddy color, and all of it has a rather unpleasant odor (as well as being poisonous), this odor being its chief drawback.

Even in the 1940s, only a small amount of oil was obtained through the use of hydraulic presses, testifying to the extremely decentralized and localized nature of oil production, as an adjunct to other peasant activities. Since the oil was both lighter and much more valuable than the raw nuts, it made sense to make oil in many small and primitive presses, rather than carry the nuts some distance to a large modern press.

Tung oil was traditionally packed for the China market in wickerwork baskets lined with specially prepared oiled paper; sturdier wooden casks were also used, but absorbed some of the oil. More recently, recycled kerosene cans were also commonly employed, since kerosene ("oil for the lamps of China") was, from the early twentieth century, a bulk import—perhaps the only bulk import from abroad—into nearly all parts of China. Used mainly for lighting, kerosene was substantially less expensive than vegetable oils, and it paid for itself by enabling peasants to carry on handicrafts after dark.

With the rapid growth of the export market, Hankow and Shanghai became the main collecting points for tung oil, with a much smaller amount flowing out through Hong Kong. From minor tributaries to major and thence into the Long River, the oil flowed downstream to Hankow or Shanghai. Since 10,000-ton oceangoing ships could reach Hankow in most seasons, some oil was exported directly from that inland port. Hankow also shipped a good deal of oil to Shanghai, and for the oil produced in the lower Yangtze basin, Anhwei and Chekiang provinces particularly, Shanghai was also the principal destination. Had the war and war-induced substitutes not intervened, tung oil would almost certainly have had a bright future. Indeed, so valuable was the product that in the 1930s efforts were made to experiment with tung plantations along the Gulf Coast of Florida, Mississippi, and Louisiana, but DuPont's chemists made them unnecessary just as they were beginning to produce a little oil.

Rice, salt, silk, tea, tung oil—none of these were ever exclusive to the Yangtze Valley, but the centers of production of all of them have been located throughout this vast region. Their abundance, variety, and quality have depended not entirely on the fertile soil and moderate climate of the area, nor even on the industriousness of the Chinese people applied to these endowments. Without the capacity to move these products, to bring them to market, there would have been little incentive to increase and diversify production beyond that necessary to meet immediate needs. Silk, tea, and tung oil might never have evolved past crude handicrafts—and even as it is, the stamp of handicraft industry is still clearly readable today.

Prior to railroads and motorized highways, bulk transport almost always meant transport by water, and here the Yangtze river system has been crucial to the development of China, not only to its economic life but also to its social and political life. Without the Grand Canal—that man-made extension of the Yangtze River—to carry the tribute grain of central China to the north, Peking could hardly have survived as China's capital for 700 years.

The reach of the Yangtze River Valley thus extends well beyond its own topographical limits, to both north and south China—and farther. Even prior to the modern age, the Yangtze Valley traded internationally: silk and tea, of course, but also porcelains and other products. Over the past couple of centuries, as distant parts of the world have come into ever closer contact, as webs of commerce and dependency have grown, the Yangtze River Valley has become part of a world economy. Silk, tea, and tung oil have been important commodities of world trade. One imagines Hunanese tea pickers, unaware of England's existence, silently, anonymously present in late-afternoon London drawing room conversations, among company oblivious to the origins of its beverage. In remote yet intimate ways, clipper ships, Ceylonese tea plantations, and the international chemical industry are a part of the Yangtze Valley.

In the next chapter, we turn from the products themselves to the craft and crews by which they were carried up and down the Yangtze River system.

8

JUNKS AND JUNKMEN

Shen Ts'ung-wen was born in 1903 in the west Hunan county seat of Feng-huang (Phoenix) to a soldier's family once of modest means but by then quite poor. Phoenix, in a rich tung-oil region, was part of the internal frontier—picturesque but backward and hardly touched by modern life, where richly romantic myths and mystical images flourished and where aboriginal Miao people still spoke their own language and followed their own ways. Shen joined a local ragtag army as a boy of fifteen, and for several years drifted about the region. But he was also reading widely on his own, and beginning to write. By the mid-1920s, he was in Peking and Shanghai, rubbing shoulders with an urbane and politicized intellectual elite but determined to pursue the writer's craft in his own nativist way. No one in modern Chinese literature has been more prolific or had a stronger regionalist identification than Shen Ts'ung-wen. In *West Hunan* (1943), a collection of essays about the places he knew so well, Shen describes the waterfront scene in Ch'ang-te, on the Yuan River. It is well to keep in mind that larger rivers and busier ports could be found throughout the Yangtze Valley, yet they would exhibit many of the features Shen here depicts:

> Geography books say that Ch'ang-te is the major river port for western Hunan, where export and import goods are exchanged. Tung oil, lumber, ox hides, pig gut, bristles, tobacco, quicksilver, gall nuts, and opium are exported from eastern Szechwan and eastern Kweichow as well as western Hunan, loaded onto boats of every sort and shipped toward Hankow. Packaged salt, dyed yarn, cotton piece goods, matches, kerosene, medicines, wheat flour, sugar, and every kind of light consumer good or daily necessity are imported in return by downriver boats. Here they are repacked to be delivered by boats of different sizes to all the

major and minor river towns along the tributaries of the upper Yuan River.

Along both banks of the river are boats large and small that seem to the casual eye of the outsider pretty much the same. But in fact, their shapes are not at all alike; each has its particular character and represents in its own way the region from which it comes.

The most obvious of boats is the three-masted square-bow boat. These are visitors from afar, having come from the Long River across Tung-t'ing Lake, with salt as their main cargo. Mostly they come no farther, and do not proceed into the upper Yuan. Naturally enough, people call them "salt boats," but the boatmen themselves call them "big carp heads."

In this region, however, the magnificent and imposing "Hung River oil boats" are undisputed kings. Most of these boats have a square bow and raised poop. They are brightly colored, sometimes embellished with gold paint, and are fitted with a stern house for the master's family. Downbound, they can carry three or four thousand barrels of tung oil; on the return trip they load two thousand bolts of cotton cloth or a full consignment of salt. Manning the sweeps are anywhere from twenty-six to forty men, along with thirty to sixty trackers. They must wait for spring flood in order to get underway between Hung River [a town about 275 river miles farther up the Yuan] and Ch'ang-te. During the high-water season, they can make three to five round trips, and the rest of the time they sit idle, moored in large flotillas—truly the monarchs of the river.

The masters are mostly men from Ma-yang [an upriver town, not far from Hung River], and many have the surname "Hsi." They are canny about local society and know who's who; they often ally with big merchants by marrying into their families. When a passenger of some standing comes aboard, the master invites him for a cup of wine while telling him all about his boat, about the powerful generals, rich merchants, and celebrated prostitutes he has carried throughout the Yuan River valley—in short, all about the "history" of the region. Aboard ship, the master's outfit is unremarkable, but ashore he wears a long gown reaching below the knee, covered by a bluish feathered silk jacket, a small felt or silk hat on his head, and at his waist a leather purse filled with silver dollars and fastened with a heavy silver chain. He wears untanned leather boots in which he walks with deliberate strides. Hard drinkers, good gamblers, and open-handed, when they throw a brothel party, they pull silver dollars from their purses with abandon.

The crew are almost all tall, strong, and brave men, with keen, fierce eyes—fine singers, swimmers, fighters, cursers. On the water they are like fish; ashore, around women, they are horny as young goats, and they get just as excited during a night's gambling.

Though there are a lot of people on board, each has his own task and there is never any confusion. When weighing anchor and getting underway, they always beat drums and gongs, burn spirit money and incense at the bow, cook pork as an offering to the spirits, and light long strings of firecrackers—all to show that men and spirits are in harmonious cooperation, and to call for a safe journey under a lucky star.

The most popular book in the river valley today is the litho-graphed almanac, printed on Pao-ch'ing paper and sold by itin-erant peddlers. According to custom, every boat has a copy of the *Imperial Almanac*. The boat people have many taboos, and the almanacs are treasured guides to action. Accidents occur often on the river, and each man wants to lessen his own responsibility: heaven must dispose all things. Doing things by the almanac brings a certain peace of mind and reduces quarrels.

Shen Ts'ung-wen here clothes in vivid language the sojourning merchant, the specialization of junk design and construction, the clannishness of oil-boat masters (*lao-ta's*) "old bigs," and the finely divided subcultures of each trade. But above all Shen evokes variety, each boat and crew adapted to its particular task, even though to the uninitiated they may look much alike. If a second-class city like Ch'ang-te exhibits such variety, how much greater the variety of the Long River system as a whole.

Junks

Fortunately, there exists a work that presents this astonishing variety in remarkable fullness and detail. George Raleigh Gray Worcester (1890–1969), employed for thirty years on the Yangtze by the Chinese Maritime Customs Service as River Inspector, made it his consuming passion to collect all the information he could about the junks and sampans of the entire river sys-tem—not only the boats themselves and their uses; their construction; means of propulsion by sail, oar, or tracker; rigging, anchors, and the like; but also the junkmen, their beliefs and superstitions; the lore of the river; and the coming of the steamers and power boats that had already in Worcester's time done so much to reduce—but not eliminate—junk traffic on many of the larger waterways.

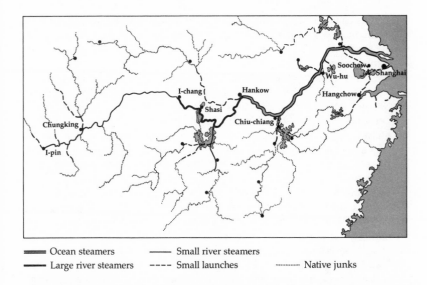

▬▬▬ Ocean steamers	▬▬▬ Small river steamers
▬▬▬ Large river steamers	---- Small launches	⋯⋯⋯ Native junks

FIGURE 8-1. Inland water transport routes, indicating the maximum vessel sizes various routes can accommodate. Steam vessels were confined by their size to major waterways. Only with the development of small internal combustion engines have most routes been open to power boats but even today they have not fully displaced traditional craft.

Of the total of nearly 9,000 navigable miles in the entire system, just about half is accessible only to native craft—junk, sampan, raft—beyond the reach of powered boats. In addition, of course, native craft could still perform short-haul tasks even on big rivers (see Figure 8-1). No accurate junk census was ever taken, but early twentieth century estimates range from 10,000 to 30,000 vessels upstream from I-ch'ang alone, with a crew population of perhaps 300,000. Although the number of junks has declined drastically in more recent years, even a casual tourist will still today see a large number and variety of native craft.

In his magnum opus, Worcester describes nearly 250 different craft, most accompanied by scale drawings, working his way region by region upriver from the estuary to the ultimate head of navigation at I-pin (P'ing-shan), 250 miles above Chungking, and including the Grand Canal, the big lakes, and the major tributaries. He also remarks that his inventory of river craft is incomplete and says of his effort, "I fear it was begun too late. Some of the finest types, as a result of the last few difficult years, have gone forever." Lurking behind Worcester's regret is recognition of change. Although it is difficult to trace the evolution of a particular feature or craft, junk design was never static, but responded to need. Some designs remained unchanged for centuries because they were well adapted to tasks that remained unchanged. But changing needs produced new designs, mostly within a well-understood repertoire of ingenious design solutions and building techniques.

These included the characteristic square bow and stern, and the absence of a keel, as well as the early development of bulkheads, watertight compartments, and the transom stern which facilitates the mounting of a rudder. One of the most visible characteristics of the Chinese junk is that the stern is higher than the bow, and that the permanent superstructure is also usually placed far aft, well behind any masts the boat may have. This leaves most of the length of the boat unobstructed for sails, tracking gear, cargo loading, etc.

Cabin location is related to another distinctive feature, not found in western ships until the coming of steam: placement of the widest part of the vessel aft of center and sometimes right at the stern. All members of the widespread *Ma-yang-tzu* junk family share this characteristic, as do several other designs whose very names indicate a similar shape: oilbottle junk, ducktail junk, red-slipper junk. Although this hull shape was adopted because it improved handling and steering, some designs were said to accentuate it for another reason—to evade transit tolls, since duty was levied according to cargo capacity, calculated by measuring the vessel's depth and breadth at the highest mast. The tallest mast was thus placed far forward on a hull shaped like "the head of a snake and the body of a tortoise," as one Chinese commentator put it.

Although no single design can represent the enormous variety of junks and sampans, perhaps the Ma-yang-tzu comes closest to a generic design, one intended to navigate the Yuan River rapids and developed in the upriver town of Ma-yang that supplied "Old Bigs" to the Hung River oil boats (see illustration on page 115). Once again, Worcester is our main source:

> All the *ma-yang-tzu* types are heavy, cumbersome, deep-draught cargo-carriers, strongly built to negotiate the long-distance voyages required of them. The size varies greatly in range from a length of 110 feet down to only 38 feet, but invariably the main characteristics are faithfully adhered to.
>
> These junks mostly ply from Hunan ports to Hankow and are also largely used to transport wood oil transhipped from I-ch'ang down river in large oil-proof baskets.
>
> This most serviceable type of junk very soon proved its worth and became deservedly popular beyond the confines of the Yuan, its river of origin.
>
> Its fame spread to the Middle Yangtze, when is not known, on which section of the river it became the recognized cargo carrier.

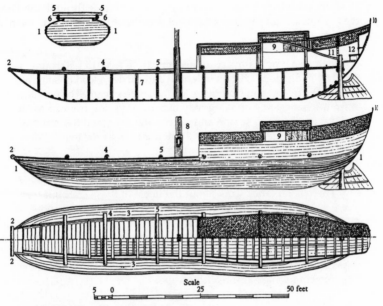

1 long and heavy wales running the length of the vessel
2 projecting cross-beam at transom bow
3 low coaming from bow to deckhouse
4, 5 projecting cross-beams holding the thole-pins for the yulohs (see p. 622 and Fig. 933, pl.)
6 transoms
7 fifth bulkhead supporting hardwood capstan
8 80-ft. *shan-mu* mast and its tabernacle, with carved halyards cleat
9 tiller-room with forward view (but in some forms the tiller may rise above this deck-house and be worked from a thwartwise gangway above it)
10 two tall pins on which spare bamboo rope is coiled
11 25-ft. tiller of balanced rudder (cf. p. 655 and Fig. 1043, pl.)
12 after-house (skipper's cabin and home)

The fully evolved Szechwan version of the *ma-yang* design, with major design features indicated. Simpler versions of this design were (and are) commonly seen.

Later it found its way into Szechwan, in which province the first of its type to be built was constructed by a Hunan merchant who took up business in Chungking. It soon demonstrated its superiority over other craft as the basic type best suited to the navigation of the rapids above I-ch'ang, though retaining the old generic name of *ma-yang-tzu*, which explains why the Hunanese name is still in general use in Szechwan for the most representative craft of the gorges, which is a modified and adapted form of the old prototype. This also accounts for the popular saying that none but a Hunan carpenter can build a true *ma-yang-tzu*.

The largest junks were engaged in long-distance trade through the Three Gorges. Cornell Plant supplies additional detail about their cost and the risks to the trip:

> The largest type of junk costs anything from 1,000 to 1,500 ounces of silver. She tops 120 feet in length and carries a load of some 60 tons up stream, and from 80 to 90 tons down stream. The passage from Ichang to Chungking may occupy anything from 25 to 60 days, according to season and state of the river, and the running expenses of such a passage will amount to from 700 to 800 [Mexican silver] dollars.
>
> The junk's crew tots up to over 100 men all told, not including the skipper and his family—usually a baker's dozen.
>
> There is no fancy work about the finest of these craft but they are suited to their job, and nothing is wasted on appearances— which may well be understood when the risks are taken into consideration. Chinese say that one junk in ten is badly damaged, and one in twenty totally wrecked, each trip. Probably not 20 percent reach Chungking unscathed, and never one without experiencing some hair-breadth escape.

If the Mayang'er comes closest to the generic junk, there were other much more specialized features or practices. One of these was the disposable junk of Szechwan, developed along the then heavily forested tributaries flowing south toward Chungking. Hastily and crudely built from inexpensive lumber, these junks made a single trip downriver and were then sold for whatever they might fetch for house building, thus obviating the difficult trip back against fast rapids and strong currents. Also made for a one-way trip were timber or bamboo rafts, particularly common in Hunan, headed downriver to be broken up in big-city lumber marts and manned by small crews who lived in makeshift cabins built aft.

Another innovation used in some junks, one not seen in the West, was a free-flooding compartment, far forward and/or aft, with holes below the water line, to allow for fast and automatic change in trim ballast as the boats pitched over heavy rapids—this practice, of course, requiring excellent watertight integrity. Such compartments were also used in oceangoing fishing boats, not for trim ballast but as live tanks in which to keep the catch fresh until reaching port.

Immediately noticeable to the eye of the observer were these "crooked-stern" and "crooked-bow" boats, also found only in Szechwan. In the 1890s, Archibald Little said of the crooked-stern junk, "It is just as though a giant had taken an ordinary junk in his two hands and wrung it a quarter round, so that the stern deck is actually perpendicular, being at right angles to the forward deck, into which the slope gradually merges." Both types of boats were used for salt transport on rapids-filled tributaries, and such peculiar designs were specifically adapted to these conditions—although, strangely, most junkmen did not understand their functions. Mixed with some authentic clues was much improbable lore about Lu Pan, the patron saint of carpenters and boatbuilders, who was inspired, some said, by the appearance of a hawk's tail feathers as it flew away from him. Another curious explanation—one that says something about Chinese values—tells of a master boatbuilder who made the careless mistake of using warped timbers; later builders then copied his example so as not to cause him to lose face.

The crooked-stern junks—in Chinese, *wai p'i-ku* (twisted buttock)—were found only on Crow River (*Wu-jiang*), which meets the Long River at Fuling, where White Crane Ridge carries low-water records going back to the T'ang dynasty. Worcester describes them as built according to a "carefully thought out plan, which is probably the outcome of centuries of trial and error":

> The crooked-stern junk has no rudder and is steered by a gigantic stern-sweep. The main purpose, therefore, of the twisted and uneven taffrail is to permit the use both of this stern-sweep and of a second, smaller, sweep on the starboard quarter. Both sweeps, though working from different planes, have nearly the same radius of action . . . and can be operated simultaneously if need be. Parallel as they are to each other and able to be used in a small compact area, there is nevertheless not the slightest danger of fouling, which would be disastrous in a rapid.

The unique crooked-bow junk—actually both bow *and* stern are biasbuilt—was confined to the T'o River and to its tributary, Salt-well River, that serves the salt and gas wells at Tzu-liu-ching (modern Tzu-kung). In the mid-1920s an estimated 3,000 such craft still plied their trade, each capable of loading about twenty-five tons of salt in reed-mat baskets of ca. 250 pounds each. This junk carried a very long stern sweep, perhaps sixty feet, as long as the junk itself and from which the Chinese name *lu-ch'uan* (oar boat) is taken. These features enabled the junk to get through one stretch of severe rapids, requiring sudden and hard turns at high speeds. Worcester describes the ticklish operation:

> The river flows down with a mighty swing, and the rocks at a distance of 2 or 3 feet seem to be flying in the opposite direction. The supreme moment has arrived, and the bowman braces himself for his important role. As the junk flashes past, a man standing on the rock neatly hands him the end of a bamboo rope which

is, at the other end, made fast to the rock. In a few seconds the bowman has cast three turns around the foremost bollard, and as swiftly starts to surge the rope, that is, he allows it to slacken in jerks. This 50-foot rope takes only about 15 seconds to run out, but the restraint has been just sufficient to alter the course of the boat from headlong collision with the ugly, jagged-looking rock.

The safety of the junk now depends entirely on the men at the sweep, which not only acts as a rudder, but can be used as a powerful lever. The five men bend all the weight of their shoulders against the heavy loom, and with a single movement wrench the junk round at the critical moment when a crash seems inevitable. To achieve this, the sweep must be put over once only and at precisely the right moment, when the junk is only a few feet off the rock. Diverted as if on a pivot, the junk now careers away in comparative safety, still at a fairly high speed, through the narrow gutterway, with the dangers fast disappearing astern.

The angled stern and bow not only make these maneuvers possible, but the bow design also facilitates tracking the boats back upstream against the current, helping to hold the proper course and prevent sheering out broadside to the current and also to prevent fouling of the tracking lines.

Two other special purpose boats are worthy of brief mention. The first was the fleet of about fifty post-boats that in the late nineteenth and early twentieth centuries carried the mail between Chungking and I-ch'ang, making faster and more dependable passage than any other type of craft. And finally there were the lifeboats, the so-called "red boats" of the Three Gorges and the upper Long River. Apparently instituted for the first time in the 1850s by a benevolent merchant who lived near New Rapids (*Hsin-t'an*), they found favor with a number of high officials (Li Hung-chang and Ting Pao-chen among them), who gave money for their maintenance and stationing at other dangerous points. In the 1880s, the service became a suboffice of the I-ch'ang Circuit Intendant. In 1899, according to Worcester, they saved 1,473 lives from 49 wrecked junks, and the next year 1,235 lives from 37 wrecks, including 33 foreigners and 285 Chinese taken off the first foreign steamer to be sunk in the river, the German-owned *Suihsing*. These figures, incidentally, suggest how many lives were lost each year prior to the introduction of the red boats. In the early 1900s, there were nearly fifty red boats on station, one or more at each danger point, manned by three or four sailors who "only receive about sixpence a day wages, but are rewarded by 1000 cash for every life saved, and by 800 cash for every corpse—irrespective whether it be male or female—so the lifeboat regulations state." Not even the most jaundiced traveler had anything but praise for the skill, bravery, and honesty of the red-boat crews. It was even possible to hire a red boat to accompany one's passage through the Three Gorges, a precaution recommended by Cornell Plant, the most knowledgeable foreign sailor of the upper river:

> The voyager on the Upper Yangtze should always be accompanied by one of these little craft. A request through one's Consul at Ichang to the Chinese officials is, as a rule, all that is necessary to procure a red-boat. When one's house-boat has carried away her tracking lines at some particularly nasty spot, and is drifting helplessly with the swift swirling current towards some jagged reef, the presence of the life-boat close at hand is certainly comforting. This luxury is not an expensive one; it costs but 500 cash per day, and if the traveller treats his red-boat crew to an occasional feed of pork, he will surely be well-served.

Traditional river craft were propelled in several ways, when not being carried by the current: sail, oar, pole, grappling iron, or tracking. Sails and rigging, a complex and technical subject, need not detain us long (the enthusiast can easily consult Worcester and Needham). On river craft, sails were most important on the wider and lower reaches of the major waterways, above all on the mid- and lower Yangtze and in the estuary, where the river was broad enough to permit maneuvering. In narrower channels, junkmen were more dependent on a favorable wind direction astern; in the Three Gorges, there were only upbound and downbound winds. The typical Chinese sail—again there is much variety in detail—is the square or trapezoidal lug sail, with a portion of the sail, the "luff", forward of the mast to help balance the larger part (see illustration on page 120). Until the twentieth century, when cotton canvas began to be used, inexpensive matting woven of bamboo or reeds was universally used as sailcloth, despite its short lifetime. After its shape, the most visible characteristic of the Chinese sail is the several battens, stiffeners of bamboo running approximately parallel to the bottom of the sail. Worcester lists the functions of these battens: to keep the sail flat, and thus permit sailing closer to the wind; to allow the sail to be quickly reefed or dropped; to permit the use of flimsy or ragged sailcloth (a typical Chinese sail was said to be one-half sail, one-quarter patches, and one-quarter holes); and to enable a crewman to go aloft, using battens as rungs.

Chinese oars are worked by pushing from a standing position, thus differing from the West, where oars are pulled from a sitting posture. River junks were (and are) often propelled by a rowing crew of six, eight, ten, or more—one man per oar, half working on each side of the vessel. In addition to these oars, however, the Chinese invented a fore-and-aft oar which extends over the stern like a sternsweep. This is the sculling oar, *yuloh* (Man-

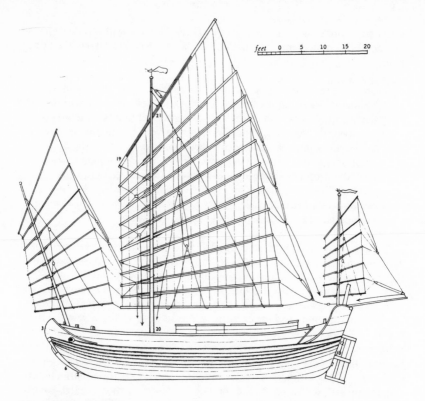

A typical junk sail layout.

darin *yau-lu*), "oscillating oar", which is moved back and forth, with the blade feathered at the end of each stroke by a quick pull on the rope attaching it to the deck, the oarman (or woman, often) working with one hand on the rope while the other moves the *yuloh*. This means of propulsion is very useful where traffic is congested, with no room for oars extending outward from the side of the boat. Small boats are often moved by the *yuloh* alone, which provides slow but steady progress with a minimum of effort.

Junkmen

Tracking—towing boats by human power—is widely used throughout China. On canals and other quiet waters, the sight of a few crewmen helping move a boat along arouses no special attention, and once started only moderate effort is necessary to maintain headway. But tracking a 120-ton Mayang-tzu through the worst rapids in the Three Gorges, against some of the most difficult currents in the world, is a feat so apparently impossible that the Western mind wonders how it could have been conceived in the first place, let alone accomplished. The origins of tracking through the Three Gorges are not well-documented, but circumstantial evidence points to the T'ang dynasty (A.D. 618–906), or possibly earlier: a Tun-huang mural, Li Po's poem about the river merchant's wife, the earliest hydrographic inscriptions at White Crane Ridge. One might also think so improbable an undertaking in keeping with the exuberant confidence of the early T'ang period, and with the growing economic importance of the entire Long River Valley.

In any case, by the Sung period (A.D. 960–1279), the practice was well established and documented, for example in the paintings of Hsia Kuei or in the travel account (in A.D. 1169) of the scholar and poet, Lu Yu, on his way to take up an official post at K'uei-chou, beside White King City at the head of the Three Gorges:

> Going up the gorges, we will use only oars and 'hundred-*chang*' towing lines and will not spread the sail. The 'hundred-*chang*' are made of huge pieces of bamboo split into four strands and are as big around as a man's arm. The boat I'm riding on, of the 1,600-bushel class, uses six oars and two hundred-*chang* lines wound on winches.

Junks headed up through the Three Gorges normally carried a basic complement of trackers as part of their regular crew, up to seventy or eighty on a large 120-ton cargo junk. These sufficed for the calmer stretches and moderate rapids, particularly if assisted by upriver winds. But, depending on the season of the year, there were many difficult passages—K'ung-ling, New Rapids, Otter Rapids, Sluice Rapids, and Windbox Gorge among others—where additional gangs of trackers were employed. Scores of junks were sometimes laid in at a mooring, waiting their turn to take on pilots and tracker gangs that might number as many as 200 or 250. In low water, it was sometimes necessary to lighten ship by offloading cargo and portaging around the rapids, at additional cost and delay.

There is no dearth of descriptions of trackers at work, so improbable and humbly daring was the notion of pitting their apparently puny strength against a heavy junk and the whole power of the river. Nearly every Westerner who passed through the Three Gorges has left a description of the trackers. They even have a place in modern American fiction, through John Hersey's portrayal in the novella *A Single Pebble*. Once again we turn to that old hand, Cornell Plant:

> Most interesting is it to watch a big junk maneuvering through some difficult passage. Seventy or eighty men ashore, hitched to

Trackers at work in the 1930s.

the stout bamboo hawser by bandoleers of cotton and line, are
straining with bent backs and swinging arms, their fingers almost
touching the ground, whilst the *tolos*, i.e., gangers, as naked as
they were born, armed with split bamboos, rush madly up and

down the double row of trackers, shouting themselves hoarse, testing each man's bandoleer as they run along by tapping on them with their bamboos with the cuteness of a grand piano tuner, and dealing out whacks on bare backs to the slackers. Away in the rear of the trackers three or four men are stationed at intervals along the tow-line, which it is their business to clear from the boulders and projecting points of rock on which it is constantly catching. It is a job involving considerable risk of bad falls and broken bones.

Perched on rocks, away out in the swift running river, several naked men may be seen, ready to wade or swim in the wake of the tow-line, throwing it clear as they go. Powerful swimmers, all of them, they perform the most daring feats, often swimming far out to the rescue of their drifting junk, with a stout bamboo line attached to them, at the risk of their lives.

At the other end of the long tow-line, away out in the rock-strewn stream, is the junk, slowly forging ahead. On her foredeck some fifteen or sixteen men stand ready to manoeuvre the great bowsweep at the word of command from the pilot, who is usually a weather-beaten grizzled old son of the Yangtze, whose experienced eye watches keenly every movement of the swirling waters, and who raps out his orders in the sharp decisive tone common to the deep sea boatswain.

At the foot of the tabernacle squats the drummer on his haunches, with the drum between his knees, on which he beats an incessant tattoo with a couple of sticks. It is the "all's well" signal to the trackers, which he instantly alters to a sharp rat-tat, rat-tat, when the tow-line, or anything untoward happens, signalling the trackers to cease pulling.

Aft, in the tiller room, on a raised platform, stands the helmsman, grappling with a fourteen-foot long tiller. He also is a pilot, and the navigating of the junk rests between him and his opposite number at the bowsweep.

The *laopan*, or skipper, usually perches on top of the deck house, from which point he watches moves. When any hitch occurs he rises to the occasion, stamping, cursing, and raving—often returned to him by the gangers, who go one better—until the skipper's mate, Mrs. Laopan, cannot stand it any longer. She comes on deck, and with a few well directed vexatious epithets ends the row. Even a Thames bargeman would be dumbfounded before Mrs. Laopan.

Plant's colorful and doubtless accurate description is nontheless too be-

Tracker's gallery or tow-path, cut into the walls of Ch'u-tang Gorge.

nign, touching only lightly on the terrible labor and great risks the trackers daily endured. Isabella Bird, that intrepid Victorian traveler (see Chapter 10), exhibited a greater sympathy for their inhuman lot:

> No work is more exposed to risks to limb and life. Many fall over the cliffs and are drowned; others break their limbs and are left

on shore to take their chance—and a poor one it is—without splints or treatment; severe strains and hernia are common, produced by tremendous efforts in dragging, and it is no uncommon thing when a man falls that his thin naked body is dragged bumping over the rocks before he extricates himself. On every man almost are to be seen cuts, bruises, wounds, weals, bad sores from cutaneous disease, and a general look of inferior rice.

In the Windbox section of Ch'ü-t'ang Gorge, the last great trial on a junk's upriver passage, before reaching somewhat easier waters above the Three Gorges, it had been necessary to cut a tracking gallery into the sheer cliff face (see photograph on page 124). There is nothing fictional about its description in John Hersey's *A Single Pebble:*

> This one-sided corridor cut from the cliffs was just high enough for trackers leaning forward on their halters, towing heavy weights, creeping almost; a man could not stand straight on his two feet in that space. In ten centuries this corridor had never been enlarged, but had been left the same height—a proper height for straining trackers . . . with a mountain of stone pressing on their shoulder blades and death off the edge to the left.

A misstep meant falling onto the rocks or into the torrent below; faulty judgment by the pilot could jerk a tracking crew out of the gallery by the hawser to which they were attached.

The tracking hawser—the lifeline of junk and tracker alike—was of woven bamboo strips, two to four inches in diameter, made in exactly the same way as larger suspension bridge cables (such as those at All-Rivers Weir) and drilling cables (such as those at Self-Flowing Wells). The core is woven of the inner part of the bamboo, and around this core are spiral-wrapped long strips of the bamboo's hard and friction-resistant outer surface layer which grip the core ever more tightly as the strain increases. The result is an extremely strong hawser of any needed length. A two-inch bamboo is three times as strong as hemp rope of the same dimension, and about half the strength of mild steel cable. Moreover, the tensile strength of the bamboo cable increases by 20 percent when wet, as opposed to loss of strength in hemp rope. These towing hawsers, as described by Archibald Little in the 1890s, were

> as thick as the arm, requiring great skill in coiling and uncoiling, which is incessantly being done, as the necessities of the route require a longer or shorter line. Notwithstanding its enormous toughness, owing to constant fraying on the rocks a tow-line only

lasts a single voyage, and when one sees deep scores cut by the tow-lines into the granite rocks along the tow-path, the fact is readily accounted for.

The hawser is fixed to a strong bulkhead or thwart on the junk, then run through a ring on the mast to elevate it above intervening obstructions. With the line laid out along the bank, each tracker ties himself onto it by means of a shoulder sling ending in a pig-tail and a wooden button (see illustration on page 127). The sling holds fast when under strain, but once slacked it immediately unfastens, freeing the tracker from the cable—a simple and effective safety device.

Next to the Old Big and his wife, the cook was the most important member of the regular crew, the pilots being local specialists who came and went and did not belong to the boat:

> Amidships, in the cockpit, reigns the cook, busy all day and half the night preparing rice and vegetables for his hungry crowd. He is also handyman, carpenter, and referee in general, an authority on most things, and altogether a most important person.

The cook's importance was more than simply practical, since in China the

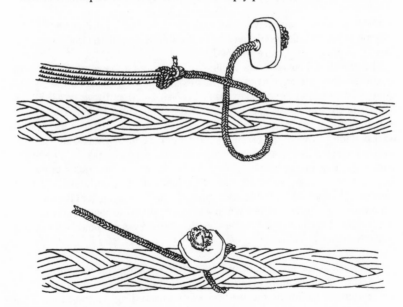

Woven bamboo tracking cable.

cooking stove is the symbolic embodiment of the family, and hence by analogy the center which defines group consciousness. Indeed, if the Old Big's wife was aboard, she too would keep a stove in their cabin, as a sign of their own family unit, within the larger group aboard the boat. It was appropriate, therefore, that the cook preside, even more than the Old Big, over the rituals of getting under way—usually firecrackers, incense, and the sacrifice of a chicken. Accounts by Westerners also regularly mention the cook as a cause of annoying delay, as he spent endless hours ashore, securing provisions and doing who knows what— arranging a little squeeze for himself, seeing friends, drinking wine—while the boat lay alongshore, waiting.

Of the junkmen and the trackers, we know very little. Downriver, particularly in the lower Yangtze and the estuary, are boat people born and raised on their vessels, from which they rarely came ashore. In this they resemble the boat people of the Fukien and Kwangtung coasts, of Hong Kong, Macao, and the Pearl River running up to Canton. These boat people, often despised and ill-treated by the general population, have been studied to some extent, but upriver, in what the foreigners used to call the "out ports," we lack even such preliminary knowledge. Shen Ts'ung-wen has told us a bit about the Yuan River men, and from other sources, other locales, we have a few fragments only. Yet all observers note the unassuming courage and apparent cheerfulness with which junkmen went about their dangerous, harsh, ill-paid, and unrelenting tasks. Plant, for example, writes:

> The junk folk, taken as a whole, are certainly a fine body of men, both in respect to physique and

Tracker's sling

temperament. They are hardy and merry and bright as a rule, nothwithstanding the arduous nature of their calling, which would try the endurance of the average mule. They are "classy" withal, in their way, the Hupeh [Hupei province] men being considered the superior breed, and those who hail from the village of Huang-ling-miao the recognized "top dogs."

Isabella Bird drew a distinction between the long-distance trackers, embarked as part of the junk's crew, and the temporary gang trackers:

These trackers may be the roughest class in China—for the work is "inhuman" and brutalising—but nevertheless they are good-natured in their way; free on the whole from crimes of violence; full of fun, antics, and frolic; clever at taking off foreigners; loving a joke; and with a keen sense of humor.

Those who crowd in hundreds to the great rapids of the season for the chance of getting a few *cash* for a haul are a rougher lot still. They bargain for the price of haulage with the *lao-pan* through gangsmen, and very often where there is much competition, as at the Hsin-t'an, get only about a penny for four hours' hard work. Their mat camps are very boisterous at night. At the lesser rapids the *lao-pan* goes ashore, dangling strings of *cash*, and as there is usually a village close by, he secures help, after some loud-tongued bargaining and wrangling, engaging even women and boys to tug at his ropes, and occasionally a woman with a baby on her back takes a turn at the dragging!

Opium was commonly smoked by the Old Big and the crew alike, particularly after mooring for the night following a hard passage through some rapids or shoal. More than one observer reported the Old Big fleeing to his cabin for a smoke, unable any longer to stand the anxiety of seeing his boat—his whole fortune and livelihood—in such dire and protracted peril.

Almost all boats were owned by their masters, there being no such organization as a shipping company. But, like other trades, the *lao-pans*—at least the more prosperous ones—belonged to junkmasters' guilds. In Shanghai, these included guilds of seagoing junkmen, rice shippers, tea shippers, and so on. In 1920s Chungking, Worcester counted twenty-two different guilds covering the river systems in Szechwan province alone. Social contacts were made and business was conducted in the guildhalls, and also in the public teahouses, which were often located on the ground floor below the guild. To avoid eavesdroppers in these crowded and curious surroundings, one negotiator would sometimes indicate prices by finger pressure on the hand of the other, their clasped hands being hidden in the folds of their long sleeves.

Shen Ts'ung-wen has mentioned the religious and ritualistic aspect of the junkmen's lives, aspects often dismissed as crude superstition. But the long-distance trackers, the crew, and the *lao-pan* as well, traveled so much that they lacked the deep community roots important to most landbound Chinese. Indeed, the *lao-pan*, whose boat it was, frequently had his family with him, and the poor trackers may not have had home or family at all—the unhappiest of fates for a Chinese—and been part of a rootless, unbelonging and expendable population, so that whatever boat they were on became a surrogate for home. Like watermen the world around, their beliefs and customs therefore took a force that landsmen find difficult to understand or appreciate. From food customs—neither fish nor dish should be tipped over while eating, nor should chopsticks be placed across a rice bowl in such a way as to suggest a junk run aground—to many dieties and myriad legends, the junkmen lived out their anonymous and expendable lives in a harsh but nevertheless richly inhabited and comprehensible world.

PART III

EVENTFUL TIME

9

HISTORY, SYMBOLISM, AND IMAGERY

History concerns the past, but the past exists only in the present. The past is not "back there" or "back when" but here and now: if the residue of the past did not exist in the present, it would be forever unknowable. A few cultures have developed a sense of the past as formal history reconstructed and written by scholars, but far more powerfully and far more widely shared is the remembered past, the imagined past, and the practiced past, transmitted in countless ways: embedded in language; in religion; in stories, legends, and myths; in poetry and song; in the visible remains of the past—buildings, inscriptions, ruins; in the transmission of skills; in traditions and customs; in symbols, attitudes, values; in behavior, social relations, ways of making a living, cuisine. In China, among the literate minority, a tradition of formal, written history developed early and was practiced continuously, but among the nine-tenths who could not read, the unconscious or only partly conscious transmission of the past took place in less prescribed and more popular ways. For them, there was no clear demarcation between the past and the present; the two commingled in a kind of permanent timelessness, like a shop in which junk and bric-a-brac and masterpieces from all periods are mixed indifferently together.

Even change was rendered customary. In John Hersey's *A Single Pebble*, Old Big curses river pilots for always wanting to find a new way through the rapids. "There is a new way every forty years," the Old Big bitterly said. "It is an old way but it is called new. River pilots wait only for their grandfathers, who know better, to die before they claim they have found a new way." And Hersey's American protagonist comes to appreciate the illiterate and unschooled head tracker: "I found that he was amazingly cultured, for he owned somewhat the same rather disturbing fund of folklore and history and myth as Su-ling [the Old Big's young wife]; I suppose what made me persist in thinking him simple in spite of this education was the fact that his learning had all been acquired orally. I guess I thought book-learning the only true enlightenment." The head tracker then surprised the foreigner by quickly and perfectly memorizing a difficult poem by a celebrated eighth-century poet.

Thus, although at first glance the educated Chinese scholar and the illiterate tracker may seem to have inhabited different worlds, to a remarkable degree they shared that "fund of folklore and history and myth" upon which were founded both the scholar's mastery of texts and the tracker's memory of an oral tradition. Along the Yangtze River and its principal tributaries, folklore and history and myth had a particular regional flavor.

In China as elsewhere, distinctive images and moods are associated with particular regions, so that their names become redolent with connotation and overtone. Such regional images, moods, and stereotypes were already taking shape by 500 B.C., at least in the minds of those northerners who produced the written records—the "classics"—upon which we depend for much of our knowledge of early China. In a Chinese version of the perennial confrontation of "civilization" with "wilderness" and "barbarism," these northerners shared a constellation of feelings about "the South," the Long River Valley, and particularly its middle reaches, the area now comprising the provinces of Hunan and Hupei but known in that early era as the exotic kingdom of Ch'u, rival to the most powerful states of the northern plains and one of the last to fall to the ruthlessly unifying Ch'in armies in the third century B.C. We know that from very early times, the south was a place of banishment; recall the northern nobleman, Ssu-ma Niu, who was exiled to the Ch'u region (Chapter 4).

Out of the rich fund of folklore and history and myth that give distinctive character to the Yangtze region, we have chosen two examples familiar to scholar and tracker alike. The first is the tragic life of a single individual, Ch'ü Yuan; the second is the richly peopled and sweeping history of the Three Kingdoms. Finally, we look briefly at the Yangtze Valley in the history of the last century or so.

Ch'ü Yuan

Exile, passion, and moral predicament surround the earliest historical figure specifically associated with the south, with the state of Ch'u. This was Ch'ü Yuan (338–278 B.C.), whose life and transfiguring suicide have been inexhaustible sources of ethical, philosophic, and poetic reflection, even to the present day. The facts can be briefly told. Scion of a noble Ch'u family and a devoted adviser to his king, Ch'ü Yuan sought to strengthen Ch'u and to ally with other states in order to checkmate the ruthless expansion of Ch'in power, rather like a European statesman in the 1930s trying to stave off Nazi Germany. Rival factions poisoned the old king's mind against Ch'ü Yuan, and his son, the new king, was even more misguided than his father had been. When Ch'ü Yuan continued his frank but unwelcome advice, he was banished forever to the southern ends of the realm. Soon after, in protest and despair, Ch'ü Yuan drowned himself in the waters of the Mi-lo River, near present-day Ch'ang-sha, the capital of Hunan province. Half a century later, Ch'in justified Ch'ü Yuan's dire warnings by overwhelming Ch'u on its march toward the unification of China.

Ch'ü Yuan was also a literary genius whose lyric poetry is the earliest in China for which we have a fully individualized author. His long poem "Encountering Sorrow" (*Li Sao*) is at the same time the impassioned—and self-justifying, self-pitying—lament of a loyal but wronged servant of the king and the grounds for his suicide:

> How well I know that loyalty brings disaster;
> Yet I will persist; I cannot give it up.
> I do not care, on my own account, about this divorcement,
> But it grieves me to find the Fair One [the King] so inconstant.
>
> I had tended many an acre of orchids,
> And planted a hundred rods of melilotus;
> I had raised sweet lichens and the cart-halting flower,
> And asarums mingled with fragrant angelica,
> And hoped that when leaf and stem were in fullest bloom,
> When the time had come, I could reap a fine harvest.
> Though famine should pinch me, it is small matter:
> But I grieve that all my blossoms should waste in rank weeds.
>
> All others press forward in greed and gluttony,
> No surfeit satiating their demands:
> Forgiving themselves but harshly judging others;
> Each fretting his heart away in envy and malice.
> Madly they rush in the covetous chase,
> But not after that which my heart sets store by.
> The age is disordered in a tumult of changing:
> How can I tarry much longer among them:
> Orchids and iris have lost all their fragrance;
> Flag and melilotus have changed to straw.
> Enough! There are no true men in the state: no one to understand
> me.
> Why should I cleave to the place of my birth?
> Since none is worthy of my service in making government good,
> I will go and join P'eng-the-Immortal in the place where he abides.

In his lyrics, Ch'ü Yuan spoke in a characteristically "southern" idiom: extravagant language, passionate emotional tone, a richly inhabited spirit world complete with seductive shaman goddesses, transparent sensuality, lush images of plants as metaphors—orchids for purity, fragrant flowers for virtue, weeds for evil. And also the brooding, untamed wilderness south of the Yangtze:

> The dark forest so endless,
> The habitation of apes and monkeys,
> The mountains so high that the sun is hidden,
> Wet with rain mists, the valleys so dark and dim.

All these themes recur again and again in the literature of the Ch'u style, a style not only different from that of the more restrained, rationalistic northerners but often repugnant and menacing to them as well. In this confrontation, one finds Chinese counterparts of the Dionysian and the Apollonian temperaments of the West.

Ch'ü Yuan thus became a many-layered symbol. In the literary tradition, his life and death became a protean archetype of personal integrity, loyalty, and dissent, and the lonely pain of the pure in heart who have been wronged by an evil world. If the ruler should heed and honor his ministers, all is well, but how should one serve—*should* one serve?—a corrupt, misguided, or incompetent ruler? If one is misunderstood and persecuted, what should one do? These are enduring issues in China, where official service was the highest calling, and where the moral demands of principle often conflicted with the equally compelling imperative of obedience to one's ruler. In the twentieth century, even iconoclastic intellectuals felt affinities with the lonely and wronged poet of Ch'u. For victims of the Cultural Revolution, tormented and exiled to the countryside, thoughts of Ch'ü Yuan were inevitable.

Yet in any age only a few have been willing to follow his example to its tragic, or perhaps futile, ending. Critics argued that fate is beyond human intervention and that if the times are out of joint, then the wise man should withdraw and await the coming of better times and a sage ruler, meanwhile nurturing his integrity. Even if such a time never comes, one will have kept one's character unsullied—and this was, after all, the case with Confucius, the "uncrowned king" never made use of by the world:

> It is best for a divine dragon to
> hide deep in a pool
> and await an auspicious cloud
> which will take him up.
> Formerly, when Confucius left Lu
> Reluctantly and tardily he began an extensive journey,

In the end he returned to his home:
What need did he have of the Hsiang River depths and its billowy
    rapids?

If one could not easily leave the court or refuse offers of service, one
might even pretend stupidity or madness:

> When Pi-kan was put to death for remonstrating with an evil
> tyrant, Chi-tzu said, "To speak, knowing one's words will not be
> put to use, is stupid. But sacrificing oneself to make the wicked-
> ness of one's prince apparent is not loyal. These are two things
> that should not be done. . . ." Whereupon he let his hair down
> his back and, feigning madness, departed. . . . The *Book of Odes*
> says, "There is no wise man who is not also stupid."

But Ch'ü Yuan's was not a tactical, feigned madness, like that of Chi-tzu or
Hamlet, but rather the extravagant madness that leads to self-destruction.

If these were the principal elements of Ch'ü Yuan lore among the educated
elite, Ch'ü Yuan was also richly celebrated in the folk tradition—the two
traditions overlapping and penetrating one another. In the folk tradition,
rites, festivals, and myths began an early accretion around an apotheosized
Ch'ü Yuan. The most famous of these, the Dragon Boat Festival (*Tuan-wu
chieh*), takes place on the summer solstice, the fifth day of the fifth lunar
month, ostensibly to search for Ch'ü Yuan's body. *Tsung-tzu*, triangular-
shaped steamed dumplings of sweetened glutinous rice wrapped in bamboo
or reed leaves, are prepared and eaten only on this occasion, and are cast
into the water to feed Ch'ü Yuan's soul. Ch'ü Yuan is also associated with
fertility rites, performed at the solstice, and with the ceremonies of rice
transplantation; he was also credited with introducing a particularly fragrant
jade-white rice throughout the central Yangtze region. One myth holds that
after Ch'ü Yuan drowned himself, his body was swallowed by a huge fish
which swam all the way across Tung-t'ing Lake and up the Long River to
the town of his birth, Tzu-kuei, in the Three Gorges, where it disgorged his
body, still intact, so that it could be properly buried.

Underlying these popular rites, festivals, and myths—most of which
involve water, fertility, and death by drowning—are earlier non-Chinese
cultural strata, which have been partly assimilated and transformed by a
Chinese overlay, much in the way that the Olympian religion of Hellenic
invaders of Greece assimilated pre-existing cult traditions or that Christianity
incorporated Near Eastern and European paganism.

Ch'ü Yuan lore, in the vexing dilemmas of the literary tradition as well as
in the water rites of the popular tradition, was bequeathed to China as a

whole from the Yangtze Valley, but it retains its distinctive southern identity. In his fine study, Laurence Schneider writes:

> In the basic story of Ch'ü Yuan, the southern countryside is cognate with his ordeal. It is both the setting and instrument of his punishment. . . . Being in the South meant being away from the metropolitan centers of power; the presence of the South's tribal peoples and its primitive ruggedness meant the absence of civilized high culture. Southern exile could mean the end of a career and a life. . . . [Later] another image of the South began to develop and infuse the lore. With each new wave of northern nomadic invasions, from the third century A.D. onward, the South was increasingly seen as a potential refuge for "exiled" Chinese ethnos and for China's high culture. . . . Implicit throughout the Ch'ü Yuan lore is a sweeping analogy between the exiled official and the exiled high culture itself. . . . The Yangtze River becomes a mythological frontier of experience, as well as a geographical frontier.

The Three Kingdoms

Even richer and more varied than Ch'ü Yuan lore in giving symbolic meanings to the Long River is the era of the Three Kingdoms, following the breakup of the Han dynasty in the late second century A.D. If one wishes to understand China, one must have some familiarity with the history of the Three Kingdoms and with the lore that surrounds it. Above all is this true on the middle and upper Yangtze where it seems every bend in the river leads to another site associated with this epoch and to the stories that have grown around it like the layers of a pearl around its grain of historical fact. If the events seem complicated and the stage crowded with unfamiliar actors, that too is part of China's reality. One might as well seek to know the Greeks without the Trojan War or the English without Shakespeare.

In the texts of scholars as in the vivid stories known to peasants, nothing equals this era of heroes, this sweeping drama on a canvas as large as China itself, with a cast of thousands playing out their destinies over nearly a century. All the great themes are here: kingdoms to be won or lost, tragedy and pathos and bathetic comedy, courage and cowardice, loyalty and deceit, shining wisdom and dull stupidity, arrogance and humility, great virtues overreaching themselves to become tragic flaws. Although the narrative begins in the north, the most important events, the most vivid memories, the most telling symbols of the Three Kingdoms era are forever associated with the Long River.

We have already spoken frequently of the first long period of unification in Chinese history, achieved by the Ch'in conquests and then raised to great heights in the 400 years of the Han dynasty (206 B.C.–A.D. 220), the temporal counterpart of the Roman Empire in the West. As in the West, the decline and fall of the Han dynasty led eventually to barbarian breakthrough and the devastation of an entire civilization. The fall of Han, its disintegration into three great regional competitors for the imperial mantle, and the eventual Pyrrhic victory of one of them over the other two is the story of the Three Kingdoms. All later Chinese, as they read or heard the stories of the Three Kingdoms, knew that just to the north, mounted nomads were about to sweep south of the Great Wall, to fall upon a China so weakened by the struggle of brother against brother that no defense was possible. The Three Kingdoms were thus the prelude and first act of a drama four centuries long, until the Sui and T'ang succeeded in reimposing imperial unity in about A.D. 600.

Upon a skeleton of factual narrative left by historians, there was soon added the flesh of fuller characterization, conversations, plausible anecdote, omens and the supernatural intervention of fate, dramatic anticipation, climax, and denouement. The main heroes became demigods or more; Kuan Yü (see below) was transformed into one of China's most popular and powerful dieties. They also became symbols of certain personality types, since the Chinese have tended to view character as ingrained and fixed, defined by traits revealed rather than developed in the course of events.

Three Kingdoms lore grew into story cycles, episodic recitations by oral storytellers—complete with voice changes, sound effects, body language, and a few props—before enthralled teahouse or marketplace audiences. Many of the episodes were also adapted to regional opera performance and to puppet theatre. At some time about A.D. 1500, these episodes were knitted together in written form to constitute the great popular novel, *The Romance of the Three Kingdoms*, attributed to a a shadowy figure named Lo Kuanchung, of whom almost nothing is known. Like other popular novels, *Three Kingdoms* retains clear evidence of its origin in the oral storytelling tradition. Chapters, called "sessions," are short enough to be told all in one sitting, and each session has its own miniature dramatic structure—ending at a moment of suspense—so that it can be enjoyed as a single episode as well as part of a larger narrative. But most revealing are the beginnings and endings of each session: "To pick up where we last left off . . ." and "If you want to know what happens, you must come back for the next episode." So intertwined have the factual and fictional strands become that it requires sustained scholarly discipline—not exercised here—to disentangle actual history from later embellishment.

To us, the Han dynasty was but China's first long imperial dynasty (206 B.C. to A.D. 220—the first of many. But to those living through it, who knew nothing of the future, the Han was synonymous with civilization itself, and its collapse threatened everything of value. In later eras, the fate of the Han dynasty reminded Chinese that even the most enduring of man's accomplishments will eventually pass away, a theme of waxing and waning struck in the opening line of the novel: "It is said of the great endeavors of the world, that the fragmented must eventually be united, and the united must at length be fragmented."

By A.D. 150, the Han was in deep trouble, not from external threats but from internal cancers. At the capital, a succession of weak emperors became the playthings of eunuchs or of the powerful male relatives of their queens. Literati and scholar-officials either chose sides, kept silent, or protested and died (thinking, perhaps, of Ch'ü Yuan). In the provinces, aristocratic lineages possessed huge landholdings along with the peasant-serfs necessary to cultivate them and private armies to protect what they had and to seize more. A miserable and desperate peasantry turned in huge numbers to the apocalyptic promises of the "Taoist" church. The millennium was scheduled for A.D. 184, these charismatic priests said: then the corrupt and sinful would be destroyed, and purified believers would enter a paradise on earth.

These ingredients came together in an explosive mixture that destroyed the Han dynasty. But the conventional ending date, A.D. 220, simply marks the dynasty's final heartbeat; it had already long been moribund. First, in A.D. 184, came the massive, apocalyptic peasant uprising known as "Yellow Kerchiefs" after the identifying headgear that the Taoist generals directed the faithful to wear as they sought to bring about the millennium. The Yellow Kerchiefs were brutally suppressed by an imperial army called back from the northwestern frontier and by the private militias of the great landholders, who then fought among themselves. The emperor was now but a pawn, held captive by one faction or another, in order to give its actions some semblance of legitimacy.

Thrown into prominence by this chaotic struggle on the North China Plain were the principal characters of the period. There was Ts'ao Ts'ao, already a high official, a man whose charismatic genius was wedded to utter ruthlessness and cunning. Chinese say "Speak of Ts'ao Ts'ao, and there he is," instead of "Speak of the Devil," but with the same sense. There was Liu Pei, a poor commoner whose claim to be a distant descendant of the royal family—"Liu" was the imperial surname, like "Romanov" in a later day—gave him a kind of legitimacy upon which he based his claim to the succession. At the start, however, Liu Pei was but one of many ambitious men on the make who gathered a following during the suppression of the Yellow Kerchiefs. He was not himself a man of unusual talent except in one crucial regard: he had the capacity to gather round him outstanding men and to hold their unswerving loyalty.

At the core of Liu Pei's following were his two "brothers," sworn to each other even in the face of death in solemn ceremony in the Peach Garden. These were the erstwhile pig butcher and hotspur Chang Fei, and Kuan Yü, on the run after having killed an oppressive official. Later, Liu Pei enlisted Chu-ko Liang, "the sleeping dragon," a strategist and tactician of supernatural ability, a gifted political advisor, and a man of surpassing integrity. These three and a host of more ordinarily talented men followed Liu Pei in good times and bad.

By A.D. 200, Ts'ao Ts'ao had gained substantial control of the old north China core area in the Yellow River Basin, and the emperor was now in his hands to rubber stamp his actions. Meanwhile Liu Pei and his followers had experienced many vicissitudes. By adroit moves from patron to patron, he had improved his fortunes, and was for a time junior ally to Ts'ao Ts'ao himself. Then he was implicated in a futile coup d'etat against Ts'ao Ts'ao and had to flee southward toward the Yangtze River with only his closest followers; even his family and Kuan Yü (who discovered only later that Liu Pei had not perished after all) were seized by Ts'ao Ts'ao. Treating Kuan Yü generously in a vain effort to win him over, Ts'ao Ts'ao rather uncharacteristically permitted him to return to his sworn elder brother, even as he sought to destroy the same Liu Pei.

By now, the geopolitical realities were clearer, and the Three Kingdoms began to take shape. As the Han empire fell apart, three huge regions emerged as the most viable bases of power. The first, of course, was north China, the Ch'in and Han heartland, now under control of Ts'ao Ts'ao and often called "Wei," after the river and the dukedom Ts'ao Ts'ao arrogated to himself. The second major region was the lower Yangtze region, including the Chiang-nan and the estuary, a region known as "Wu" that had thus far been spared the devastations of the north. Wu was under the sway of the Sun family, first the father, then his son, Sun Ch'üan. The third region, not quite yet so clearly defined but with great potential, was modern Szechwan, or "Shu" as it was then known. Surrounded by mountains and approachable only through the Long River and difficult passes, Shu offered security, haven, and fertile soil; it too had been spared destruction, but it was the least populated and least developed of the three regions. These, then, were the Three Kingdoms—Wei in north China, Wu in the lower Yangtze, and Shu in Szechwan—into which the Han empire divided as it sank into ruin.

Between Shu and Wu lay the middle Yangtze basin, the old realm of Ch'u and the home of Ch'ü Yuan. With its innumerable lakes, rivers, and marshes, the middle Yangtze was a difficult base to maintain and defend, yet it was of great strategic importance because from it one could threaten either the power of Wu downriver to the east or the upriver region of Shu.

It was here, in the middle Yangtze, that the most pivotal events of the Three Kingdoms era took place. Liu Pei had fled into this region, with Ts'ao Ts'ao and the large Wei army at his heels. The ruler of Wu, recognizing the mortal danger to himself should Ts'ao Ts'ao gain control of the middle Yangtze, contracted an alliance with Liu Pei and sent his best army commanded by his best general. The climactic Battle of Red Cliff, on the Yangtze between modern Hankow and Tung-t'ing Lake, determined the fate of China for almost a century.

Using the stratagems of Chu-ko Liang and troops supplied by the Wu ruler Sun Ch'üan—Liu Pei had only a small following at this moment—the underdog southern alliance won a victory as sweeping as it was unexpected. Ts'ao Ts'ao, in overweening arrogance, had failed to reckon on the difficulty his northern infantry and cavalry would encounter in this watery and miasmic world, and he discounted the possibility of attack by fire against his flotillas. The southerners took advantage of an easterly gale rare in that season of the year (Chu-ko Liang having heeded the apparently casual forecast of a simple fisherman and then ceremonially invoked the spirits of the wind) to drive fireboats into the northern camp, where their boats were chained together and could not escape.

Ts'ao Ts'ao's boats were burned and his forces cut to pieces and routed; with the tables now turned, Ts'ao Ts'ao had to flee for his life with only a few stalwart supporters. At this critical juncture, Kuan Yü cut off his retreat and could have killed him, but respecting the code of chivalry and remembering his adversary's former generosity—of which Ts'ao Ts'ao archly reminded him: "You have been well, I trust, since we parted?"—Kuan Yü spared his life.

Although Ts'ao Ts'ao escaped with his life, the Battle of Red Cliff ended all immediate hopes for a unified China and led to the full development of the Three Kingdoms. With Chu-ko Liang's help, Liu Pei now staked out his base in Szechwan, probing northward against the much weakened power of Ts'ao Ts'ao, and meanwhile competing with the Wu state for influence in the middle Yangtze Valley, where Kuan Yü was stationed as Liu Pei's proconsul.

At this juncture, Ts'ao Ts'ao benefited from the underlying suspicions and jealousies in the alliance between the two southern states. Sun Ch'üan tried to bribe Kuan Yü into abandoning Liu Pei, and when Kuan Yü contemptuously dismissed Sun's offer, he was seized and beheaded. Haunted like a Chinese Macbeth by the treachery of his deed, and knowing that he had destroyed the alliance upon which his own security depended, Sun Ch'üan sent Kuan Yü's head to Ts'ao Ts'ao in dishonorable supplication, hoping thereby to win favor and safety. Ts'ao Ts'ao greeted this grisly prize with cynicism and cruel irony, speaking to Kuan Yü's bodiless head: "You have been well, I trust, since we parted?"

Liu Pei, in an agony of grief and anger, determined to wreak vengeance on Wu, and would not be dissuaded by the sage Chu-ko Liang. The foolhardiness of such a campaign was irrelevant to Liu Pei and Chang Fei, both bent on redeeming the pledge made in the Peach Garden so many years before, thus placing the oath of brotherhood ahead of the long-term interests of the state. As Chu-ko Liang foresaw, the campaign was a disaster. Chang Fei was assassinated even before it began. Later, downriver, Liu Pei's poorly deployed encampments were set afire, his powerful army destroyed or routed. He was forced to return, his fortune and his honor in ruins, to White King City at the head of the Three Gorges. There he languished, dying, entrusting Chu-ko Liang with affairs of state in place of his own incompetent son. Chu-ko Liang refused the throne but agreed to assist in what he knew to be a doomed venture.

Thereafter, all was anticlimax and sad denouement. Chu-ko Liang made the best of a bad situation for a few years, even firing brief hopes with his strategic genius despite being constantly hampered by a doltish king. But Wei, led now after Ts'ao Ts'ao's natural death by his son, had regained its strength and overcame in turn Shu and Wu—before Wei itself was taken over in a coup d'état by the clan of its prime minister. The usurpers, calling themselves the Chin dynasty, imposed a fragile and short-lived unity that collapsed early in the fourth century A.D., under the onslaughts of the northern barbarians, and China lapsed into 250 years of division.

All up and down the Long River are the recollections and the relics, the myths and legends of the tragic lives and deaths, the heroes and the villains of the Three Kingdoms. By the T'ang dynasty, at least, Kuan Yü was well along in the process of apotheosis that made him the most universally worshiped deity in the folk pantheon, under the name of Lord Kuan (*Kuan-ti*) or Duke Kuan (*Kuan-kung*). Depicted in many guises but often with a ruddy face, a full beard, intense eyes, and a long spear, he became the symbol of loyalty and god of war, of wealth, of literature; protector-god of temples; patron saint of merchants, of actors, and of secret societies. By the late dynasties, he was even co-opted into the Confucian rites in an effort to regularize and channel his great popularity. Like the Ch'ü Yuan lore, Kuan-ti lore shows how intimately connected are the folk and elite traditions.

Red Cliff, scene of Ts'ao Ts'ao's great defeat, is the most famous of the many sites on the Long River associated with the Three Kingdoms. The theme of man's passionate but ephemeral efforts contrasted with the indifferent, ever-flowing river has been sounded time and time again, but never more movingly than in a pair of prose-poems (*fu*) written by Su Tung-p'o (A.D. 1037–1101). A native of Szechwan, brightest light in a brilliant literary family, Su Tung-p'o had something of the "southern" temperament, but with a brighter, more optimistic turn than Ch'ü Yuan's morbid self-absorption. Although inspired by the great battle eight centuries earlier, these two *Odes on Red Cliff* have taken on an independent existence, and Red Cliff becomes an image seen through these later images. On this occasion in the autumn of 1082—Su Tung-p'o dates it precisely—the poet and some literati friends are embarked in a small boat near Red Cliff. After setting the scene—cool evening breezes, the river below and constellations swinging overhead,

Painting by T'ang Yin (1470-1524) depicting Su Tung-po's "Odes on Red Cliff."

wine, singing—the poet listens while a guest plays a sobbing flute tune and muses sadly on life's melancholy paradoxes:

"At the time when Ts'ao Ts'ao smote Ching-chou and came east-wards with the current down from Chiang-ling, his vessels were prow by stern for a thousand miles, his banners hid the sky; looking down on the river, winecup in hand, composing his poem with lance slung crossways, truly he was the hero of his age, but where is he now? And what are you and I compared with him? . . . Mayflies visiting between heaven and earth, infinitesimal grains in the vast sea, mourning the passing of our instant of life, envying the Long River which never ends! Let me cling to a flying immortal and roam far off, and live for ever with the full moon in my arms! But knowing that this art is not easily learned, I commit the fading echoes of my flute to the sad wind."

[The poet Su Tung-p'o then replies:]

"Have you really understood the water and the moon?" I said. "The one streams past so swiftly yet is never gone; the other forever waxes and wanes yet finally has never grown nor dimin-ished. For if you look at the aspect which changes, heaven and earth cannot last the blinking of an eye; but if you look at the aspect which is changeless, the worlds within and outside you are both inexhaustible, and what reasons have you to envy any-thing? . . ."

The guest smiled, consoled. We washed the cups and poured more wine. . . [then] we leaned pillowed back to back in the middle of the boat, and did not notice when the sky turned white in the east.

The Middle Yangtze in Modern Times

As we have seen, the middle Yangtze was of great strategic importance as early as the Medieval Era. As the lower Yangtze—the Chiang-nan— became more and more the economic and cultural center of China, it was the prize that all regimes sought to control. But the middle Yangtze was a key to gaining control over the resources of the lower river. Although the Chiang-nan could be approached by marching south across the Huai River plain and more or less down the route of the Grand Canal, this avenue could be defended by land forces. But farther west, control of the upriver areas in the middle Yangtze by a hostile power posed a mortal threat to Chiang-nan, and by T'ang and Sung times (ca. 600–1200), the middle Yangtze was itself becoming an increasingly important economic region. The modern scholar Wang Gungwu sums it up:

Although vulnerable to attack, the middle Yangtse [sic] was never easy to hold and control, whether the effort was made from [the Yellow River in] the north or from the lower Yangtse area in the east. Control from the east, of course, meant only the political unification of a great area of southern China. Conquest from the north, however, seemed always to lead to the unification of China. Control of this region was therefore a critical factor in the balance between unification and division.

We saw these realities play themselves out for the first time during the Three Kingdoms era, and they did so repeatedly in later eras. An outstanding example was the Mongol invasion of the Southern Sung, which took its principal route down the Han River to the Yangtze. The Mongol seige of Hsiang-yang, main Sung fortress on the Han, took five years (A.D. 1268–1273) and included the use of explosive bombs, primitive cannon, and catapults so large it required a hundred men to operate them. These same realities have been operative in the nineteenth and twentieth century—in the T'ai-p'ing Rebellion, the Revolution of 1911, and Chiang Kai-shek's Northern Expedition of 1926–1927.

The T'ai-p'ing Rebellion (1850–1864) was to China what the contemporaneous Civil War was to the United States—an enormously destructive conflict pitting North against South, which nearly overthrew the established government and replaced it with a radically different regime. These civil wars left indelible marks on both countries, and many Chinese, like many Americans, retain an abiding interest in the issues surrounding these conflicts. In each, there is a constant flow of books and articles, scholarly and popular, concerning the internecine war and its deeper meanings. We can here only touch glancingly on the T'ai-p'ing T'ien-kuo (Heavenly Kingdom of Great Peace) as it relates to our themes of the Long River.

At the heart of the T'ai-p'ing movement was a peculiar but powerful amalgam of traditional, radical, and supernatural beliefs enunciated by a prophetic visionary named Hung Hsiu-ch'üan (1814–1864). Hung Hsiu-ch'üan, born near Canton into a poor Hakka family, showed promise as a scholar and several times as a young man tried unsuccessfully to pass the civil service examinations. Depressed by repeated failure, he suffered a psychotic episode—later said to have lasted forty days—during which he experienced hallucinatory visions. Some years later, he accidentally came in contact with Protestant missionaries in Canton, and from their tracts he was inspired to interpret his visions as having taken place in Heaven, in the presence of God, who identified him, Hung, as the younger brother of Jesus Christ and called upon him to rid China of demons. Hung interpreted this mission to mean the expulsion of the Manchu rulers of the Ch'ing dynasty.

Hung Hsiu-ch'üan rallied round him a group of mostly poor and marginal

Painting by the contemporary artist Fu Pao-shih, showing the enduring vitality of the Red Cliff theme.

men and women fired with his vision. Hung and his closest followers worked out a plan for the *T'ai-p'ing T'ien-kuo*, the Heavenly Kingdom of Great Peace, a strict theocracy to be led by the Heavenly King (Hung himself) and second-level kings named for the cardinal directions. In addition to a national uprising to expel the Manchu "devils," T'ai-p'ing ideology called for such revolutionary measures as abolition of private property, full equality of the sexes, and a merging of civil and military organizations.

If Hung's Society of God Worshippers had been content to remain on their mountaintop in Kwangsi province, they might have been ignored, but these were true believers whose dynamic, goal-oriented movement sought followers, not without notions of class struggle, among the poor and dispossessed:

> The upper crust owes us dough,
> Folks in the middle better wise up.

But underdogs, follow me!
It beats plowing no-good land with a rented ox!

Once the T'ai-p'ing came into direct conflict with the authorities, there was no turning back. Philip Kuhn describes how in 1852 they crossed their Rubicon and moved "over a crucial divide: out of the Kwangsi river systems and into the Yangtze tributary network. It was during the crusade to Nanking that the Taiping Kingdom transformed itself from a relatively small, provincial rebellion into a vast movement that swept up treasure and recruits from broad reaches of central China."

The T'ai-p'ing swept up and over the Miracle Canal and into the Hsiang River Valley, continuing northward downriver, using boats and rafts of all kinds to enhance their mobility, bypassing large towns and cities which they lacked the manpower, patience, and weapons to beseige. Gathering adherents as they went, spirited T'ai-p'ing armies swept aside the often larger but poorly led and dispirited Imperial forces sent against them. They sailed across Tung-t'ing Lake, seizing a large armory and 5,000 boats before entering the Yangtze River, and sailing downstream to the Wuhan cities (Hankow, Wu-ch'ang, Han-yang), which they sacked—enriching themselves with a million ounces of silver and 10,000 more vessels in the process—and then abandoned. Later, Wuhan would change hands three more times, each time with more destruction added to earlier damage. On down the river the T'ai-p'ing forces went, apparently unstoppable, until they reached Nanking, where they established their capital.

Shanghai was thrown into a panic. A secret society, the Small Swords, even took over the city for a time, leading the foreigners to organize a militia and to begin collecting customs revenue, but the T'ai-p'ing did not aggressively seek to drive all the way to the estuary, probably because they did not wish to provoke an armed response from the foreign powers now entrenched in this fast growing treaty port.

Instead, the T'ai-p'ing sent an expedition northward toward Peking; for a time it continued the victorious course of the rebellion, but as its columns became further extended and the population less receptive, imperial forces were able to turn it back. After their unsuccessful effort to invade the north, the Taiping settled down in control of the middle and part of the lower Yangtze Basin.

The eventual suppression of the T'ai-p'ing by the forces of the Ch'ing Empire—with some assistance near the end from Americans and British military officers, especially the famous Charles "China" Gordon, later to die in Africa at the seige of Khartoum—is a long and tortuous story which need not be told here. The reinvigorated Ch'ing effort was undertaken not by the dynasty's incompetent regular military forces but by new regional armies recruited, trained, and financed by provincial governors, to whom they were personally responsible. These were able and dedicated men—Tseng Kuo-fan, Li Hung-chang, and Tso Tsung-t'ang were only the most eminent among many—and it is ironic that in increasing their provincial power these men unintentionally accelerated the disintegration of the very centralized authority they sought to defend and uphold.

However that may be, one of the cornerstones of Tseng Kuo-fan's policy was to gain the riverine equivalent of "control of the seas," since security of the T'ai-p'ing base and the supply of their capital at Nanking could be assured only by dominating the region's rivers and lakes. In the beginning, neither side had any specialized war vessels or naval tactics: boats were used as a means of transporting supplies or troops or as fighting platforms. Soon they began to mount small cannon, and in the larger lakes and wider rivers, where there was room for maneuver, the two sides began to develop fighting tactics. The T'ai-p'ing employed small, highly maneuverable boats—none of course were powered save by sail or oar—called "fast crabs," while Tseng's forces used larger boats in formations designed to make them difficult to attack. In seesaw campaigns lasting several years, Tseng's squadrons finally overcame the T'ai-p'ing "navy," an accomplishment that might still have eluded him had not jealousy and mistrust among T'ai-p'ing leaders themselves erupted into such murderous conflict that all aspects of rebel strategy were seriously compromised.

Suspecting the East King of planning a coup d'etat, the Heavenly King, Hung Hsiu-ch'üan, called in the North King and Assistant King. On September 2, 1856, in an awful night of carnage, the East King and perhaps 20,000 adherents were killed; soon Hung came to mistrust the North King as well, and he too was assassinated. Assistant King Shih Ta-k'ai, perhaps the most stable personality among the top leadership and an able military leader, took his army out of Nanking in disillusion and fear for his own safety, and for seven years roamed through the countryside. In Nanking, most of the surviving leaders, including Hung, lived increasingly in paranoia and the pleasures of their large harems, the ideals of the movement and its vision of a radical, egalitarian theocracy souring into cynicism or mad fanaticism.

In regaining control of the middle river, Tseng limited T'ai-p'ing mobility, and squeezed them between his upstream forces and Li Hung-chang's armies in the Chiang-nan. Incredibly, a few able leaders still remained on the T'ai-p'ing side, and many believers remained loyal. T'ai-p'ing fortunes waxed then waned again, and many battles were yet to be fought before Nanking fell in 1864 and Hung Hsiu-ch'üan, now entirely mad, committed suicide in the depths of his palace in 1864. Meanwhile, the previous year, Tseng had finally run Shih Ta-k'ai's wandering army to ground in western Szechwan province, and destroyed it on the shores of the River of Golden

Sand, which Shih had been unable to cross. The logic of the Yangtze River, from Szechwan to Shanghai, finally prevailed against the T'ai-p'ing.

The T'ai-p'ing Rebellion and its suppression ravaged large areas of China's most productive region, some of which took decades to recover. Entire towns or cities were razed by one side or the other, and sometimes by both. The toll of lives was terrible, with overall estimates running between 20 and 30 million fatalities from all causes, more deaths than China suffered in the War of Resistance against Japan (1937–1945).

As in so many instances in Chinese history, control of the middle Yangtze was the key to the lower river, and without the resources of the lower river no northern regime could fully consolidate itself, or, perhaps, long survive. By overcoming the T'ai-p'ing and the other rebellions of the mid-nineteenth century, the Ch'ing dynasty survived, albeit in worse and worse shape, more and more assaulted from without, for another fifty years.

The same realities came into play during the twentieth century. The Revolution of 1911 began in Wuhan, sparked off by regional disaffection in Szechwan and Hupeh provinces, and the final collapse of the Ch'ing dynasty—virtually certain sooner or later in any case—was sealed by the defection of the central and southern provinces. The Revolution of 1911, which brought an end not only to the Ch'ing dynasty but to the dynastic system itself, is associated above all with the name of Sun Yat-sen. Born just a year after Hung Hsiu-ch'üan's palace suicide, growing up not far from Hung's native place, and surrounded by T'ai-p'ing lore in much the way a boy raised in Mississippi might be surrounded by the tales and emotions of the Civil War, Sun Yat-sen had often thought of himself as carrying on Hung's mission to drive out the Manchus and establish a new China. It was Sun's plan to make China's capital at Nanking, a plan frustrated by his principal rival, who had a strong army and insisted on staying in his own base of power in the Peking area. But the Nationalist Party under Sun and under his successor Chiang Kai-shek remained committed to Nanking as the proper and legitimate capital of China.

During the early 1920s, Sun and his allies, which then included the Soviet Union and the fledgling Chinese Communist Party, built a revolutionary base in Kwangtung province, centered on Canton. Sun died of cancer in 1925, at age 58, with his dreams of a modern Chinese nation still unfulfilled; but from the revolutionary base, Sun's self-appointed heir Chiang Kai-shek led the forces of the Nationalist Revolution on the "Northern Expedition," still in alliance with the USSR and the Chinese Communists. This campaign followed routes with which we are now familiar: across the two passes leading into the Yangtze watershed, then up the Hsiang and Kan rivers toward the big lakes and the Long River. Like the T'ai-p'ing before them, the forces of the Northern Expedition swept away their opposition, this time warlord troops rather than the Ch'ing bannermen, and established themselves in the middle and lower Yangtze.

Once again the revolutionary forces hesitated before Shanghai, so as not to embroil the foreigners and expand domestic struggles into foreign war. Just as T'ai-p'ing rivals bled one another in 1856, so on April 12, 1927, Chiang Kai-shek initiated "Party purification," unleashing a white terror in Shanghai and wherever else his power reached against the Chinese Communists, against the labor movement, against student leaders, and against liberal activists in general. Remnants of the Chinese Communist Party, not quite destroyed, fled to the countryside, where, under Mao Tse-tung and others, they began to develop that rural revolutionary strategy that would carry them to surprising victory in 1949. But in the mid-1930s, Chiang Kai-shek dislodged the Communists from their rural bases in central China and pursued them throughout their epic retreat, the Long March, that eventually took them to the barren reaches of northern Shensi province. As he pursued the Communists toward the River of Golden Sand, Chiang Kai-shek swore to destroy them just as Tseng Kuo-fan had destroyed the T'ai-p'ing armies of Shih Ta-k'ai seventy years earlier. Now the historical metaphor was stood on its head: where Sun Yat-sen took upon himself the fulfillment of Hung Hsiu-ch'üan's revolutionary mission, Chiang Kai-shek, Sun's successor, took as his exemplar Tseng Kuo-fan, destroyer of the Heavenly Kingdom of Great Peace.

Nanking became Chiang Kai-shek's capital in 1928, and the center of his power was always in the middle and especially the lower Yangtze Valley—until the Japanese invasion in 1937 drove him farther and farther upriver, first to Hankow, and then past Red Cliff, past the Three Gorges and White King City to his wartime capital at Chungking. Once again, as with Liu Pei during the era of the The Three Kingdoms and so many other times in Chinese history, Szechwan provided haven for a regime driven from the crucial arenas of northern and eastern China.

The Long River does not "make" history in the conventional sense, but the history of China is incomprehensible without an understanding of that river, both as geographical fact and collective memory.

SOME WESTERNERS ON THE LONG RIVER

No familiar names of Western explorers on the Long River come to mind, no one like Sir Richard Burton on the Nile, like Stanley and Livingstone on the Congo, or even the ill-starred Mungo Park on the Niger. Perhaps none had Burton's mercurial brilliance and literary skills, or Sir Henry Stanley's flair for self-advertisement. Perhaps it was because China was politically as well as geographically inaccessible until war and the Unequal Treaty settlements began to open the country in the mid-nineteenth century; even then it was wracked by the T'ai-p'ing and other internal rebellions. And surely there was something paradoxical in the notion of "discovering" a river along which lived hundreds of millions of people with a continuous high and literate culture stretching back perhaps as far as the Trojan War. How could one "discover" Red Cliff and the Three Gorges?

Yet the same urges that fired Burton and Stanley "to roam in untrodden ways where mere adventure might be dignified by geographical service" sent men and women to China as well as to Africa, India, and the New World. Such adventuring was also legitimated by the missionary impulse to serve God in the uttermost corners of the world, and if dangers—even death—were encountered, so much the greater proof of one's capacity for sacrifice. And finally, of course, such adventuring was directly or indirectly, intentionally or unintentionally, linked to imperial ambitions and to the scramble for colonies or spheres of influence, for which "geographical service" served as indispensable intelligence.

Prior to the nineteenth century, and excepting Marco Polo and other medieval travelers, the only Europeans in China were Catholic missionaries—Jesuits, Lazarists, Dominicans, and Franciscans—and an occasional Russian. None of these left behind anything very extensive concerning the Yangtze, nor could they be said to have "explored" the river. China was virtually closed to Westerners for a century, excepting only the small Portuguese colony of

Macao, and seasonal trade limited to Canton only. Indeed, it was a crime for a foreigner to enter the country and for a Chinese to teach his language to such a person.

These conditions changed with the two so-called Opium Wars, (1840–1842 and 1856–1860), with mainly British and token French forces on the one side and Chinese on the other (the United States remained technically neutral). At the end of each of these conflicts, China was compelled to sign a battery of agreements known collectively as the Unequal Treaties, not only with the British and the French, but also with the United States, Russia, and (later) Germany and Japan. As periodically extended and amended, the Unequal Treaties remained in force for almost exactly one hundred years and were not finally abrogated until 1943, in recognition of China's heroic resistance against Japan in World War II and thus signifying her elevation as one of the "Big Four."

The earlier of the two treaty settlements opened five coastal treaty ports, including Canton and Shanghai, to foreign residence and trade. China also ceded the island of Hong Kong to England at this time. (The colony was enlarged by the addition of Kowloon in the second treaty settlement, and finally the so-called New Territories were leased to Great Britain by China in 1898 for a term of 99 years. This lease, which expires in 1997, set the deadline for the return of the entire Hong Kong colony to Chinese sovereignty.) Nevertheless, prohibitions upon travel in the interior remained in force. One clause, "most favored nation," stipulated that a concession granted to *any* of the treaty powers automatically applied to *all* treaty powers—with Chinese authorities hoping that such a provision would reduce competition among the foreigners to outdo one another.

In the second treaty settlement, prohibitions to inland travel were removed, and Chinese authorities were made responsible for the safety of such travelers. Ten additional treaty ports were opened to trade, including Nanking, Hankow, and two other Yangtze River ports. It was further stipulated that since foreigners might reside in such treaty ports, the powers would have the right of gunboat as well as commercial navigation on inland waters. Moreover, the country was opened to missionaries, who were now permitted to travel at will throughout the empire, and to be at all times protected by the Chinese government—a provision often impossible to enforce against popular anti-Christian sentiment. Missionary cases, usually called "outrages" by the foreign community, were enormously troublesome throughout the nineteenth century. The French, presenting themselves in the 1860s as the protectors of Catholicism in China (despite anti-Catholic measures at home) and insisting that the Chinese government *not* establish direct relations with the Vatican, also demanded that the Chinese government permit the Catholic church to own property and to guarantee the return of all property that had ever belonged to it, referring specifically to those missions that had been established by Matteo Ricci and his successors in the seventeenth and eighteenth centuries.

Until the the second treaty settlement, the Catholic church in China had maintained a tenuous but stubborn toehold as an illegal, underground religion. It had been proscribed in 1724 by the Yung-cheng Emperor, except for a few authorized clerics in imperial service at Peking. At this time there were roughly 300,000 converts in China, declining by the end of the century by perhaps half or two-thirds, served by forty or so foreign clerics and twice that number of Chinese priests. Despite the risks, religious orders continued to smuggle priests into China and to smuggle a few Chinese out for training and ordination. Foreign priests had to be secreted at all times, usually in the homes of believers, going out only at night or in covered sedan chairs or boats. This was a harsh and dangerous business. If discovered, foreign priests might be attacked by hostile mobs or bandits. Official punishment might range from deportation to imprisonment to execution. Chinese Catholics often came in for even severer treatment.

The most active mission arena was the southwest, comprised of Szechwan, Yunnan, and Kweichow provinces, where vicariates apostolic had long existed in Chungking and Chengtu, both under the French Société des Missions Étrangères. Rough estimates—the only ones available—suggest that in the early nineteenth century, there were perhaps 70,000 Chinese Catholics in these three provinces. This region was far enough removed from Peking so that the prohibitions rested a bit more lightly there than in the eastern provinces; but by the same token, the protections of the second treaty settlement were less well-known and enforced. Although some Chinese Catholics had renounced their faith, as directed by imperial edict, many others remained loyal despite repeated persecution.

Against this background, a few Westerners embarked upon explorations of the Yangtze River, and their books began to appear before a curious public. These explorers were not, of course, the first nineteenth-century Europeans to travel on the Yangtze River. In 1841–1842, an Anglo-French naval force had penetrated far enough to blockade the Grand Canal, thus demonstrating the capacity to strangle the capital by preventing vital grain shipment, and to take Nanking under its guns. There the first of the Unequal Treaties, the Treaty of Nanking, was concluded in 1842. A decade later, during the T'ai-p'ing Rebellion, several Europeans visited the dissident capital at Nanking, and left behind fascinating accounts of their experiences. But these men had little interest in the Yangtze River itself, except as a means of access to the interior. Even more reticent were the Catholic missionaries who began to take advantage of the concessions wrung from the second treaty settlement but tried to remain invisible, like their illegal predecessors, by wearing native dress and going concealed in sedan chairs or boats.

Thomas W. Blakiston and Captain William Gill

The earliest systematic accounts of the river in English were those of Thomas W. Blakiston (1832–1891) and Captain William Gill (1843–1881). Blakiston's trip took place between February and July 1861. Gill's expedition consumed about nine months, from late January to early November 1877.

Thomas W. Blakiston was the second son of John Blakiston, baronet and major with a distinguished military career in India, Java, and elsewhere in the East. Thomas was educated to follow his father's calling, and after service in the Crimean War (where his brother was killed), he was sent in 1857 as part of a scientific expedition to explore western Canada and the Rocky Mountains, thus developing his talents as explorer and naturalist. By 1859 he was in China, commanding a detachment of artillery at Canton, which was then occupied and administered by the British.

In Canton, Blakiston wasted no time in seizing the opportunities provided by the second treaty settlement, immediately proposing a privately funded expedition to explore the middle and upper Yangtze, despite the continuing T'ai-p'ing Rebellion in the lower reaches of the river. Equally important was the desire to exercise as soon as possible the right of transit stipulated in the treaties, and to "open the Yang-tsze Kiang to trade." The remainder of Blakiston's plan was to ascend the upper Yangtze through and beyond the Three Gorges and past Chungking, as far as its confluence with the Min River at I-pin, thence northward to Chengtu, where one might follow the imperial route overland to Tibet and thence to northern India via Lhasa.

Blakiston's party was taken on board ships of an eight-vessel squadron— "a respectable little fleet" of hermaphrodite steam-and-sail vessels—no longer required for war service and commanded by Vice-Admiral Sir James Hope, who had been wounded in the engagement off Tientsin. The squadron set out from a Shanghai "deep in mud and deluged with rain, hardly an appearance to justify the appellation of 'The Model Settlement'" on February 12, 1861. The squadron dropped off a consul at newly opened Chinkiang, and proceeded to Nanking, the T'ai-p'ing capital, where the group spent a leisurely week:

> As the weather was fine, the Taipings not quite so bad as they had been represented and the country well stocked with game, we made daily excursions either within or without the walls, passing the time very pleasantly.

Despite being entertained by one of the kings, it was nevertheless plain that the T'ai-p'ing, deliberately or by default, had lost whatever foreign sympathy they once had:

> A year or two ago the Taipings had many friends, particularly among Protestant missionaries, by whom they were looked on as

Christians; but the bubble has burst on nearer scrutiny, and now it is equally the fashion to abuse them.

Before leaving Nanking, the expedition encountered the steamship *Yang-tsze*, chartered to the Shanghai trading firm of Dent and Co. and flying the United States flag, which was headed upriver and "thus had the honor of being the first merchant-vessel at Hankow."

The squadron continued on to the Wuhan cities, where Hope presented his credentials to the Governer of Hupei, and arrangements were made for the forward journey. After describing the bustling commercial activity of Hankow, despite the ravages of having been four times captured, looted, and lost by the T'ai-p'ing, Blakiston concludes:

> But what need I say more of this great emporium of commerce? When we visited it, not an European—excepting a disguised priest or two of the Romish church—was within hundreds of miles of it; now [1862], merchants and missionaries follow their avocations without secrecy, and a vessel of war lies off the town to remind the Celestials of the promise they made at Tien-tsin.

Beyond Hankow, accompanied only by a single gunboat and the flagship, Blakiston's group was now embarked on a Chinese junk engaged in Hankow to take the party as far as I-ch'ang, at the mouth of the Three Gorges.

They were finally left entirely on their own at Yueh-chou (Yo-chow), at the mouth of Tung-t'ing Lake and a major exchange point for traffic headed up or down the Hsiang, the Yuan, and the Tz'u rivers. The party consisted of four Europeans—Blakiston, Lt. Col. H.A. Sarel, Dr. Alfred Barton, Rev. S. Schereschewsky—four Sikhs, and three Chinese. Despite his Russian name, Schereschewsky, the interpeter, was a member of the American Episcopal Board of Foreign Missions. One of the Chinese served Schereschewsky as tutor-informant, Chinese language secretary, and go-between, a position called "mandarin," "writer," or "pundit" in nineteenth-century China-coast parlance.

The trip to I-ch'ang, accompanied all the way by river porpoises, the shift to two smaller passenger boats, the passage through the Three Gorges with descriptions of the river, stops along the way, natural resources, flora and fauna—all this is told in a lively, discursive style, for Blakiston was clearly a man of wit and judgment as well as strong powers of observation. In a typical passage, Blakiston both admires the Chinese and condescends to them:

> The Chinese seem to practise this river navigation to perfection, and it is amusing to observe the remarks about the "clumsy and awkward native boats," and the "primitive mode of navigation,"

which one sees so often in print in England. I have seen something of boat voyaging in North America, where it is carried to great perfection, but I am free to confess that the inland navigation of China beats it, to use a trans-Atlantic expression, "all to pieces." The only way in which we can hope to overreach the Chinese on their inland waters is by the powerful agency of steam, and that no doubt is destined soon to work a revolution on the Yang-tsze Kiang. It will be by our steamers and mercantile enterprise rather than by our arms and missionaries that we shall humanize Celestials.

The party was surprised to find many Catholic Chinese in the river towns, and repeated an estimate—undoubtedly too large but bespeaking a considerable following—of 100,000 for the entire province and perhaps 3,000 in Chungking; Blakiston was moved to compare very favorably the Catholic cleric's lifelong dedication and adoption of Chinese ways deep in the interior with the Protestant missionaries:

> Located among the European and American communities at the open ports on the coast, the latter live in all the ease and comfort of civilized society, surrounded by their wives and families, with dwellings equal, and often much superior, to what they have been accustomed to in their own country.

After their arrival in Chungking (April 28, 1861), where Blakiston formed a very sanguine estimate of current and potential commercial activity, the expedition found itself in danger for the first time on its travels. The city was restless and full of ill-disciplined local troops, ostensibly being marshalled to put down unrest in the province, but not far removed from bandits or rebels themselves. Several boarded the two junks in a curious but threatening mood. No one west of Tung-t'ing Lake seemed to have heard of the second treaty settlement; the local prefect advised against entering the city, and one of the two French Catholic priests in the city, long schooled to sense danger in the air, sent two urgent messages to the boats:

> I hear that the Chinese soldiers will certainly murder you and pillage your boats. They have determined to commence the attack during dinner [at his residence, to which the Europeans had been invited]; they intend to destroy my house. I think it, therefore, prudent to defer the invitation till to-morrow, until the mandarins have taken measures for your safety.

The group did enter the city on the following day, and were not molested, but the very real potential for trouble was borne home.

A few days later, they pressed upriver beyond Chungking, their plans now uncertain because of risks both real and unpredictable. Arriving at P'ing-shan, a little beyond I-pin and the true limit of commercial navigation on the Long River on May 25, Blakiston's group had a hostile though not truly dangerous reception. Nevertheless, an attempt to reach Chengtu was clearly ill-advised, and after some brief, unrealistic thoughts of a direct overland trek from I-pin to Tibet, the expedition reluctantly decided on May 30 to turn back. The return trip, with water levels in the river much higher than during the winter and early spring ascent, was virtually without incident. The group was welcomed safely back in Shanghai on July 9, 1861, after a journey of about five months.

In his accounts of these travels, Thomas Blakiston followed a practice common among nineteenth-century English explorers of presenting the more technical matter—river surveys and charts, meteorological readings, geological samples, flora and fauna, etc.—in specialized publications, especially those of the Royal Geographical Society, then writing a somewhat more popular book for the general public; the book nevertheless contains a good deal of fairly technical information scattered throughout the text and in a number of appendices.

This was an era when books of travel and exploration carried very long subtitles. Blakiston chose the following: *Five Months on the Yang-tsze; with a Narrative of the Exploration of its Upper Waters and notices of the Present Rebellions in China.* Published shortly before the camera became standard equipment on such expeditions, the book is illustrated by accurate etchings prepared from Barton's sketches.

Before returning to England, Blakiston visited Japan, including the northern island of Hokkaido, then known as Yezo. In 1863, having resigned his commission, he returned to Hokkaido via Russia and Siberia, and made his residence in Hakodate, where he entered the lumber business. He now had time to indulge his passion for birds (in his book, he reported sadly that "my ornithological collection on the Yang-tsze number but a very few specimens"). He explored Hokkaido at his leisure, paying particular attention to its birds and their regional affinities, of which he prepared several authoritative catalogs and treatises.

After more than twenty years in Japan, Blakiston retired from his business, traveled in Australia and New Zealand, and then moved to the United States, where he ended a long bachelorhood in 1885 by marrying Anne Dun of Ohio, by whom he had a son and a daughter. After some years in New Mexico, he died in San Diego on October 15, 1891, but was buried in Columbus, Ohio—presumably in the Dun family plot.

William John Gill was born in Bangalore, India, in 1843. Like Blakiston,

An etching from Blakiston's *Five Months on the Yang-tsze*. In Witches Gorge.

eleven years his senior, his father was a career military officer (Madras army), and he too was educated for a military career. Assigned to the royal engineers, he was returned to India for duty in 1869. In 1871, a distant relative left him a "handsome fortune which enabled him to gratify his desire for exploration." His first expedition took place in 1873, an eight-month divagation in Persia. The attention garnered from this difficult and dangerous trip, the account of which was later published under the title *Clouds of the East*, led him to stand twice, unsuccessfully, for Parliament.

In 1876, he was ordered to Hong Kong, and there he obtained leave to travel in China. By this time, fifteen years after Blakiston's trip, much had happened. The great rebellions within China proper—the T'ai-p'ing and the Nien—had been suppressed some years earlier, and only the remnants of the Moslem uprisings still required attention. A new emperor, a mere boy known by the title *Kuang-hsü*, had been enthroned in 1875, as the outcome of palace intrigues that left the shrewdly ruthless and unenlightened Empress Dowager in effective control of the Forbidden City. In some provinces, powerful regional officials continued the process of "self-strengthening," i.e., the adoption of western military technology, rudiments of scientific learning, and language study, all in the interests of building up China so that she might more effectively resist further encroachment and turn the tide against the foreign powers. Their efforts were strongly opposed by conservatives and xenophobes, who saw good only in past precedents and believed that humiliation and the erosion of traditional values would inevitably result from such whoring after barbarian ways. These conservatives would have agreed with their descendants in the 1980s in their concern for "spiritual pollution."

Meanwhile, the foreign powers, led by Great Britain, sought to follow what they called "the cooperative policy"—having obtained the desired treaty rights, they now wished the central government to be strong enough to enforce them *and* to be held responsible for doing so. To this extent, then, representatives of the Foreign Office tended to be unsympathetic to the fumings of "old China hands" in the mercantile community, who held the Chinese government in contempt and were convinced that only "firmness"—gunboat diplomacy—exercised directly upon local officials in their bailiwicks would overcome obstructions or avenge "outrages."

Call them outrages or justified resistance to unwanted intruders, friction between foreigners and Chinese was frequent and periodically boiled over into violent attack. Virulent and often obscene anti-missionary propaganda was widely distributed, and violence against missionaries and Chinese converts was common. During this period, the bloodiest and most flagrant of these attacks was the Tientsin Massacre of 1870, directed against French Catholics in that important northern city, where foreign military presence was pronounced and anti-foreign feeling ran high. Angered partly by rumors that the nuns were killing orphans in order to use their organs in blood rituals and partly by the arrogance of a French official on the scene, a mob set upon the mission, killing ten nuns, two priests, and two French officials. Several churches, Protestant and Catholic, were destroyed. As usual, the affected foreign power received an official apology and an indemnity; the responsible officials were executed, and others were beaten or banished.

But a few years later, when Gill was beginning his journey in 1876, the big news among the foreign community was the murder of Augustus Margary (1846–1876). This must have made a deep impression on Gill, since both had been born in India and had been schoolmates at Brighton College. Margary's fate was bound up with recurrent British efforts to see if a feasible trade route might be found to link India with China, particularly to tap the rich resources of the southwest provinces of Szechwan, Kweichow, and Yunnan. Blakiston had been skeptical:

> It appears to me that beyond the fact of an overland communication between India and China, and its use by baggageless travellers, little practical good is likely to result from the expenditure of any amount of life and capital on such a venture.

His skepticism did not daunt others, however, and in 1875 it was proposed to explore a route from the Burmese town of Bhamo, head of navigation on the Irrawady, across Yunnan province, and thence northward into the Yangtze Basin. Until the Moslem rebellion in Yunnan (1855–1873), quite a flourishing frontier trade had existed between Yunnanese and Burmese traders, and some preliminary explorations had been undertaken by the British from Burma. This remains today a difficult and problematic area—on the Burmese side, it is part of the infamous Golden Triangle, where much of the world's heroin supply has its source.

Augustus Margary, a young consular official with experience in several China posts, was sent out from Shanghai to meet an expedition under Colonel Browne coming up from Burma, and was then to serve as interpreter and guide for the China portion of the trip. He proceeded up the Yangtze, crossed Lake Tung-t'ing, and thence ascended the Yuan River—where Shen Ts'ung-wen was later to describe the boats of Ch'ang-te. The Yuan River led him into Kweichow province, and onto the trails southward into Yunnan and finally to northern Burma. Margary found "the people everywhere charming, and the mandarins extremely civil," but he also disregarded their cautions concerning lawlessness and anti-foreign sentiment in the southwest, where the Moslem rebellion had only recently been quelled. Margary reached Bhamo safely, traversing a part of the route that in the late 1930s became the Burma Road, and then began the trip back with Browne's party.

Shortly after their re-entry into China, however, Margary's advance party was ambushed and Browne's larger following party was also attacked.

Margary and most of his small party were killed on February 21, 1875, but Browne's party repulsed their attackers without casualty. The precise details, including the fixing of responsibility, were never satisfactorily determined: various explanations blamed bandits, aboriginal hill tribes, the Burmese government, and inflammation of anti-foreign feeling by local Chinese gentry perhaps abetted by the county magistrate.

Since the Browne-Margary expedition had secured official Chinese travel permits, the British held the imperial government responsible for Margary's death, with particular culpability falling on the acting governor of Yunnan. The result was the Chefoo Convention of 1876, which fine-tuned the unequal treaties in several respects, and opened a number of additional treaty ports, including Chungking. As a side effect, the mission of apology sent to London evolved into China's first overseas diplomatic undertaking and eventually to legations in foreign countries.

Gill's trip began as had Blakiston's, by an ascent of the Yangtze. He left Shanghai in January 1877, in company with Edward Colborne Baber, an interpreter and consular official who had been a member of the commission investigating Margary's death and was now on his way to set up a consulate in newly opened Chungking; Gill's plans beyond Chungking were still unformed. Gill and Baber proceeded as far as Hankow by steamer—such service was now on regular schedule—and then proceeded by junk up to I-ch'ang and through the Three Gorges to Chungking. Rather unusually, their junk was commanded by a formidable woman who had survived or kicked out several husbands, and had both knowledge and temper sufficient to run a *kwa-tzu* herself.

After a short stay in Chungking, Gill set off alone for Chengtu, with only a retinue of coolies to carry his gear and, occasionally him, in a sedan chair. Thus far, Gill's trip had added only color and story to regions previously described. But from Chengtu, Gill set out, also without European guide, companion, or interpeter, on what he called "a loop-cast towards the Chinese alps," that is, northward out of Chengtu, passing through Mien-yang, up and over the Great Snowy Mountain (*Ta Hsüeh-shan*) at over 13,000 feet, thence to Sung-p'an and down the Min River back to Chengtu. Sir Henry Yule remarks:

> His success on a journey in which he has had no forerunner, and had no companion,—that from Ch'eng-tu to the north,—shows that he carried in his own person the elements of that success,— patience, temper, tact, and sympathy.

This route remains today a remote and difficult track: in the mid-1930s,

Mao Tse-tung led the forces of the Chinese Communist Party on their Long March through a part of this same route to Sung-p'an and over the Great Snowy Mountain; it was one of the most difficult passages of that dramatic march, and many men were lost to its dangers.

Back in Chengtu after his six-week "loop-cast" in late spring and early summer, Gill was forced by unsettled conditions to give up tentative plans to head north to the Silk Road or into Tibet to Lhasa. Joined now by a British consular official named Mesny, who knew Chinese and had had long experience in Kweichow province, Gill and his companion decided to follow the Old Tea Road toward Tibet, as far as Batang, high on the River of Golden Sand, then follow the river southward into Yunnan province to Ta-li, thence westward to the Irrawaddy and the town of Bhamo.

This, too, was largely terra incognita. Two rather peculiar French priests, Huc and Gabet, had traveled in Tibet a few decades earlier, and in 1850 Huc had published a startling work describing their journeys, a period of residence in Lhasa, and the road out as far as their re-entry into China. Although the book made a considerable splash in geographical circles, suspicions soon arose—justifiably it turned out—that Huc had included at least as much fantasy as fact and that his work was quite unreliable as a guide to further exploration.

Gill and Mesny left Chengtu on July 10, 1877, with sixty coolies, sedan chairs, mules, and ponies, and made a westward zigzag course toward the mountain town of K'ang-ting, at an elevation of 8,300 feet, crossing on the way the iron-chain suspension bridge at Lu-ting across the Ta-tu River made famous during the Long March in 1935. Gill's detailed description of this bridge, constructed in 1705, tallies perfectly with Mao Tse-tung's account contained in Edgar Snow's *Red Star Over China* (1938). From K'ang-ting to Batang, on the Chin-sha Chiang (River of Golden Sand), the party never descended below 8,000 feet, and was mostly above 10,000 feet, with many ups and downs in between. Towering over their trail were peaks soaring to 20,000 feet and more. Gill's account, in addition to careful topographical route maps, also includes much descriptive and linguistic information on the non-Chinese inhabitants—Tibetans, Lolo, and others—encountered on the way. Unfortunately, the Chinese names for these people were quite imprecise, so that it is difficult today to be certain which tribes or peoples are being described.

Batang is the frontier town a little downstream from the point at which the Sino-American rafting team abandoned the river in the summer of 1986. Both here and in K'ang-ting, where Tibetans far outnumbered Chinese, who had official authority but not much actual power, Gill and Mesny encountered French Catholic priests.

The next leg of the journey took the two Englishmen south to Ta-li, the major city of western Yunnan, where more non-Chinese peoples were to be found but where the Chinese were once again clearly dominant. From Ta-li, they followed the route used six centuries earlier by Marco Polo and two years earlier by Augustus Margary. On November 1, 1877, Gill and Mesny reached Bhamo, whence Gill began the long trip back to England. From Shanghai to Bhamo, the journey had consumed nine months, six months of it beyond Chungking and Chengtu, in the Tibetan marches, and in Yunnan. This was a major extension of knowledge, building on Blakiston's travels, but going far beyond it.

Gill did not long remain in England, however, but soon undertook various missions for the military intelligence service to which he was now assigned. In 1881, he was sent to Egypt to assist in improving security around the newly opened and already vital Suez Canal and in the laying of telegraph lines from Cairo to Constantinople. In the Sinai Peninsula, Gill and his companions were set upon, robbed, and murdered by Bedouins; Gill's remains were recovered and buried in St. Paul's Cathedral.

The book that resulted from Gill's travels in China was entitled *The River of Golden Sand: The Narrative of a Journey Through China and Eastern Tibet to Burmah*, originally brought out in two volumes in 1880 by John Murray, Blakiston's publisher (in 1969, a facsimile reprint was published). Volume 1 takes Gill to Chengtu, before his "loop-cast"; Volume 2, where the greatest amount of new information is to be found, covers the rest of the trip. The work is illustrated with many etchings from original drawings; and careful route maps, with elevations noted, accompany the more exploratory sections of the book. The value of the work is further enhanced by a long and informative introduction by Colonel (later Sir) Henry Yule (1820–1889), himself a noted traveler, translator of Marco Polo, and the most learned chronicler of exploration in China and inner Asia.

Isabella Bird and Other Women

Isabella Bird (1831–1904) was sixty-four years old when she arrived in Shanghai in January 1896. The urge for adventure, discovery, and exploration was not limited to men, and no Victorian woman possessed it more deeply than Isabella Bird. She was one of a remarkable group of "Victorian lady travellers," as Dorothy Middleton, their collective biographer, has called them. To the most difficult reaches of every continent except Antarctica these women went:

> From about 1870 onwards more women than ever before or per-
> haps since undertook journeys to remote and savage countries;
> travelling as individuals, and for a variety of reasons, they were
> mostly middle-aged and in poor health, their moral and intellec-
> tual standards were extremely high and they left behind them a
> formidable array of travel books.

While superficially these journeys might seem to be the women's counterpart of men's explorations, Middleton draws a sharp distinction between the two:

> Though this outburst of female energy is undoubtedly linked with the increasingly vigorous movement for women's political and social emancipation, it was neither an imitation nor a development of the male fashion for exploration which was such a feature of Victorian times. Whereas the famous lone travelers among the men were followed up by expeditions of ever greater size and complexity, the women did not inspire such an outcome. . . . Travel was an individual gesture of the house-bound, man-dominated Victorian woman. Trained from birth to an almost impossible ideal of womanly submission and self-discipline, of obligation to class and devotion to religion, she had need of emotional as well as of an intellectual outlet. This she found, often late in life, in travel . . . [and] she was able to enjoy a freedom of action unthinkable at home.

Yet despite the distinction drawn by Middleton, several of the lady travelers aspired to fellowship in the all-male Royal Geographical Society, the symbol of membership in the elite circle of explorers. Beyond Isabella Bird's undeniable accomplishments, which by 1892 already far surpassed those of many male Fellows, it was, finally, her determination and the great public acclaim accorded her that led the R.G.S. to make a few exceptions, though it was not until 1913 that women were admitted on the same basis as men. The issue caused considerable grumbling (Curzon fumed, "Their sex and training render them equally unfitted for exploration . . . and the genus of professional female globe-trotters . . . is one of the horrors of the latter end of the nineteenth century") and some sexist wit in the pages of *Punch*:

> A lady an explorer? A traveller in skirts:
>   The notion's just a trifle too seraphic:
> Let them stay and mind the babies, or hem our ragged shirts;
>   But they mustn't, can't, and shan't be geographic.

But if the Victorian lady travelers were the most visible and articulate among women in far-off places, they were not alone. As Jane Hunter's research shows, the Protestant missionary movement appealed to many of these same urges among nineteenth- and early-twentieth-century women, married and single. For the most part, these women were anonymous and silent, yet by 1890 they constituted sixty percent of the mission force in China, serving as teachers, health workers, and in particular ministering to

Isabella Bird in mandarin costume, from her own book.

the needs of Chinese women in a social structure virtually beyond the reach of men. Unlike Isabella Bird and her sisters, who came and went, these women spent many years in the lands to which their faith had sent them. These women, particularly married women—including those who married in the field—found themselves

> caught between the confident ideology and the troubling vulner-
> ability of the American home. . . . Throughout their lives, they
> balanced their initial loyalty to the evangelical mission of woman's
> sphere with their anxious efforts to reinforce its sacred core, the
> home.

Isabella Bird was perhaps the most famous and perhaps also the most prototypical of these lady travelers. She was "not everyone's favourite, inspiring in about equal proportions admiration, exasperation and that kind of idolatry which women of vigorous personality command from their less strong-minded sisters. Her emotions were violent, her health precarious and her energy phenomenal." Raised in a prosperous but strict evangelical household, Isabella was a fretful and sickly child who grew into an outwardly conventional, frail spinsterhood, devoting herself to her widowed mother and younger sister, Henrietta.

She was past forty when she made her first trip, with many misgivings, to Australia and New Zealand in 1872. She did not linger long in this outpost of the British Empire, but embarked for Hawaii, then still called the Sandwich Islands. There she found for the first time vigorous health and true fulfillment, riding, hiking, spending an ecstatic night on the very edge of Mauna Loa's active volcanic crater. All this she poured out in letter after letter to her sister "Hennie . . . whose function in life was that of lodestar to Isabella's wanderings, fire-keeper for Isabella's return and inspiration for Isabella's best writing."

From Hawaii, Isabella Bird sailed to San Francisco, crossed the Sierras with a stop at Lake Tahoe, then spent six wonderful, tempestuous months in the Rocky Mountains, above Denver. There she met a handsome, charming, moody mountain man, Jim Nugent, a man, she said, "any woman might love, but no sane woman would marry." Despite his frequent drunkenness and violent temper, Isabella had to restrain herself from falling in love with a man who appalled her Victorian upbringing but deeply appealed to the wild and passionate side of her nature. After her departure from the U.S. in 1874, Jim Nugent was killed in a gunfight.

Back in England, Isabella Bird became a best-seller with her first two travel books, on Hawaii and on her American adventure. In the latter book, notes the biographer Pat Barr, with quiet and deadly decorum, the whole bizarre and passionate adventure of Colorado is defused and expurgated for the Edinburgh drawing rooms to which Isabella returned, and Rocky Mountain Jim, shorn of all his volatile and sensual glamour is relegated to an object fit only for the moral zeal and compassion of a good Christian woman.

She also turned down a proposal of marriage by Dr. John Bishop, the Birds' family doctor, and a gentle and thoroughly civilized man, the utter opposite of Jim Nugent. She then fled to the Far East, where she spent nearly a year in Japan (mainly in Hokkaido and among the Ainu), in Hong Kong and Canton, and in Southeast Asia (Saigon, Singapore, Malaya). Two more books emerged from these travels.

Then, in 1880, her beloved Henrietta died. Prostrate with grief for her sister and her own alter ego, she now accepted Dr. Bishop's proposal, and in 1881, at the age of 50, she married. Isabella was nearly as devoted to her generously understanding husband as she had been to her sister, and she spent equally little time with him. "I have only one formidable rival in Isabella's affections," John Bishop said, "and that is the high tableland of Central Asia." But this companionable marriage lasted only five years before it ended with her husband's death. Now

> her activity became compulsive and her adventures progressively more arduous, as if with the snapping of all close emotional ties she was left with no alternative but to pursue, in ever-widening circles, a fulfilment which eluded her. . . . With every journey her immunity to cold became more complete, her appetite less fastidious, her tolerance of discomfort almost an addiction.

Turning more than ever toward religion, she determined to visit mission stations in the farthest reaches of the world. While one cannot disentangle such zeal from travel for its own sake—religious concerns are present in her later books but description is still their core—this phase saw her most ambitious efforts: to India, Turkey and Persia in 1889–1890, and Korea, Japan, and China in 1894–1897.

Her journey up the Long River began like most—by steamer as far as I-ch'ang, then by *kwa-tzu* through the Three Gorges to Wan-hsien. Here, however, she struck off on a route rarely if ever previously traveled by a Westerner. Leaving the river, she proceeded overland in a northwesterly direction, to the mission station at Pao-ning, where the China Missionary Society had an important station headed by the hearty, athletic Bishop Cassells. This was a route upon which she may have been the first European; certainly she was the first to write about it. In Pao-ning she endowed the small Isabella Bird Memorial Hospital. From Pao-ning, she continued on to Mien-yang and thence to Chengtu, but then determined to go farther, into the eastern edge of the Tibetan marches. The peak of her adventure, and peril, came on a 12,500 foot pass, at night in a driving snowstorm:

> The men were groaning and falling in all directions, calling on their gods and making expensive vows, which were paid afterwards by burning cheap incense sticks . . . yet they had to be prevented from lying down in the snow to die.
>
> Several times I sank in drifts up to my throat, my soaked clothes froze on me, the snow deepened, whirled, drifted, stung like pin points. But the awfulness of that lonely mountain-side cannot be conveyed in words. . . . I have fought through severe blizzards in the Zagros and Kurdistan mountains, but on a good horse and by daylight, and not weakened by a blow. On the whole, this was my worst experience of the kind.

Yet this woman of sixty-five survived to go even a bit farther into Somoland before returning to Chengtu to follow the Min and Yangtze back down to Shanghai "sweltering in a 'hot wave,' sunless and moist" in late June 1896. If this was a return to civilization, it was a civilization she felt as bondage, whether in Shanghai or in England, and she always experienced worse health in such comfortable surroundings than in the wilderness. She soon completed her book, *The Yangtze River and Beyond: An Account of Journeys in China, Chiefly in the Province of Sze Chuan and Among the Man-tze of the Somo Territory*, published as were all her earlier works and those of many other explorers by her friend John Murray (1899). She signed herself "Mrs. J.F. Bishop (Isabella L. Bird). F.R.G.S." For a couple of years, she remained bustlingly active, restless, energetic.

With the turn of the century and her own 70th year, however, her health began a progressive decline. Not well enough, she thought, to stand London any longer, she grasped for her accustomed panacea—travel—and was packing for China when she became too ill to go on. She died in Edinburgh on October 7, 1904, her famed digestion still intact despite failing heart and lungs, "with her luggage corded and labelled for a strange port on the other side of the world."

Archibald Little, Cornell Plant, and the Coming of Steam

Archibald John Little (1838–1908) was an "old China hand." Unlike Blakiston, Gill, Baber, Margary, and Mesny—all military men or consular officials—Little was a merchant. He arrived in China in 1859 and was to make China his home for nearly fifty years, until his final departure in 1907.

During his early years, he appears to have pursued a number of enterprises at various ports, but he then became increasingly determined to bring steam navigation to the upper Yangtze, beyond I-ch'ang and through the Three Gorges to Chungking. He became a prominent treaty port figure, as did his wife, who was one of the founders of the anti-footbinding movement. Like other old China hands, he lobbied both in China and at home for "firm" policies, including the frequent use of gunboats, "to teach the Chinese a salutary lesson." His condescending affection for the Chinese in general was often matched by his specific contempt for Chinese officials and sometimes for representatives of his own government, whom he considered supinely indulgent toward the defects of the Chinese imperial government. Both Mr. and Mrs. Little wrote books on China—travel, description, essays. According to one description, his appearance conformed to stereotype: portly, muttonchop mustaches, pith helmet, and all.

The Chefoo Convention (1876) had opened Chungking to consular residence, and E.C. Baber had accompanied Captain Gill upriver in the following year in order to set up the post. But the convention had not quite opened the city to foreign trade: it stipulated that such arrangements *might* be considered, once steam vessels had succeeded in ascending so far up the river— a transparent effort by Chinese negotiators to concede and withhold at the same time, since even foreign authorities (e.g., Blakiston) were doubtful that steam navigation of the Three Gorges was possible. Commerce could move downstream more rapidly and cheaply than in the other direction, but risks of loss were also greater. Upstream, with the voyage taking weeks or months, freight charges were so prohibitively high that only high-priced luxuries could profitably be sold. According to one estimate in the late 1880s, it cost more and took longer to get a ton of cargo from Hankow to Chungking than from London to Hankow. From Chungking to Chengtu, another 50 percent was added to the cost.

Attracted by Szechwan and the southwest, both for its rich resources, its potential as a market, and for the opportunity it might provide to extend British influence, Little accepted the challenge of pushing steam navigation through the Three Gorges. Indeed he made it his obsession. In 1887, he formed a company in London, The Upper Yangtse Steam Navigation Co., Ltd., with a capital subscription of £10,000, to build a ship on the Clyde, which was sent out to Shanghai in pieces and assembled there. This 175-foot stern-wheeler, named the *Kuling*, sailed upriver to I-ch'ang in 1889, with the intention, he wrote,

> of ascending to Chungking, and so getting the place opened to foreign trade as a treaty port; but I reckoned without my host in the shape of the British Government and their then representative in China, Sir John Walsham. These refused to coerce the Chinese

Government in any way, and so the *Kuling* was eventually sold and the scheme abandoned.

Little gave short shrift to Chinese objections, which, apart from free-floating reluctance to allow further penetration by foreigners, involved well-founded fears of mob action. There had been serious anti-missionary riots in Chungking in 1886, Hunan province was a chronic hotbed of anti-foreignism, and almost every year saw similar violence somewhere in China. Although Chinese officials could not foresee the future, they had good reason to believe that worse was to come, as indeed it did. The Chinese also worried about loss of transit duties, about further harm to the junk trade through loss of livelihood for tens of thousands of junkmen and trackers, and about physical damage caused by collision or swamping of native craft by the wake of steamships. Flouting of Chinese customs and beliefs and disrupting the spirits were also invoked. In desperation, one official even warned that monkeys in the Three Gorges, their serenity disturbed by noise and smoke, might throw rocks down upon the offending steamships.

As Little noted, he was unable to obtain the necessary passports. But not all foreigners saw matters as he did. Sir Robert Hart, Inspector General of the Chinese Maritime Customs and for forty years the most influential and impartial foreigner in China, found Little insensitive and exasperating. As so often both before and after, Hart arranged a solution, but he suspected he was being "fleeced by Master Archie!" After much annoying negotiation, the Chinese government bought the boat for £18,000, with an additional £5,400 for a wharf-site owned by Little in I-ch'ang. (The Chinese government also made a profit on the *Kuling* by selling it to Li Hung-chang's China Merchants Steam Navigation Company. For many years after, it worked the Hankow/I-ch'ang run. In return, the government agreed in 1890 to open Chungking to foreign trade, but for the time being only in native vessels.)

Little persisted, nevertheless, taking up residence in Chungking for a time. (Isabella Bird described him as the only foreign merchant in that city when she passed through.) In 1895, after China was disastrously defeated by Japan in the first Sino-Japanese War, a minor clause in the Treaty of Shimonoseki finally opened Chungking fully. Little seized this opportunity and had built in Shanghai a much smaller craft than the *Kuling*, the seven-ton teakwood launch *Leechuan*, with a top speed of nine knots. With Little in command, Mrs. Little aboard, and a crew of five, the *Leechuan* set off on February 15, 1898 from I-ch'ang, accompanied by a Chinese gunboat, extra trackers, and a red lifeboat with its own crew. The first rapids pilot, unused to a power boat, collided with a ferry; his successor tried to flee from such an outlandish and unpopular expedition, as did other Chinese in the entourage. Despite this and other serio-comic adventures, on March 8 the *Leechuan* moored below Chungking to allow for a celebration to be organized by the foreign community of about sixty; among the Chinese, curiosity was even more powerful than resentment, and firecrackers added to the hullaballoo of welcome.

But Little's ascent was an accomplishment of greater symbolic than practical significance. The *Leechuan* was neither a cargo nor a passenger carrier, and it had been quite unable to make the passage under its own steam. Gangs of up to 300 reluctant trackers had been required in the most difficult spots, and elsewhere they had had to secure cable to the shore and winch the boat up.

The second passage by steam vessels (though not by steam power alone) was accomplished in May 1900 by two British gunboats, the *Woodlark* and the *Woodcock*. Meanwhile, Archibald Little, by no means satisfied with mere symbolic victory, was ready to try for commercial success, for which he went on the stump at home by speaking before chambers of commerce about British policy and his own plans. The *Pioneer*, a much larger ship than the old *Kuling* but like it built in England and shipped out to China for assembly, was a side-wheeler of 180 feet, capable of 14 knots. To skipper the *Pioneer*, Little engaged S. Cornell Plant, whom he had met at the Oriental Club in

British gunboat in the Three Gorges (1920s).

London. Plant had not previously been to China, but he had had considerable river experience on the Tigris and Euphrates.

In mid-June 1900, the *Pioneer* set off from I-ch'ang on the first commercial voyage through the Three Gorges. Carrying a full load of passengers and cargo, the passage to Chungking took a little over seven days. Trackers were not used, but at one critical point the ship was stalled for three days before getting over with the aid of hawsers to the shore. Worcester tells of the fate of the *Pioneer*:

> The voyage was a great success; but unfortunately it was the only commercial trip she made, for owing to repercussions from the Boxer troubles she was commandeered by the British Consul for use as an evacuation ship and eventually sold to the British Government. She served as a river gunboat under the name HMS Kinsha for more than 20 years, but was finally sold into Chinese hands and served to carry chickens from Ningpo to Shanghai.

The *Pioneer* was Little's last hurrah, though if he made as much money selling that vessel as he had with the *Kuling*, he may have done very well.

In the same year, 1900, a German firm sought to crack the commercial possibilities of western China and also to open a niche into the de facto British sphere of influence in the Yangtze Valley. Their ship, the *Suihsing*, was the largest yet—over 200 feet. This length was perhaps her undoing, for while attempting passage of K'ung-ling Rapids on her maiden voyage, during the low water season in December 1900, she was unable to maneuver properly. Plant wrote that she "struck on the submerged Pearl Rocks. A great hole was ripped in her side, she became unmanageable and, after drifting down stream for about half a mile, dived headforemost to the bottom, where she now lies 23 fathoms deep." This total loss of a brand new ship stalled further commercial efforts for several years.

New efforts were undertaken by Cornell Plant, who in effect received the baton from Archibald Little after the latter's departure from China in 1907 and his death in the following year. Plant had spent the intervening years trading in native vessels and carrying out careful surveys of the various hazards between I-ch'ang and Chungking. Failing—for understandable reasons—to attract foreign investors to this hitherto fruitless project, Plant raised money from Chinese sources, forming the Szechwan Steam Navigation Company. Plant's innovation was to build, in England, a powerful vessel, the 115-foot *Shutung*, which was not designed to carry much cargo itself but to work as a powerful tug, with a specially designed cargo-and-passenger barge lashed alongside. This same arrangement has been successfully used ever since, and is still frequently seen in the Gorges.

Plant had found a feasible solution, and from the *Shutung*'s first trip in

October 1909, the era of more or less dependable service began. During the navigation season, April to December, the *Shutung* averaged two round trips a month, and was almost always fully booked. In 1914, a more conventional second vessel, the *Shuhun*, was put in service, and after World War I, other companies entered service, which had become far more dependable. Even so, passage was far from uneventful.

> The little "Shu-tung," with her flat lashed alongside—the "twins," as they were often called—kept running throughout the season, warping over those rapids which she could not cross, by the aid of her powerful capstan and a steel wire rope attached to the shore, getting badly bumped occasionally, and always attended by hair-breadth escapes. Nevertheless, favoured by the mighty dragon, she kept going.

The modest and self-effacing Cornell Plant served also as River Inspector for the Chinese Imperial Maritime Service and compiled an authoritative navigator's guide to the river between I-ch'ang and Chungking. He trained pilots, both Chinese and foreign, and he felt much responsibility for their performance. He helped to design the system of river signals so that shipmasters would know of the approach of up- or downbound vessels and could take appropriate action. Particularly dangerous were downbound junks, which had very little maneuvering capacity in the swift current. Steamers, up- or downbound, had to give way to avoid collision, often thereby putting themselves in serious jeopardy.

He also authored one of the most charmingly written and illustrated accounts of this portion of the river, *Glimpses of the Yangtze Gorge* (1921), in which, typically, he hardly mentions his own role in developing communications on the upper river. Ivon A. Donnelly, his friend and the illustrator of this little book, remarks:

> Having devoted the greater part of his life to studying and overcoming the dangers and difficulties which attend navigation of this river, Captain Plant is the ideal man to write a book on this subject. Very reticent by nature—loved by Chinese and foreigners alike—he has at last been persuaded to give the public the benefit of his vast knowledge.

When Plant retired from the Customs Service, the Chinese government— the generally ineffectual government of the early Republican period following the overthrow of the Ch'ing dynasty in 1911—expressed its gratitude for his service by building a bungalow for him and his wife overlooking

Cornell Plant

Hsin-t'an ("New Rapids"). G.R.G. Worcester noted the recognition paid him by passing river craft:

> Here amid scenes familiar to him and his wife, he planned to live within sight and sound of the most spectacular and formidable of all the rapids. No steamship ever struggled up over the astonishing gradient, or careered down the roaring boiling reach unseen by the old sailor, who would watch their progress from his window. The custom grew up of saluting him in passing with a blast on the whistle, and he would reply with a wave of his handkerchief.

In 1921, the Plants, who had not been back to England since their arrival in China, decided to make a visit before returning to their home above the rapids. They were given a warm send-off all down the Yangtze, but Cornell Plant fell ill with pneumonia and died aboard ship before reaching Hong Kong. Mrs. Plant, bereft and overwhelmed with grief, also died as the ship entered port; the couple were buried in Hong Kong, in Happy Valley.

Ken Warren and the River Rafters

If the latter nineteenth century was a time to fill in the blank spaces on the world's map, the latter twentieth century has been a time to climb every peak and raft every river, not simply to seek conquest over nature's severest challenges but to do so in ever more novel or in ever more minimalist ways: to stand atop the highest peak on every continent, to ski down Mount Everest, to climb free-style unroped, to kayak wild rivers, to sail the oceans not only alone but blind. These self-imposed limitations seem to say that nature itself is not enough, that man will not simply prevail but totally dominate. If the aura of such feats is thereby enhanced, they may also trivialize the earth's awesome places. Hillary's ascent of Everest in 1953 inspired millions; today it hardly rates back-page mention, and climbers deplore the amount of debris left on the mountain by previous parties.

As recently as 1984, no one had traversed the entire length of two of the world's greatest rivers, the Amazon and the Yangtze. In that year, the Amazon fell to a Japanese rafter, who went from the river's source high in the Andes all the way to its Atlantic estuary. This left only the Yangtze. Or, more properly speaking, this left the Yangtze above I-pin; from I-pin to Shanghai the Yangtze is a highway, the Three Gorges no challenge at all to a modern rafting expedition.

Some years earlier, Ken Warren had already determined to conquer the Yangtze. Its source had been more or less definitively surveyed only in 1976, about the time Warren was making the first raft trips from the sources of the Ganges down its two major confluents. With these accomplishments safely logged away in 1977, Warren, then 50 years old, set his sights on the first 2,000 miles of the Long River, down to I-pin. Nine years later, in 1986, he found himself at 15,000 feet on the Tibetan Plateau, ready to begin.

Ken Warren, an experienced river outfitter and hunting guide from Portland, Oregon, is a controversial figure. With a personality as powerfully intimidating as his 6'4", 220-pound physique, Warren inspires loyalty and engenders resentment in about equal proportions. Driven to achieve his goals, he is one of those men determined not only to lead any group of which he is a member but to be its visible center. During his years of preparation for the Yangtze, Warren met and married his second wife, Jan, whose dedication to the project at least equaled his own. On those few occasions when even Ken Warren despaired of their efforts to get the trip financed, manned, and under way, it was Jan Warren who insisted upon driving ahead.

After much tribulation and many reverses, the Warrens finally put the expedition together. It had devoured all the money they could raise and their own resources as well, forcing bankruptcy in 1985. The Chinese wanted $1,000,000 before issuing the necessary permits, but lowered their demand when Warren offered to add three Chinese to the group and again when it appeared that the whole thing might fall through; finally $325,000 was agreed upon, and ABC Television became one of the sponsors of the expedition. Not all of the nine Americans and three Chinese (plus the Warrens) in the primary group were experienced outdoorsmen or rafters. On July 5, 1986, the expanded party—now numbering 29, including various cameramen and auxiliaries—arrived in Canton, with ten tons of equipment.

On July 21, the group set out in kayaks, since the rivulets near the source were too shallow for the seven rafts to be used later. The plan was for Jan Warren and the support group to make periodic rendezvous along the way with the rafters, for resupply, repair, medical care, and evacuation (if necessary). To do so she would travel overland by truck, in long-distance detours over roads that barely deserved the name. The overland resupply effort was an adventure in itself.

All this noisy preparation had aroused great nationalistic concern in China. We recall (Chapter 1) that a young Chinese photographer from Chengtu, Yao Mao-shu, had sought to join Warren's group, but had been turned down because Warren already had three Chinese members. Yao's response was to attempt in June 1985 a one-man dash down the river, an effort that cost his life in one of the early rapids. But Yao Mao-shu became an instant national hero, a patriotic martyr to keeping the symbolic ownership of the river in Chinese hands. Now, a year later, as Warren's Sino-American team was setting in, no fewer than six Chinese groups were either on the river or preparing to begin. Only two were serious undertakings, but even these were hastily thrown together. One was sponsored by Yao Mao-shu's home

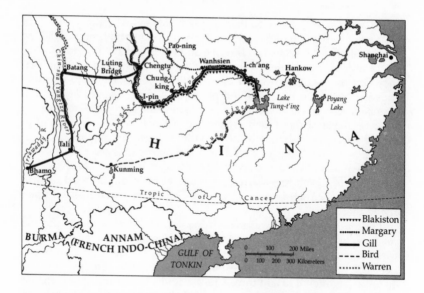

FIGURE 10-1. Map showing routes of the explorers (the trip upriver from Shanghai to central China is not shown on the map).

province, Szechwan; the other was the Long River Scientific Expedition. The members of these expeditions had very little river experience.

From the start, problems plagued the Sino-American expedition. A photographer, David Shippee, was soon afflicted with high-altitude pulmonary edema and died on August 4. Relations between Warren and several members of the group grew increasingly strained and acrimonious, over both decisions of substance and Warren's domineering style. The rafts were ungainly and progress was much slower than anticipated—and also more monotonous, since the river (called here the Tuotuohe and T'ung-t'ien) was meandering across flat terrain, without much incident or challenge. Beneath the surface lay anxious anticipation about the river ahead and festering resentment about Warren's leadership.

Things came to a head with the rendezvous at the frontier county seat of Yü-shu, on the edge of the plateau, just before heading into serious rapids. The group learned that one of the Chinese expeditions—they weren't sure which—had lost several men in the river ahead. In a bitter and angry confrontation with the Warrens, four members of the group packed up and left. One of them later told Michael McRae, "I left because I did not want to be part of Ken Warren being famous. I did not think he deserved to be the first white man down the river." Warren's reported reaction was that "at some time they would have quit anyhow. They just did not have the guts."

One of the Chinese rafting teams shooting Tiger-Leaping Gorge in an enclosed capsule.

The four-raft group that set out from Yü-shu was more cohesive as well as smaller than before. They soon entered white water rough enough to be interesting but not particularly dangerous. But by the time they passed the town of Dege on a tributary slightly off the River of Golden Sand, they were heading into peril. Batang, where Capt. William Gill had passed through more than a century earlier, was their next rendezvous with Jan Warren's supply team.

The Dege-Batang stretch defeated the team, seriously damaging their rafts and repeatedly throwing rafters into the water. Warren tenaciously wanted to continue, despite the almost certain knowledge that worse yet was ahead, particularly the terrible rapids at Tiger-leaping Gorge, below Batang. But the battered group, exhausted and unwilling to continue without reconnoitering ahead, refused to go on. One member of the team began a hike out to seek help. Two days later, Warren himself, carrying an 80-pound pack, ascended the river's cliffs and, seeing what was ahead, simply turned toward Batang. It took him six days, and soon after he arrived, relieving his wife's terrible anxiety, a rescue party brought in the rest of the team. Even then, Warren was willing to continue, to join one of the Chinese teams at Tiger-leaping Gorge, but, as McRae puts it,

> the ravaged expedition had neither the time nor the strength to go on. Several nights later, under a brilliant full moon, the three rafts that had been left upriver were spotted drifting, unmanned and ghostlike, past Batang.

Ken Warren later remarked, "I'd always said the Yangtze would be the toughest river in the world to run." He went on,

> but I thought it would be just very, very big water and we'd tie the boats together. The Colorado has some big water, but not like this. . . . I've never seen another river that just churns like a cauldron of whitewater, twisting, turning. And sizewise it's also the biggest I've seen. It's rockier, the turns are sharper, there are more large drops. . . . This was the biggest whitewater anyone has tried to run.

Of the Chinese expeditions, at least one and perhaps two made it through Tiger-leaping Gorge, although the Luoyang group lost one man there and four altogether. Unlike the Sino-American team, the Chinese groups used fully enclosed capsules, further protected by inner tubes and tires lashed to the outside. Only one or two team members were selected to risk this passage, with the rest of the group portaging around the gorge. Once past the worst passages, they returned to more conventional rafts.

On November 12, 1986, the Chinese press reported the arrival of the Luo-yang group in the estuary of the Yangtze River, and pronounced them the first to traverse the entire length of the river. About two weeks later, the Long River Scientific Expedition also arrived. The distinction of running the Yangtze from source to mouth thus did, in the end, remain in Chinese hands.

THE RIVER
CHANGED FOREVER?

Those who know Mao Tse-tung only as the ruthless architect of the Chinese revolution may learn with some surprise that he was a poet of more than middling talent. More surprising still—Mao was full of surprises—was the fact that he wrote poetry in the style of the Sung dynasty, a millennium before his own time and an era firmly within "the feudal past." Can one imagine anything comparable from Lenin or Stalin? Ronald Reagan or Margaret Thatcher writing in the manner of Chaucer or John Donne?

Mao was also capable of the grand gesture, among which were his long swims across the Yangtze River at Wuhan in 1956, under the arches of the nearly completed first bridge across the river. Mao exalted his physical prowess, the bridge, and the future dam—all of them triumphs of human will over the river—in a lyric entitled "Swimming." The first stanza alludes to history, to Ch'ü Yuan and the Three Kingdoms, but then Mao turns to the present and the future:

> The bridge soars from north to south and
> > Nature's moat becomes a thoroughfare.
> Still to come is the western river's wall of stone,
> > Cutting through the mists and rain of Witches Gorge
> And raising calm lakes in steep ravines.
> > If the Goddess were still alive
> She'd be amazed at how the world has changed.

The notion of a dam on the Long River by no means originated with Mao Tse-tung. Sun Yat-sen envisioned a dam in the gorges as part of his hugely ambitious plans for China's development. Such ideas were discussed from time to time during the 1920s and 1930s, and some preliminary explorations were made. The dream of a dam even figured in John Hersey's novella, *A*

Single Pebble, in which the protagonist, a young American engineer, brashly new to China in the 1920s, embarks on a *kwa-tzu* for an upriver journey through the Three Gorges to survey possible locations for such a project. In Witches Gorge, in the same region referred to by Mao, he found the place:

> There it was! Between those two sheer cliffs that tightened the gorge a half-mile upstream, there leaped up in my imagination a beautiful concrete straight-gravity dam which raised the upstream water five hundred feet. . . . Ingenious lift-locks at either side carried junks up and down on truly hydraulic elevators. The power plant was entirely embedded in the cliffs on both sides of the river. The strength of the Great River . . . created a vast hum of ten million kilowatts of light and warmth and progress flowing out through high-hanging wires over six widespread provinces. Away through pipelines flowed, too, unimaginable numbers of acre-feet of water, irrigating lands that after the harvest would feed, let me say, seventy-five million Chinese. . . . Beyond the tall barrier, junks sailed forward with their wares, to Chungking and farther, as on a placid lake.

But in the end the young engineer, stunned and sobered by the gulf separating his callow notion of progress from a deeper Chinese attachment to the ways of nature, abandons the dream not as technically impossible but as somehow profoundly wrong:

> How could I, in the momentary years of my youth, have a part in persuading these people to tolerate the building of a great modern dam that would take the waters of Tibet and inner China, with their age-old furies, on its back, there to grow lax and benign? How could I span a gap of a thousand years—a millenium in a day? . . . [I began to] wonder whether a dam was the right thing with which to start closing the gap.

Hersey's young engineer doubtless learned some important lessons on the river and came away from his experience with greater sensitivity to cultural difference. In the 1920s and 1930s such enormous undertakings were far beyond the capacity of Chiang Kai-shek's government, and, just as in the past, one had to take the river pretty much as it was. But many Chinese were quite prepared to tamper with nature, a nature that exacted such a toll in labor and lives. For all his newfound humility, Hersey's engineer patronizes the Chinese still by assuming—indeed somehow admiring—a preference for patient endurance rather than for change. But if that image seemed true, it was because no alternatives were then feasible, and for most ordinary folk in China, change usually meant change for the worse. Yet when Chinese are realistically convinced that things *can* change for the better, they are as quick as any people to make those changes.

Although the Yangtze River is normally less malevolent than the Yellow River, its floods have been tremendously destructive, and this danger still remains. Traditionally, efforts to control such floods were limited to dike-building and diversion into the lakes and marshes below the Three Gorges. During years of abnormally heavy rainfall, these measures proved pitifully inadequate. Statistics for the "100-year flood" of 1870—one which might be expected once a century—are not available, but the "30-year" flood in the summer of 1931 inundated 8.5 million acres of farmland and cost 150,000 lives; millions were left homeless. For three weeks, water stood several feet deep in low-lying Hankow. In 1954, under comparable conditions, the new government saved Hankow through an aggressive strategy of river diversion and frantic strengthening of the dikes, but elsewhere 30,000 lives were lost and flooded areas were nearly as great as in the 1931 flood. Even "small" floods, occurring every few years, do substantial local damage.

Alongside flood control, which tries to cope with too much water, is the problem of irrigation, addressed to deficiencies in the water supply. The third purpose of most dams is the generation of hydroelectric power. China is estimated to possess greater potential for hydropower than any other nation in the world, and almost half that potential capacity is found in the Yangtze Valley, along the main river and its tributaries. And finally, of course, navigation and shipping is a major concern on larger rivers, and above all on the Yangtze.

Ever since the establishment of the Peoples Republic of China in 1949, that government has undertaken flood control, power projects, and irrigation works throughout the country, including the Yangtze Valley. Some of these projects are quite substantial, even on an international scale, and they have involved the kinds of controversies, foul-ups, delays, and cost overruns all too familiar in such undertakings elsewhere, including the United States. They also involve intense political controversy, because water is so critically important to life and to livelihood, because water is no respecter of political boundaries, and because water requires large-scale projects. Quite frequently, one region will reap the benefits of a water project, while another must bear its costs and burdens.

In China, where all low-lying land is densely occupied and intensively cultivated, dam projects are likely to displace large populations and submerge forever fields and towns, ancestral graves and temples to the spirits of the land. In one large dam-reservoir project on the Han River (Danjiang-kou, built between 1958 and 1974), over 350,000 persons had to be relocated. Finding places for displaced people in a land already so crowded is extremely difficult, all the more so because they wish to remain together in the kinship and village units which have been so much a part of their lives. Usually, however, they must be dispersed. Project refugees are already devastated, economically and emotionally, by the loss of their fields and homes and communities, and they expect, at the very least, compensatory treatment by the government. Meanwhile, natives of the proposed resettlement areas resent alien newcomers being dumped in their midst, and they, too, are likely to demand special treatment if they are to bear these added burdens.

These projects, numerous though they have been, have only begun to meet the most pressing needs. Flood control measures are still minimal. Despite the enormous hydroelectric potential of the Yangtze Valley and China's chronic energy shortage, only 3 percent of that capacity is even now in use. Some work had been done on the Long River itself—improving navigation in the Three Gorges by blasting out the worst obstructions, improving the channel markers and signal systems, shortening the river's meanders north of Lake Tung-t'ing, enlarging diversion areas for flood control, reinforcing dikes, etc. But on the scale of this great river, all these undertakings are mere tinkering and the fundamental character of the river was changed by them hardly at all.

Three great projects—one nearly completed and the other two still in the planning stages—will have a fundmental impact on the river. If all these projects are completed, the Long River will have been changed forever.

The Dams: Gezhouba and Three Gorges

Gezhouba, the multipurpose dam which has been under construction since late 1970 and is now nearing completion, sits just above I-ch'ang at the very gates of the Three Gorges. This was not the original idea. According to the master plan set down in 1958, a high dam in the gorges was to come first, with regulating dams below it to be built later. A new and powerful bureaucracy, the Yangtze Valley Planning Office (YVPO), was to oversee this and other projects along the river. But the high dam project was dauntingly large and complex. Furthermore, early in the planning stage, the disasters of the Great Leap Forward and the Cultural Revolution effectively put the high dam idea on the shelf.

In 1968, with the worst excesses of the Cultural Revolution winding down, Hupei province took the initiative by proposing a low dam at I-ch'ang. Taking advantage of a still-confused command structure, provincial authorities did an end run around the Yangtze Valley Planning Office by going up a different chain of command, that of the Ministry of Water Conservancy, which was happy to increase its own clout in the central government. Hupei representatives argued their case on several grounds: that the project was entirely within the province and would therefore be comparatively simple administratively (though, in fact, management became badly snarled); that the dam could provide desperately needed electric power for the central Yangtze

Basin, and particularly for the major industrial complex at Wuhan; that some flood control could be provided below the dam and navigational safety improved above it. One crucial argument was that, as a low dam, water levels would be raised very little, and hence almost no one would have to be relocated. Finally, advocates argued that Gezhouba could serve as a goose to lay some golden eggs—to help generate capital for the high dam through the sale of electric power and fees from boats passing through its locks.

These arguments won the day, and construction was begun—no accident, in that era of personality cult—on Mao Tse-tung's birthday, December 26, 1970. During the first couple of years, things were a mess. Planning had been hastily done, design flaws quickly emerged, concrete quality was substandard. Worst of all, the management committee was ineffectual and often deadlocked. At Chou En-lai's order, construction was halted from 1972 to 1974. When construction was resumed, the worst of the problems were ironed out, though some completed work had to be torn out in order to be redone properly. Management organization was revamped also, with the YVPO now much more prominent. Since late 1974, progress has been fairly steady, with some design changes incorporated along the way. The first phase of the dam was declared complete in 1981, and, in mid-1987, the second phase is nearing completion (see Figure 11-1).

This is a big, complex dam. Crossing two natural islands, the total length of the structure is 1.6 miles, with a height of 130 feet above the riverbed. A series of spillways discharge excess water, with smaller sluicegates specifically designed periodically to flush silt from behind the dam. Electric power

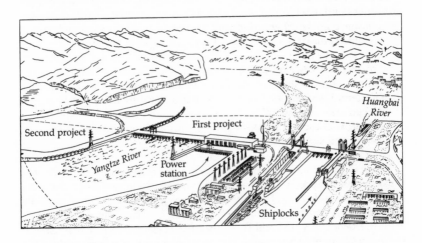

FIGURE 11-1. Perspective drawing of Gezhouba dam, lock, and hydropower complex.

comes from two large generating stations, one at either end of the dam. The northern station was completed in Phase I and is now on line; the southern, and larger, station is still under construction as part of Phase II. Two locks, the larger about the size of the biggest locks on the Panama Canal, are capable of raising or lowering boats by seventy feet in about twenty minutes. When both phases of the dam are complete and designed and hydroelectric generating capacity (2.7 million kilowatts) comes fully on line, Gezhouba will rate as the twentieth largest hydropower dam in the world, in addition to performing its other functions. China has never released cost figures, but estimates of direct construction costs are in the $1.5 to $2.0 billion range, at Chinese rates for labor and materials.

In the spring of 1981, power generation began, the locks were opened to traffic, and Phase I was pronounced complete. Three months later, in early July, the heaviest rains in thirty years hit Szechwan province, causing tremendous damage. In that province, about 1,500 lives were lost, 30,000 were injured, and over 150,000 were rendered homeless. Over 1.5 million acres of farmland were inundated, and Chengtu was badly flooded. Holding their breath, engineers knew that Gezhouba would be tested at close to its maximum rated capacity by the torrents cascading through the Three Gorges. Would the dam hold? Early on the morning of July 19, waters crested at the dam. For a few hours, 95,000 cubic yards of water *per second* passed through the spillways, accompanied by surge waves twenty feet high. By afternoon, the crest had passed and the dam had survived without serious harm. On July 24, navigation through the shiplocks was resumed.

Impressive as Gezhouba is, the Three Gorges Dam project will dwarf it, assuming that it is indeed built. If the project goes ahead to full-scale completion, it will be the biggest dam and the largest engineering project in the history of the world. According to Lieberthal and Oksenberg,

> In terms of size alone, it will dwarf any dam in the United States and will be larger than the Brazilian dam at Itaipu, the largest dam built to date. In addition, the dam would be unique in that no other major dam in the world copes simultaneously with flood control, major hydropower generation, large amounts of shipping, and serious silt problems.

Since Three Gorges Dam was first seriously proposed in the 1950s, enthusiasm for the project has waxed and waned, and even today the issue appears to be undecided. Publicly, the Chinese government and mass media say that a final decision has not yet been made, but then they often go on to extol the benefits which will flow from the project "when it is finished." Meanwhile, survey and design work continues, and travelers on the river can easily see where preliminary work is being done.

The debates about this project are not aired in public, however, and only with considerable probing can one uncover the profound and wide-ranging controversies that have swirled about Three Gorges Dam from its very inception. Disagreement has attended every facet of the project: technical feasibility, the silting problem, costs vs. benefits, financing, resettlement of displaced populations, environmental impact, and so on. Since public opinion is not a factor in any direct and immediate way, these controversies are carried on largely in camera, through the major agencies of government (Yangtze Valley Planning Office [YVPO], Ministry of Water Resources and Electric Power, Ministry of Communications, State Scientific Bureau, etc.)—each of which tends to have its bureaucratic preferences—and through the territorial entities (provinces, municipalities, etc.) which will be most affected by decisions concerning the project. Perhaps needless to say, issues of principle quickly become intertwined with organizational and political concerns: How will *our* organization (province, municipality) make out? Which decisions will increase our influence, and which decrease it? If things go badly, who will bear the responsibility and who will take the blame? Whose ox will be gored?

YVPO has consistently championed Three Gorges Dam, with some of the other bureaucracies opposing it, or agreeing only if their considerations are met. Downstream provinces, especially Hunan and Hupei, are strongly in favor since they appear to be the principal beneficiaries; meanwhile, Szechwan province has been opposed because it was slated to receive little of the electric power (they would prefer numerous smaller plants on the headwaters of the many rivers in the province), and in addition, Szechwan was to be responsible for handling most of the refugees. On the other hand, Chungking municipality favors the dam but only if it raises water levels sufficiently so that 10,000-ton barges can reach the city.

If Three Gorges Dam is to be built, it will soak up a big chunk of the funds available for capital construction nationwide, and it will do so for a decade or two before the first payoffs begin to appear. No one can confidently estimate total cost—or even agree how to calculate costs—but some guesses are in the four- or five-billion-dollar range. Skeptics observe that cost estimates at comparable stages of other large projects have proved almost always to be far too low, and they wonder if the money might be better spent on smaller, less risky projects which have an earlier and more dependable return on investment.

Three Gorges Dam—assuming it is to be built—will not be located in Witches Gorge, where Mao's poem and Hersey's novel had placed it. Instead, it will be sited farther downstream in the third gorge, Hsi-ling, anchored in the ancient pre-Cambrian granites of the Huang-ling anticline. (See Figure 11-2.) Just off Sandouping, a small village on the south bank of the river, lies a half-mile-long island whose core is solid bedrock. Here the proposed

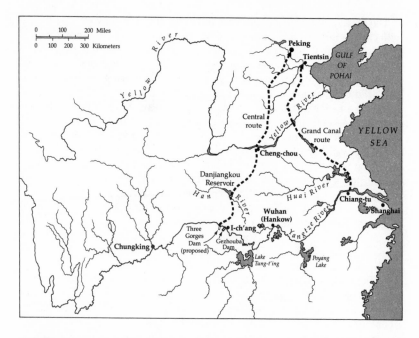

FIGURE 11-2. Map showing location of Gezhouba, proposed Three Gorges Dam, and routes for the Southern Waters North project.

dam will span the river. No place else in the gorges offers a comparably stable foundation, as periodic landslides like those that created New Rapids testify: in 1985, almost three million cubic yards of rock and earth fell into the river in that same zone of extreme instability.

One of the most crucial design decisions has to do with the height of the dam, and hence the depth of the water that can be impounded behind it. Reservoir depth in turn determines how much power can be generated, how much land will be flooded, and how many people will have to be resettled. Meanwhile, of course, costs escalate as the height of the dam increases. Maximum proposals are for a dam of 200 meters (656 feet) with a reservoir 180 meters (580 feet) deep at the dam site. This would exceed North America's largest dam, Grand Coulee, in height (by a hundred feet) and length (by 2,000 feet). Designed hydroelectric capacity for a 200-meter dam would be 25,000 megawatts, almost triple that of Grand Coulee, and twice that of the world's largest hydroelectric power dam, Itaipu, on the border between Brazil and Paraguay. A dam of this size would back up a reservoir more than 250 miles, and Chungking would have its desired water depth for 10,000-ton barges.

Scaled-down proposals have also been suggested, down to a minimum dam height of 140 meters (450 feet) and reservoir depth of about 120 meters (385 feet). Such a dam would cost less and displace many fewer persons, but it would also seriously reduce generating capacity, flood control capability, and upstream navigation benefits. Chungking municipality opposes this minimum proposal as failing fully to meet its transport needs. At any height, silt-handling and navigation locks will require special solutions. Raising and lowering 10,000 vessels by 500 feet or so is a major operation to say the least.

All the way back to Chungking, water levels would be markedly raised. In human terms, all the river towns in the Three Gorges, and all the historical and cultural sites associated with this part of the river, would be submerged. White King City would be a hundred feet or more below the surface. If one of the higher dam proposals were followed, both Wan-hsien, the first important city above the Three Gorges, and Chungking would lose much of the older, poorer, and lower-lying parts of their towns. But both these very hilly cities appear willing to suffer such loss in return for the benefits they hope to reap.

A 200-meter dam would inundate 115,000 acres of farmland and, more importantly, require resettlement of at least 1.5 million people. This is such a thorny problem that there has even been talk of creating a new province carved out of eastern Szechwan and western Hupei, a province whose first mission would be to resettle these refugees from Three Gorges. A lower dam would make a big difference on this score. At the minimum of 140 meters, 11,000 acres and 200,000 persons would be directly impacted. Displacement of even this latter number of people would be, of course, unthinkable in the United States and most other western nations.

Southern Waters North

In the late 1950s, while some planners were giving thought to the Three Gorges Dam, others were considering yet another way to make use of the enormous amounts of water in the Yangtze system. Since north China is chronically water poor, why not divert some of central China's abundant supply northward? Central China receives about twice the rainfall of the North China Plain, and the volume of water in the Yangtze is nearly ten times as great as that in the Yellow River. North China is deficient in water not only for agriculture but equally for urban use in industry and by the growing number of city dwellers. Furthermore, north China's water supplies are much more intensively used than those of the Yangtze Valley, and as the cities draw off more and more water, less is available for agriculture. Ground water supplies are being dangerously depleted, and the prospect of increasing salinization of the soil is a real one. Nearly 80 percent of the water in the Yellow River is utilized, and such intensive use produces friction between upstream water consumers, who get first crack at it, and downstream populations, for whom the flow is much diminished by the time it reaches them. Meanwhile, less than 10 percent of the Yangtze's much more abundant waters are similarly used.

Several transfer routes have been proposed, but only two are realistic candidates. The Central Route would run from Gezhouba (or Three Gorges Reservoir, when and if it became available) northward across the Danjiang-kou reservoir, the Yellow River, and the North China Plain, to its destination in the Peking-Tientsin region. The long-term advantage of this alignment is that once the route has been established, the landforms would permit gravity transfer, without the need for costly pumping to move the water. This route, which requires extensive tunneling, would be costly to construct initially, but is said to still be under consideration.

Meanwhile, the Eastern or Grand Canal Route is already being developed, with first-phase construction having begun in 1983; this explains the considerable effort of recent years on the rehabilitation of the Grand Canal. In fact, the Eastern Route does not exactly conform to the Grand Canal throughout its entire length, but makes use of the string of lakes between the Yangtze and Huai rivers. The advantage of this route is that much of the channel is already in place, although the northern sections, from the Huai to the Yellow River and from the Yellow River to Tientsin, still require much work. The bad news is that fourteen very large pumping stations will be required to impel the water northward and up the 120-foot rise toward the bed of the Yellow River. As part of the plan, a tunnel will be created to carry the southern waters *under* the bed of the Yellow River. From that point northward to Tientsin, gravity will do the job, then pumping will be required again to get water to Peking.

The project, with a target completion date of 1990, is intended to serve transport and irrigation needs along the way, in addition to sending water to the north. One of the major transport objectives is to move coal southward to fuel industries in Shanghai and Chiang-nan, thus providing important relief for the overtaxed north-south trunk rail lines. In order to handle 2000-ton bulk carriers from Shantung province south to the Yangtze River, a large double lock is being built at Huai-an, near the Huai River, and the canal is being widened to 250 feet and dredged to a depth of 15 feet.

The national media in China have carried only blandly enthusiastic accounts about Southern Waters North, with occasional assurances that "because this is a big project, we must go slowly" to assure that unwanted side-effects are kept to a minimum. Even if both routes are completed, however, the water needs of north China will by no means be fully met. Instead, these projects will help to alleviate some shortages in major cities (especially Peking and Tientsin) and will provide some irrigation water in a belt adjoining the canal.

It may be that there is very little opposition to this project, far less perhaps than in the case of Three Gorges Dam. If so, this would be surprising to an American familiar with the intense conflict generated by interregional water transfers, actual or proposed. One has only to think of the Colorado River. The Colorado River has been so ruthlessly exploited by California and Arizona that it no longer has a mouth, all water having been taken off before it reaches the Gulf of California. Meanwhile within California, periodic proposals are made to expand what might be called a "Northern Waters South" project in order to benefit agriculture in the Central Valley and the great Los Angeles urban agglomeration by drawing water from the northern part of the state. All such efforts are accompanied by the most intense efforts by each side, the one to accomplish the project, the other to stall or prevent it.

Whatever the similiarities or differences, the experiences of the two nations underline the crucial importance of water. The Chinese often characterize water-deficient areas as regions in which "water is more precious than [cooking] oil." In the long run and for the nation as a whole, it may be that water, and how water is handled, will in fact be more important than oil— petroleum—in determining the success or failure of efforts to build a strong, modern, and prosperous China.

AFTERTHOUGHTS

As I prepare to see this book go out into the world on its own, two thoughts come to mind. One is about writing the book and the other is about the subject of the book.

Only as I finish writing do I feel finally that I know what it was that I was writing about, and about my relationship to it. I am even more acutely aware now than when I began of how vast a subject I staked out, and how very small and fragmented are the essays that make up this book. Each of the essays is itself but a superficial introduction to a subject, some of which I may try someday to explore at greater depth. Nor do these fragmented pieces fit together in a finished mosaic. Instead, they are widely spaced, seemingly—perhaps—scattered at random. Yet I hope that these essays form for the reader, as they do for me, implicit patterns in which interconnections and mutual influences can be read, so that these various themes enrich and deepen one another. My goal, as I said at the outset, quoting Levenson, is "to restore the whole in comprehensible form," but knowing that it is, ultimately, the reader who must do the comprehending, who must make sense of it all.

This is, perhaps, a turgid way of saying what Robert Graves said with sly wisdom in "The Devil's Advice to Story Tellers":

> Assemble, first, all casual bits and scraps
> That may shake down into a world perhaps;
> Nice contradiction between fact and fact
> Will make the whole read human and exact.

My thoughts about the Yangtze River involve that simultaneous awareness of change and continuity of which Su Tung-p'o wrote in the first of his *Odes on Red Cliff*: "For if you look at the aspect which changes, heaven and earth cannot last the blinking of an eye; but if you look at the aspect which is changeless, the worlds within and outside you are both inexhaustible."

In the perspective of natural time, a kind of time-lapse photography, the Long River comes into being along with the collision of continents, the seas recede, the Szechwan Basin emerges, the Three Gorges cut through the damming mountains, the lakes and marshes of central China take shape, rise and fall with the seasons, and gradually fill up. The Central China Plain flattens out, and the inexorable pushing out of the land shapes the future site of Shanghai. It is literally, as the Chinese proverb has it, from "blue sea to mulberry field."

The evolution of human life and of increasingly complex human society marks the emergence for the first time of a self-conscious actor who can, with awareness and design, seek to use and modify natural processes. In what has been, even within recent geological time, no more than an instant, human action has profoundly influenced the course of nature.

Natural processes are changed—accelerated, slowed, or diverted—by human action. Until fairly recent times, most such effects have been the result of innumerable and imperceptible actions taking place over long periods of time: deforestation that exposed the land and increased erosion and siltation, paddy fields that encroach upon lakes and marshes, canals that interrupt drainage patterns. In modern times, however, human beings have developed the capacity to produce such changes within a few years through dramatic and large-scale projects—reservoirs, dams, and the like. In either case, however, the ramifications and the side effects of such action have not been well foreseen or controlled.

From these perspectives, the Yangtze River does indeed seem to be changing in "the blinking of an eye"; perhaps within the lifetime of the readers of this book it will have changed forever. Yet from the other perspective, it seems to have gone on forever. Until the last two decades, changes in the river during a generation or two were so trivial as to be insignificant. Despite all the history enacted on its waters, along its banks, or within its valley, despite memories of Ch'ü Yuan and Red Cliff, the endless current remains attentive above all to the swing of the monsoon seasons, to rainfall and snowmelt and drought. It remains utterly indifferent to human concerns. Perhaps, as T.S. Eliot suggests, it is waiting:

> . . . I think that the river
> Is a strong brown god—sullen, untamed and intractable,
> Patient to some degree, at first recognised as a frontier;
> Useful, untrustworthy, as a conveyor of commerce;
> Then only a problem confronting the builder of bridges.
> The problem once solved, the brown god is almost forgotten
> By the dwellers in cities—ever, however, implacable,

Keeping his seasons and rages, destroyer, reminder
Of what men choose to forget. Unhonored, unpropitiated
By worshippers of the machine, but waiting, watching and
    waiting.

                            "The Dry Salvages"

NOTES AND COMMENTS

In order not to burden the text unduly with footnotes and bibliographic references, I have indicated for each of the chapters the principal sources upon which I have relied, unless that information is clearly contained in the text. Readers who wish precise citations to primary or secondary sources are invited to write directly to the author, in care of the Department of History, Stanford University, Stanford, CA 94305.

Background information can be found in a good textbook. One of the best surveys from early times to the nineteenth century is Charles O. Hucker, *China's Imperial Past* (Stanford, Calif.: Stanford University Press, 1975), or its abridgement, *China to 1850* (Stanford, Calif.: Stanford University Press, 1978). The last century or so is ably covered by John K. Fairbank, *The United States and China*, 4th ed., enlarged (Cambridge, Mass.: Harvard University Press, 1983).

Perspectives

I draw from the introduction to Braudel's work. The teacher referred to was Joseph R. Levenson; the quotation is found in his essay in L.P. Curtis, ed., *The Historian's Workshop* (Berkeley, Calif.: University of California Press, 1970).

Chapter 1: The Lay of the Land

For more information on the rafting expeditions, see Chapter 10. The most accessible of Molnar and Tapponier's writings on the geology of Asia is "The Collision between India and Eurasia," *Scientific American* (April 1977). Maps 1-1 and 1-2 come from this source. General geographic and climatic descriptions can be found in many works, e.g. T.R. Treagar, *A Geography of China* (Chicago: Aldine, 1965). See also Caroline Blunden and Mark Elvin, *A Cultural Atlas of China* (New York: Facts on File, 1983).

Chapter 2: A Tour of the River

More detailed sources concerning parts of the river may be found under the relevant chapters. A lavishly illustrated general survey of the Yangtze was published a few years ago in China: Jiang Liu, *Changjiang: The Longest River in China* (Peking: Foreign Languages Press, 1980). Unquestionably the best traveler's guide to the river is Judy Bonavia, *A Guide to the Yangzi River*, (Hong Kong: China Guides Series, 1985). The long quotation from Edgar Snow comes from his autobiography, *Journey to the Beginning* (London: Gollancz, 1959).

Chapter 3: The Three Gorges

The fullest geologic survey of the river in English is now more than fifty years old: G.B. Barbour, "Physiographic History of the Yangtze," *China Geological Survey: Memoirs*, Series A, No. 14 (Peiping, 1935). A very useful general source (in Chinese) has been prepared by the Yangtze Valley Planning Office, *A Brief History of Water Management on the Yangtze River* (Peking: Water Resources and Electric Power Publishing House, 1979). The term *wu*, usually translated "witch," as in Witches Gorge, is an ancient term, pregnant with mystery. Because *wu*—usually women—were possessed by spirits during trance states, they are more properly shamans than witches. In ancient China, such cults were particularly strong in this region, but were deplored and feared by northerners. See Arthur Waley, *The Nine Songs: A Study of Shamanism in Ancient China* (London: Allen and Unwin, 1955). Vivid descriptions of the gorges come from one who knew them intimately: Cornell Plant, *Glimpses of the Yangtze Gorges* (Shanghai: Kelly and Walsh, 1921). Plant also prepared *Handbook for the Guidance of Shipmasters on the Ichang-Chungking Section of the Yangtze River* (Shanghai: Maritime Customs, 1920). A detailed, technical article on the history of hydrological measurement along the upper river, featuring the stone fish at White Crane Ridge, appeared in the Chinese journal *Wen-wu* in August 1974.

Chapter 4: A Historical and Regional Reconnaissance

Despite the great wealth of new and unprecedented archaeological discoveries, Edward H. Shafer's *Ancient China* (New York: Time-Life Books, 1967), remains a graceful and informed survey of early China. Ssu-ma Ch'ien, who wrote his monumental *Records of the Historian* in the second century B.C., aimed to cover everything from China's earliest beginnings to his own day. Large portions of his work have been translated by Burton Watson. Wall-building was not a new idea. From about the sixth century B.C. on, the feudal states of the later Chou period built walls against each other and against the northern "barbarians." The Great Wall, as completed by the first emperor of Ch'in, incorporated many segments of these already existing walls.

The most important theoretical and descriptive work on regional systems in China has been done by Prof. G. William Skinner of Stanford's Anthropology Department. See in particular the work he edited, *The City in Late Imperial China* (Stanford, Calif.: Stanford University Press, 1977).

Chapter 5: Migration and Settlement

The description of Li Ao's trip draws heavily on Edward Schafer, *The Vermilion Bird: T'ang Images of the South* (Berkeley, Calif.: University of California Press, 1967). The extract from Li Po's poem on the road to Szechwan is taken from Arthur Waley, *The Poetry and Career of Li Po, 701–762 A.D.* (London: Allen and Unwin, 1950). The quotation concerning plank or gallery roads is taken from Joseph Needham, *Science and Civilization in China*, vol. 4, part III (Cambridge, England: Cambridge University Press, 1971). Part III is itself a 931-page volume entitled *Civil Engineering and Nautics*. I have drawn heavily on this work in several chapters of the present book. Some of Needham's material, from this and other volumes, has been presented in more popular and accessible form in Robert Temple, *The Genius of China: 3,000 Years of Science, Discovery, and Invention* (New York: Simon & Schuster, 1986). The classic work on Chinese population during the later dynasties is Ho Ping-ti, *Studies on the Population of China, 1368–1953* (Cambridge, Mass.: Harvard University Press, 1959). An authoritative work on some aspects of migration is Herold J. Weins, *Han Chinese Expansion in South China* (New Haven, Conn.: The Shoestring Press, 1967). G. William Skinner's work (e.g., *The City in Late Imperial China*) is important in understanding many of the dynamics of China's demographic history; he has recently published a technical case study: "Sichuan's [Szechwan's] Population in the Nineteenth Century: Lessons from Disaggregated Data," *Modern China*, Vol. 8, No. 1 (June 1987).

Chapter 6: The Grand Canal

Despite the great importance of the Grand Canal, no satisfactory general history of this great work presently exists in any language; many articles can be found, but cannot be cited here. *The Grand Canal of China* (1984) is a popular illustrated account published in Hong Kong by the *South China Morning Post*. A survey of the Grand Canal and its history was presented serially by *China Pictorial*, from July to December 1986. Much more information, based on Chinese sources, is contained in Hoshi Ayao, *The Ming Tribute System*, Mark Elvin, trans. (Ann Arbor, Mich.: University of Michigan Center for Chinese Studies, 1969); see also Blunden and Elvin, *A Cultural Atlas of China* (cited in Chapter 1). Much technical information is available, passim, in Joseph Needham, *Science and Civilization in China*, vol. 4, part III (Cambridge, England: Cambridge University Press, 1971). Information on canal-building in the United States, for comparative purposes, can be found in John S. McNown, "Canals in America," *Scientific American* (July 1976). The chronically depressed Huai-pei region and its impoverished population are vividly described in Elizabeth J. Perry, *Rebels and Revolutionaries in North China, 1845–1945* (Stanford, Calif.: Stanford University Press, 1980). The poem and the predator-protector model are drawn from her work.

Chapter 7: Merchants, Commerce, and Products on the Move

The problem of merchants and the place of commerce in China has been and continues to be a much debated issue; the fundamental issue is whether or not China's development is in some sense comparable to that of Europe, or whether the two are fundamentally different. Not all scholars would agree with the analysis presented here. Mark Elvin's *The Pattern of the Chinese Past* (Stanford, Calif.: Stanford University Press, 1973) engages these issues; the characteristics of the medieval economic revolution are drawn from Blunden and Elvin, *A Cultural Atlas of China* (cited in Chapter 1). A different view is taken by William T. Rowe, *Hankow: Commerce and Society in a Chinese City, 1796–1889* (Stanford, Calif.: Stanford University Press, 1984); the drawing of the Shansi-Shensi Guildhall is taken from this work. The description of the guildhall and guild activities in Chungking comes from Archibald Little, *Through the Yangtze Gorges: or, Trade and Travel in Western China*, 3rd ed., rev. (London: Sampson Low, Marston & Co., 1898).

Most of the technical data on rice production come from M.S. Swaminathan, "Rice," *Scientific American* (January 1984). An authoritative survey of Chinese agriculture during the past 500 years is Dwight Perkins, *Agricultural Development in China, 1368–1968* (Chicago: Aldine, 1969). The depiction of rice-transplanting (Fig. 7) is found in *Keng Chih T'u* (*Plowing and Weaving*), an eighteenth-century agricultural handbook. Even more comprehensive is the 1637 encyclopedia of technology, Sung Ying-hsing (tr. by E-tu Zen Sun), *T'ien-kung k'ai-wu: Chinese Technology in the Seventeenth Century* (University Park, Pa.: Pennsylvania State University Press, 1966); Figs. 8 and 9 come from this source.

A classic chapter in the social history of salt is Ho Ping-ti, "The Salt Merchants of Yang-chou: A Study of Commercial Capitalism in Eighteenth-Century China," *Harvard Journal of Asiatic Studies* (1954). Li Jung's mid-nineteenth century description of the salt wells in Szechwan province was translated by Fang Tu Lien-che, "An Account of the Salt Industry at Tzu-liu-ching," in Nathan Sivin, ed., *Science and Technology in East Asia* (New York: Science History Publications, 1977).

In addition to *T'ien-kung k'ai-wu*, one of the best brief accounts of the technology of silk, from egg to fabric, may be found in William Willets, *Chinese Art* (Harmondsworth, England: Penguin, 1958). Some of the information presented here was gleaned during my trips to China. So also was some of the information on tea. An engaging and informative history of clipper ships and tea trade is William F. Baker, *Running Her Easting Down* (Caldwell, Idaho: Caxton Printers, 1974); the best treatment of the international opium and tea trade, and Great Britain's Asian empire, is Peter Ward Fay, *The Opium War, 1840–1842* (New York: Norton, 1975).

No history of tung oil has been written, but during the 1930s a number of quite detailed articles appeared, reflecting the rapid growth of that product as an item of international trade. Since most of these appear in relatively inaccessible journals, I do not cite them here.

Chapter 8: Junks and Junkmen

The most comprehensive study of junks, junkmen, and river lore is that of G.R.C. Worcester, *The Junks and Sampans of the Yangtze* (Annapolis: Naval Institute Press, 1971). This is a superb revision of four volumes published by the Chinese Maritime Customs Service between 1940 and 1948. Worcester also built and collected scale models of junks, which are on display at the Kensington Science Museum in London. Many of these subjects are also treated in Needham, vol. 4, part III. For a richly illustrated appreciation of the Chinese junk, see Derek Maitland, *Setting Sails: A Tribute to the Chinese Junk* (Hong Kong: *South China Morning Post*, 1981). The description of the crooked-stern junks is taken from Archibald John Little (cited in Chapter 7). Cornell Plant's advice concerning red boats is found in *Glimpses of the Yangtze Gorges* (cited in Chapter 3). Extracts from the travel diary of Lu Yu have been translated by Burton Watson, *The Old Man Who Does as He Pleases: Selections from the Poetry and Prose of Lu Yu* (New York: Columbia University Press, 1973). Isabella Bird's account of her trip upriver is *The Yangtze Valley and Beyond* (London: John Murray, 1899). The works of Little, Bird, and Plant are cited extensively in Chapter 10.

Chapter 9: History, Symbolism, and Imagery

We are fortunate to have a superb study of Ch'u Yüan and the lore which has grown up around him: Laurence A. Schneider, *A Madman of Ch'u: The Chinese Myth of Loyalty and Dissent* (Berkeley, Calif.: University of California Press, 1980). My discussion of Ch'u Yüan draws heavily on Schneider's work. The translation of "Li Sao" is based on that found in Cyril Birch, ed., *Anthology of Chinese Literature* (New York: Grove/Evergreen, 1965), vol. I. See also Arthur Waley, *The Nine Songs* (cited in Chapter 3). The historical record is contained in Ssu-ma Ch'ien's great work of the second century B.C., *Shih-chi (Records of the Historian)*. The issue of suicide had deep personal meaning for Ssu-ma Ch'ien, who had been ordered castrated by Emperor Wu for his outspokenness. Suicide was the expected response, but Ssu-ma Ch'ien chose to remain alive to complete his historical writings.

The most accessible version in English of the novel of the Three Kingdoms

(*San-kuo yen-i*) is Moss Robert's superb abridgment, *Three Kingdoms, China's Epic Drama by Lo Kuan-chung* (New York: Pantheon, 1976). A full translation of this very large novel (120 chapters) was done by C.H. Brewitt-Taylor in the 1920s and was reprinted in 1959. Su Tung-po's "Odes on Red Cliff" are translated in Birch, *Anthology of Chinese Literature*, vol. I. Wang Gungwu's assessment is taken from his "The Middle Yangtze in T'ang Politics," in Arthur F. Wright and Denis Twitchett, eds., *Perspectives on the T'ang* (New Haven, Conn.: Yale University Press, 1973).

The Hakka are an ethnic Chinese minority of later migrants into south China, especially the provinces of Fukien and Kuangtung. Earlier settlers resented them and discriminated against them. The Hakka, with their own distinctive dialect of Chinese, usually occupied marginal lands and pursued low-status trades. Some of their customs differed from those of the majority, e.g., the feet of Hakka women were left unbound. The T'ai-p'ing poem was quoted in Philip Kuhn, "The Taiping Rebellion," *The Cambridge History of China* (Cambridge, England: Cambridge University Press, 1978), vol 10, part I.

The best accounts of the "Long March" of the Chinese Communists are to be found in Edgar Snow's 1938 classic *Red Star Over China*, available in many editions, and in Harrison Salisbury, *The Long March: The Untold Story* (New York: Harper & Row, 1985).

Chapter 10: Some Westerners on the Long River

The main sources used in this chapter are the works of the travelers themselves. (1) Thomas W. Blakiston, *Five Months on the Yang-tsze; with a Narrative of the Exploration of its Upper Waters, and Notices of the Present Rebellions in China* (London: John Murray, 1862). (2) William Gill, *The River of Golden Sand; the Narrative of a Journey through China and Eastern Tibet to Burmah* (London: John Murray, 1880). (3) Archibald John Little, *Through the Yang-tse Gorges, or Trade and Travel in Western China*, 3rd. ed., rev. (London: Low Marston & Co., 1898). (4) Mrs. John F. Bishop (Isabella Bird), *The Yangtze Valley and Beyond: An Account of Journeys in China, Chiefly in the Province of Sze Chuan and among the Man-tze of the Somo Territory* (London: John Murray, 1899). (5) Cornell Plant, *Glimpses of the Yangtze Gorges* (Shanghai: Kelly and Walsh, 1921) and *Handbook for the Guidance of Shipmasters on the Ichang-Chungking Section of the Yangtze River* (Shanghai: China Maritime Customs, 1920). Worcester, *Junks and Sampans*, also contains much information on Little, Plant, and the steam navigation of the upper river. Isabella Bird's life and travels have been chronicled by Pat Barr, *A Curious Life for a Lady: The Story of Isabella Bird* (Garden City, New York: Doubleday, 1970); and by Dorothy Middleton, *Victorian Lady Travellers* (New York: E. P. Dutton, 1965). Women missionaries are treated by Jane Hunter, *The Gospel of Gentility: American Women in Turn-of-the-Century China* (New Haven, Conn.: Yale University Press, 1984).

The fullest account of Ken Warren's rafting expedition is a highly critical article by Michael McRae, "Mutiny on the Yangtze," *Outside* (May 1987). Chinese magazines, notably *China Reconstructs* and *China Pictorial*, also carry stories on the Sino-American and Chinese teams that were simultaneously on the river. ABC Television produced two one-hour films on the expedition, which were broadcast in April and May 1987.

Chapter 11: The River Changed Forever?

The most complete information on the two dams and the Southern Waters North project is found in two unpublished papers by American scholars: (1) David M. Lampton, "Water: Challenge to a Fragmented Political System" (June 1983), 51 pp. and (2) Kenneth Lieberthal and Michel Oksenberg, *Bureaucratic Politics and Chinese Energy Development*, Chapter 6, "The Three Gorges Dam Project" (August 1986), pp.249–327. An abridged version of Lampton's paper appeared in *China Business Review* (July–Aug. 1983). Illustrations, diagrams, and some technical information is contained in Chen Gengyi, ed., *Large Dams in China* (Beijing: Ministry of Water Resources and Electric Power, 1980). Occasional articles have appeared in *Beijing Review*, *China Reconstructs*, etc.

ABOUT THE AUTHOR

Lyman P. Van Slyke was born and raised in the iron-mining region of northern Minnesota and attended Carleton College. His introduction to Asia and to the San Francisco Bay Area began in 1952, as a junior officer in the U.S. Navy during the Korean War. He entered the University of California at Berkeley in 1955, receiving his M.A. in 1958 and his Ph.D. in Asian history, with an emphasis on modern China, in 1964.

Between 1960 and 1965, Professor Van Slyke and his family spent three years in Taiwan, where Chinese became his second language and, for a time, the first language of his two sons and one daughter. In 1963, he joined the Stanford faculty as a member of the History Department. He helped to establish and continues to administer the Inter-University Program for Chinese Language Studies in Taipei and currently serves as Director of Stanford's Center for East Asian Studies, a position he has held twice previously. In 1984 he won the Dean's Award for Excellence in Teaching.

Professor Van Slyke has served on the boards of a number of professional and scholarly organizations. His previously published research has centered on the twentieth century, particularly in the areas of Sino-American relations and the history of the Chinese Communist Revolution. Author of the well known book, *Enemies and Friends: The United Front in Chinese Communist History*, and editor of *The Chinese Communist Movement*, and *The China White Paper*, all three of which were published by the Stanford University Press, he has also written many articles for journals and scholarly publications.

Since his first visit in 1975, Lyman Van Slyke has made twelve trips to China and has traveled widely in many parts of that country, leading several groups on behalf of the Stanford Alumni Association's Travel/Study Program. He lives on campus with his wife, Barbara, a psychotherapist, harpsichord player, and early music enthusiast. His own hobbies include jogging, vegetable gardening, shooting pool, and watching the sports in which he once engaged.

INDEX

China Missionary Society, 168
Ching-chiang diversion basin, 22
Ch'ing-t'an. See Rapids, Green
Chin-sha Chiang. See River of Golden Sand
Chou En-lai, 185
Chuang-tzu (Taoist philosopher), 82
Chu-ko Liang (strategist), and the Three Kingdoms, 19, 141–43
Ch'u (region), 45–46
Ch'ü Yuan, as a symbol, 134–38, 141
City, White King (Pai-ti ch'eng), 31, 143, 189
Climate, of China, 10–14
Clouds of the East (Gill), 160
Coal, transport, and the Grand Canal diversion route, 190
Communist Party, Chinese, 25, 79, 150–51, 163
Confucianism, 81, 82, 84, 143
Confucius, 46, 134, 136
Convention, Chefoo, 162, 170
Cooks, on junks, 126–27
Cultural Revolution, 53, 136
Culture: early Chinese perceptions of, 45–46; nuclear-area theory of origins, 45; spread of Chinese, 44–47
Current, through the Three Gorges, 32, 34–38
Cutty Sark (tea clipper), 105

Dam, 181–89; Danjiangkou, 183; Gezhouba (Yangtze River low), 20, 28, 184–86; social effects of, 183–84; Three Gorges, 28, 52, 186–89; Yangtze River low, *see* Dam, Gezhouba
Delta, of the Yangtze, 23–24, 55
"Devil's Advice to Storytellers, The" (Graves), 192
Diking, effect of, 21–22
Diplomacy, gunboat, 160, 170
Ditch, Han. *See* Han-kou
Donnelly, Ivon A., 174
Drill, churn, for salt, 95, 97
Dynasty: Ch'in (221–206 B.C.), 48, 60, 62, 65; Ch'ing (1644–1911), 50, 51, 63, 76, 94, 148–50; Chin (Gold), 63, 143; Han (206 B.C.-A.D. 220), 47, 48–49, 139–45; Ming (1368–1644), 51, 63, 73, 94; Shang (1500–1000 B.C.), 44–45; Southern Sung (1100–1300), 50; Sui (581–618), 50, 65, 67; Sung (960–1279), 50, 60, 83–84,

121; T'ang (Middle Empire) (618–907), 39, 50, 51, 70–71, 83–84, 121; Yuan (1280–1386), 50, 71

Earthquake, T'ang-shan (1976), 8, 10
Eliot, T.S., 193–94
Elvin, Mark, 83
Empire, Middle. *See* Dynasty, T'ang
"Encountering Sorrow" (*Li Sao*) (Ch'ü Yuan), 135
Erosion, and topography, 12–14
Europe, tea in, 102
Expedition, Long River Scientific, 178, 180

Fault, K'ang-ting, 17
Fay, Peter Ward, 103
Festival, Dragon Boat (*Tuan-wu chieh*), 137
Fish, carvings of, as water-level markers, 38–39
Five Months on the Yang-tsze (Blakiston), 158
Flood, 183, 186; and the Grand Canal, 76–77, 78; in the Three Gorges, 19
Flood control, 21–22, 183, 184
France, and Chinese Catholicism, 153–54
Fuling, hydrographics at, 38

Gabet (French priest), 163
Gas, natural, from the salt wells, 95
Gate, K'uei, 32
Geology, and the Yangtze, 8–10
Geosyncline, Cathaysian, 10
Gill, Captain William, 155, 158, 160–64, 169, 179
Glimpses of the Yangtze Gorge (Plant), 174
Gordon, Charles "China," 148
Gorge: Bellows, *see* Gorge, Windbox; Ch'ü-t'ang, 19, 30, 31–32, 125; Hsi-ling, 19, 20, 30, 31, 33–35, 39, 187–89; Ta-ning River, 29; Three-Gates (*San-men hsia*), 71; Windbox (Bellows), 32, 121, 125; Witches, *see* Gorge, Wu; Wu (*Wu-hsia*; Witches), 19, 30, 31, 181–83
Gorges, Three. *See* Three Gorges
Grain: shipments of, up the Grand Canal, 67–68, 73–74; system of tribute, 74–75, 76
Granary, Sui, 74
Grand Canal (Great Transport River), 23, 54, 65–80, 145; as an aqueduct, 80; blockade of, 154; costs of, 74, 76;

CREDITS

Cover — Art is a detail from "The Great Yangtze River" (long horizontal scroll) by Chang Dai-Chien. Reproduced courtesy of Chang Chun and Eugene Wu, director of the Harvard-Yenching Library.

Page 9 — Figure 1-1: Adapted from "The Collision Between India and Eurasia" by P. Molnar and P. Tapponier. Copyright © 1977 by *Scientific American*.

Page 57 — Figure 5-1: Based on Jiang Liu, *Changjiang: The Longest River in China* (Peking: Foreign Languages Press, 1980).

Page 61 — Figure 5-2: Adapted from Joseph Needham, F.R.S., *Science and Civilization in China*, vol. 4 (London: Cambridge University Press, 1971). Copyright © Cambridge University Press. Used by permission.

Pages 70, 71 — Figures 6-1 and 6-2: Adapted from maps in Mark Elvin, *The Ming Tribute System* (Ann Arbor: University of Michigan, Center for Chinese Studies, 1969).

Page 78 — Photograph reproduced by permission of EOSAT.

Page 101 — Photograph of painting courtesy of the Peabody Museum of Salem.

Page 106 — Illustration by Max Millar in William F. Baker, *Running Her Easting Down* (Caldwell, Idaho: The Caxton Printers, Ltd., 1974).

Page 113 — Figure 8-1: Based on Harold J. Wiens, "Riverine and Coastal Junks in China's Commerce," *Economic Geography* XXXI (1955).

Page 115 — Illustration from Needham, *Science and Civilization in China*, vol. 4. Copyright © Cambridge University Press. Reprinted by permission.

Page 120 — Illustration of junk sail layout from G.R.G. Worcester, *Junks and Sampans of the Yangtze*. (Annapolis, Maryland: U.S. Naval Institute, 1971). Copyright © 1971, U.S. Naval Institute.

Page 122 — Photograph by Dmitri Kessel, courtesy *LIFE Magazine*. Copyright © 1956, Time Inc.

Page 124 — Photograph by the author.

Pages 126, 127 Illustration of tracking cable and tracker's sling from Worcester, *Junks and Sampans of the Yangtze*. Copyright © 1971, U.S. Naval Institute.

Page 172   Photograph from Le Palud, *The Yangtze Gorges in Pictures and Prose* (Shanghai: Kelly & Walsh, Ltd.).

Page 175   Photograph by Donald Mennie from Gretchen Mae Fitkin, *The Great River* (Shanghai: North-China Daily News & Herald, Ltd., Kelly & Walsh, Ltd., 1922).

Page 179   Photograph courtesy *China Pictorial*, Beijing, China.

Page 185   Figure 11-1: Based on an illustration appearing in *The Atlas of Geo-Science Analyses of Landsat Imagery in China*, Chen Shu Peng, editor (Beijing: Science Press, 1986).

Page 202   Photograph by Chuck Painter, Stanford News and Publications.

Series Editor: Miriam Miller
Production Coordinator: Gayle Hemenway
Art Direction: Andrew Danish
Book Design: Jeffrey Whitten
Cover Design: Copenhaver Cumpston